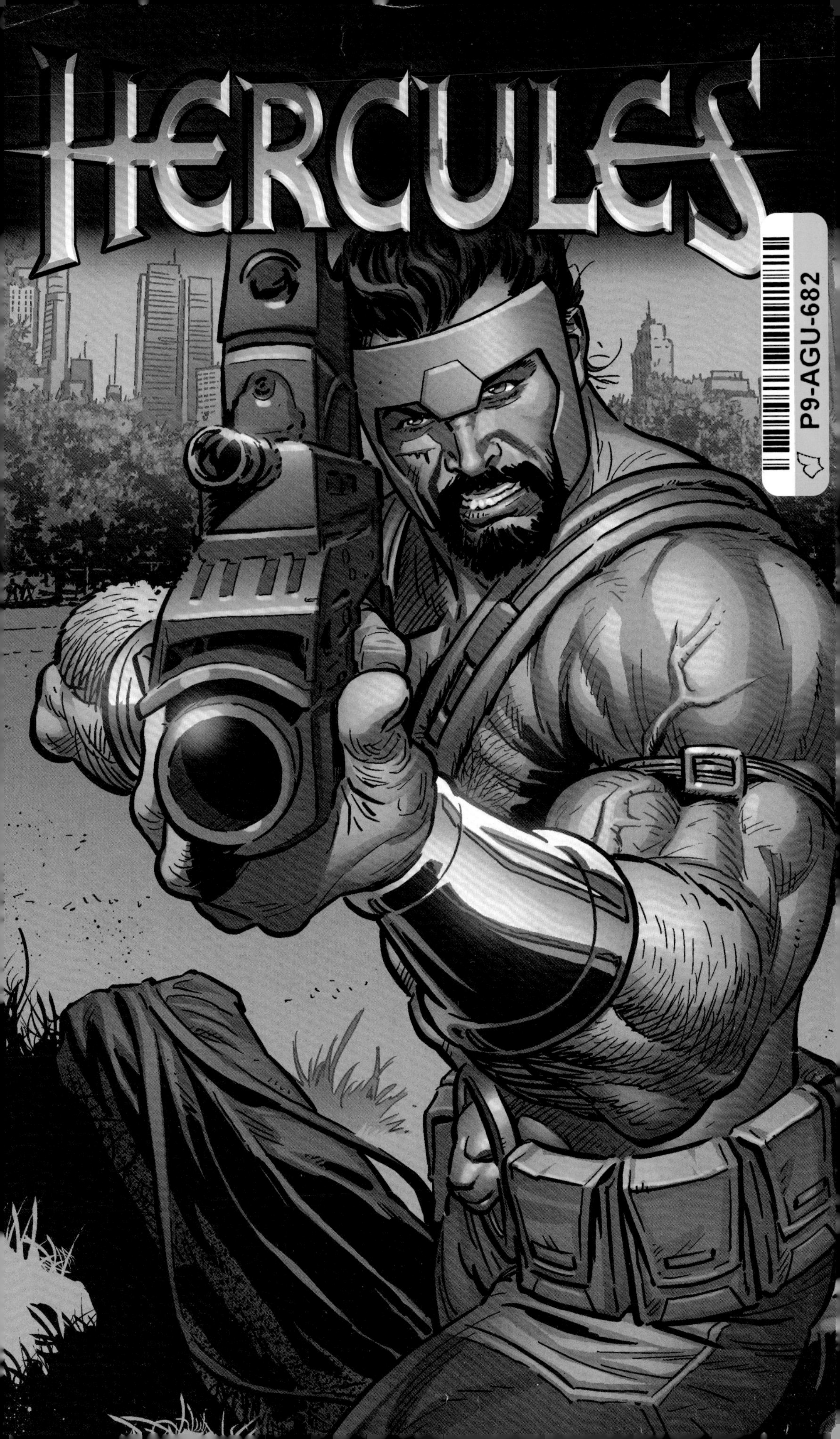
HERCULES

HERCULES
STILL GOING STRONG

DAN ABNETT
WRITER

LUKE ROSS (Nos. 1-5) WITH **EMILIO LAISO** (No. 2) AND
GORAN SUDŽUKA & **DALIBOR TALAJIĆ** (No. 6)
ARTISTS

GURU-eFX
COLOR ART

VC's JOE SABINO
LETTERER

CLAY MANN & **CHRIS SOTOMAYOR** (Nos. 1-2),
JAY ANACLETO & **RICHARD ISANOVE** (Nos. 3-4) AND
JAY ANACLETO & **ROMULO FAJARDO JR.** (Nos. 5-6)
COVER ART

CHRISTINA HARRINGTON
ASSISTANT EDITOR

KATIE KUBERT
EDITOR

HERCULES CREATED BY **STAN LEE** & **JACK KIRBY**

JENNIFER GRÜNWALD
COLLECTION EDITOR

SARAH BRUNSTAD
ASSOCIATE EDITOR

ALEX STARBUCK
ASSOCIATE MANAGING EDITOR

MARK D. BEAZLEY
EDITOR, SPECIAL PROJECTS

JEFF YOUNGQUIST
VP, PRODUCTION & SPECIAL PROJECTS

DAVID GABRIEL
SVP PRINT, SALES & MARKETING

ADAM DEL RE
BOOK DESIGNER

AXEL ALONSO
EDITOR IN CHIEF

JOE QUESADA
CHIEF CREATIVE OFFICER

DAN BUCKLEY
PUBLISHER

ALAN FINE
EXECUTIVE PRODUCER

HERCULES: STILL GOING STRONG. Contains material originally published in magazine form as HERCULES #1-6. First printing 2016. ISBN# 978-1-302-90033-5. Published by MARVEL WORLDWIDE, INC., a subsidiary of MARVEL ENTERTAINMENT, LLC. OFFICE OF PUBLICATION: 135 West 50th Street, New York, NY 10020. Copyright © 2016 MARVEL No similarity between any of the names, characters, persons, and/or institutions in this magazine with those of any living or dead person or institution is intended, and any such similarity which may exist is purely coincidental. **Printed in Canada.** ALAN FINE, President, Marvel Entertainment; DAN BUCKLEY, President, TV, Publishing & Brand Management; JOE QUESADA, Chief Creative Officer; TOM BREVOORT, SVP of Publishing; DAVID BOGART, SVP of Business Affairs & Operations, Publishing & Partnership; C.B. CEBULSKI, VP of Brand Management & Development, Asia; DAVID GABRIEL, SVP of Sales & Marketing, Publishing; JEFF YOUNGQUIST, VP of Production & Special Projects; DAN CARR, Executive Director of Publishing Technology; ALEX MORALES, Director of Publishing Operations; SUSAN CRESPI, Production Manager; STAN LEE, Chairman Emeritus. For information regarding advertising in Marvel Comics or on Marvel.com, please contact Vit DeBellis, Integrated Sales Manager, at vdebellis@marvel.com. For Marvel subscription inquiries, please call 888-511-5480. Manufactured between 4/15/2016 and 5/23/2016 by SOLISCO PRINTERS, SCOTT, QC, CANADA.

10 9 8 7 6 5 4 3 2 1

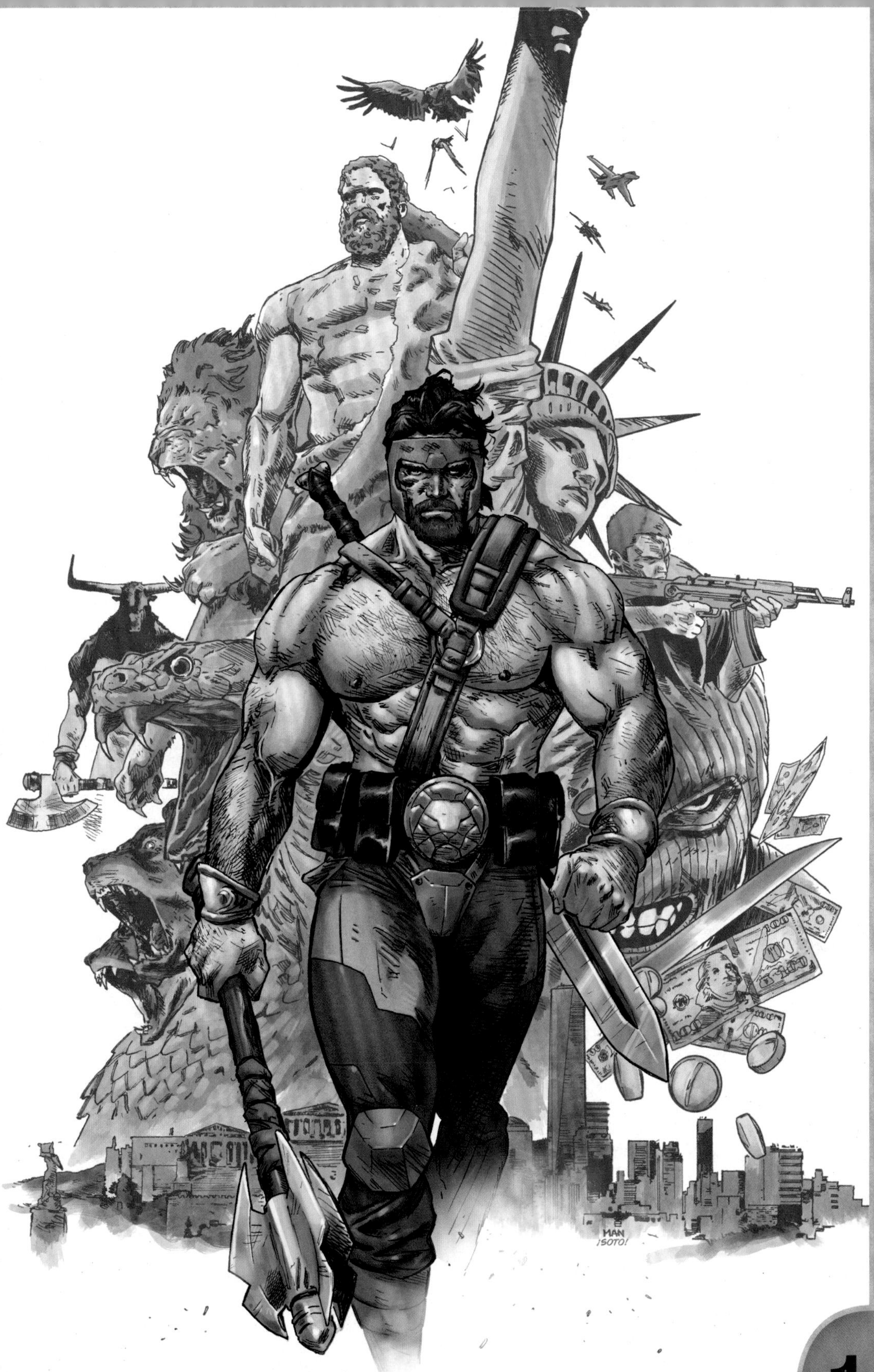
MAN
¡SOTO!

STILL GOING STRONG

1

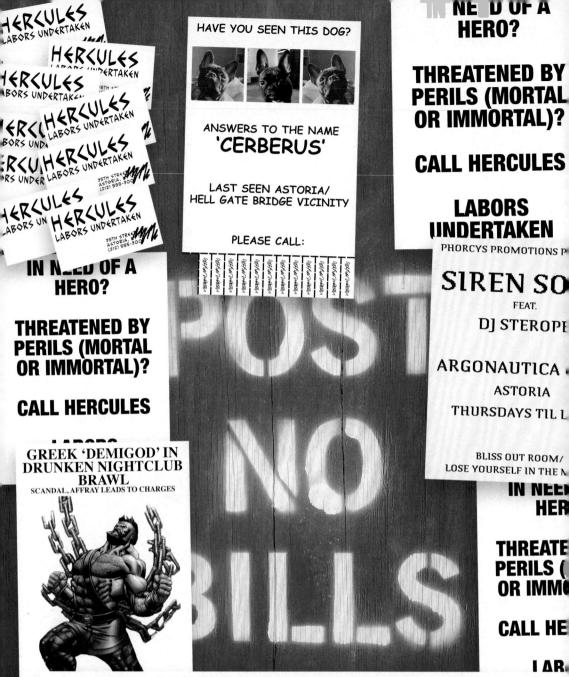

HERCULES
LABORS UNDERTAKEN

HERCULES
LABORS UNDERTAKEN

HERCULES
LABORS UNDERTAKEN

HERCULES
LABORS UNDERTAKEN

HERCULES
LABORS UNDERTAKEN

HERCULES
LABORS UNDERTAKEN

HERCULES
LABORS UNDERTAKEN

35TH STREET
ASTORIA,
(212) 555-30

HAVE YOU SEEN THIS DOG?

ANSWERS TO THE NAME
'CERBERUS'

LAST SEEN ASTORIA/
HELL GATE BRIDGE VICINITY

PLEASE CALL:

IN NEED OF A
HERO?

THREATENED BY
PERILS (MORTAL
OR IMMORTAL)?

CALL HERCULES

GREEK 'DEMIGOD' IN
DRUNKEN NIGHTCLUB
BRAWL
SCANDAL, AFFRAY LEADS TO CHARGES

IN NEED OF A
HERO?

THREATENED BY
PERILS (MORTAL
OR IMMORTAL)?

CALL HERCULES

LABORS
UNDERTAKEN

PHORCYS PROMOTIONS P

SIREN SO
FEAT.
DJ STEROPE

ARGONAUTICA
ASTORIA
THURSDAYS TIL L

BLISS OUT ROOM/
LOSE YOURSELF IN THE M

IN NEE
HER

THREATE
PERILS (
OR IMMO

CALL HE

LAB

IN ANCIENT DAYS, HERCULES WAS THE GREATEST HERO OF ALL. THROUGH
HIS DEEDS AND COURAGE, HE BECAME FAMOUS AND BELOVED ACROSS THE
KNOWN WORLD. HE WAS THE WORLD'S FIRST SUPER HERO, AND SET THE
STANDARD FOR ALL HEROES THAT CAME AFTER HIM.

BUT IN THE MODERN WORLD, IMMORTAL HERCULES HAS DONE LITTLE BUT
ENJOY HIS FAME AND CELEBRITY. HE HAS BECOME NOTORIOUS FOR HIS
DRUNKEN ANTICS, HIS UNRULY BEHAVIOR AND HIS DEBAUCHED LIFESTYLE.
THE SUBJECT OF GOSSIP AND SCANDAL, HE HAS BECOME AN IRRELEVANCE.

IS IT TIME FOR HIM TO RETIRE AND FADE AWAY, OR CAN HE FIND HIS FORM
AGAIN, CLEAN UP HIS LIFE, AND REMIND THE WORLD--A WORLD FULL OF
ASTONISHING MODERN HEROES--THAT HE WAS THE FIRST OF THEIR KIND...
AND IS STILL THE GREATEST CHAMPION THE WORLD HAS EVER KNOWN?

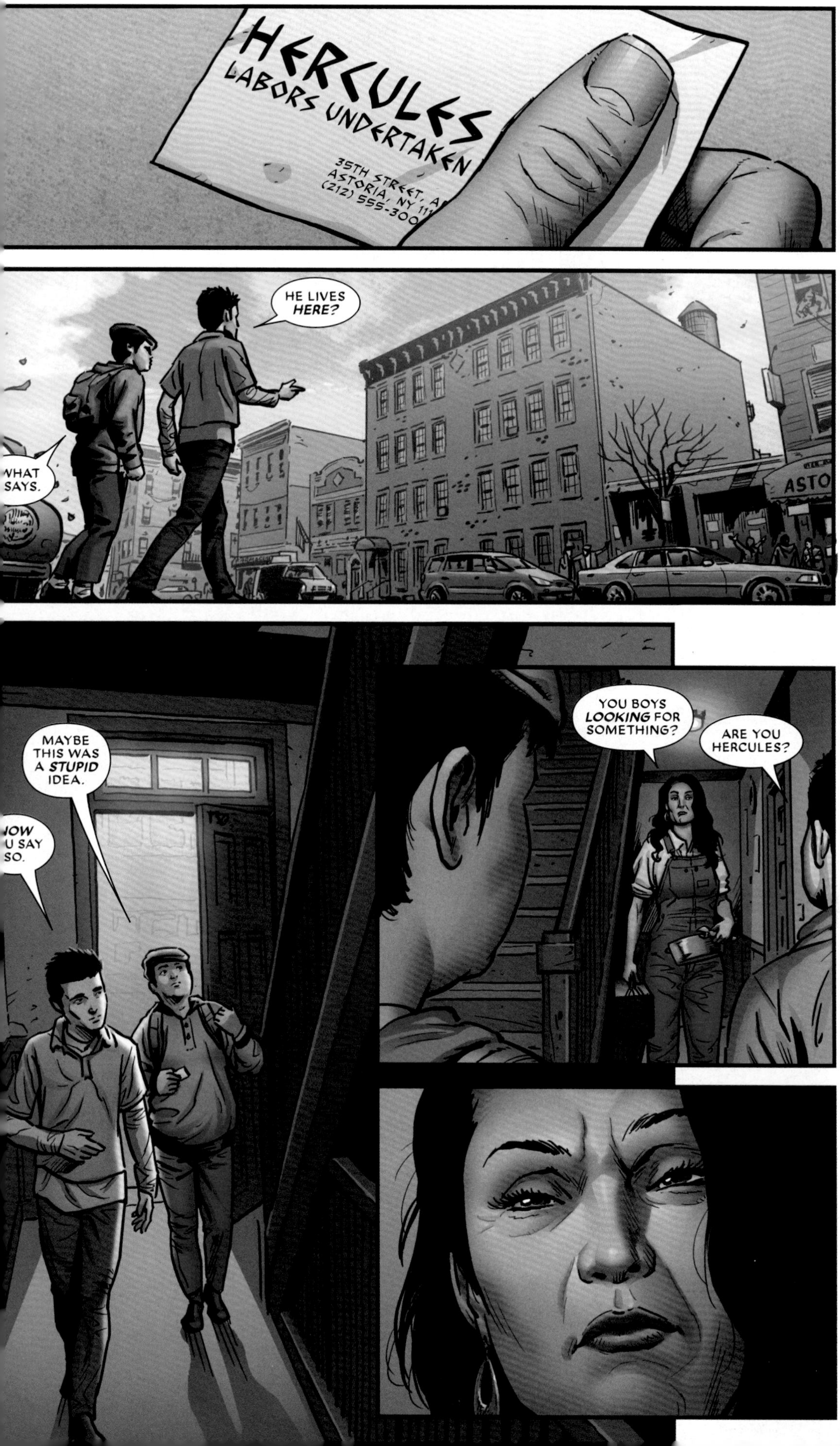

HERCULES
LABORS UNDERTAKEN
35TH STREET, A
ASTORIA, NY 11
(212) 555-300
HE LIVES HERE?
WHAT
SAYS.
MAYBE THIS WAS A STUPID IDEA.
NOW
U SAY
SO.
YOU BOYS LOOKING FOR SOMETHING?
ARE YOU HERCULES?

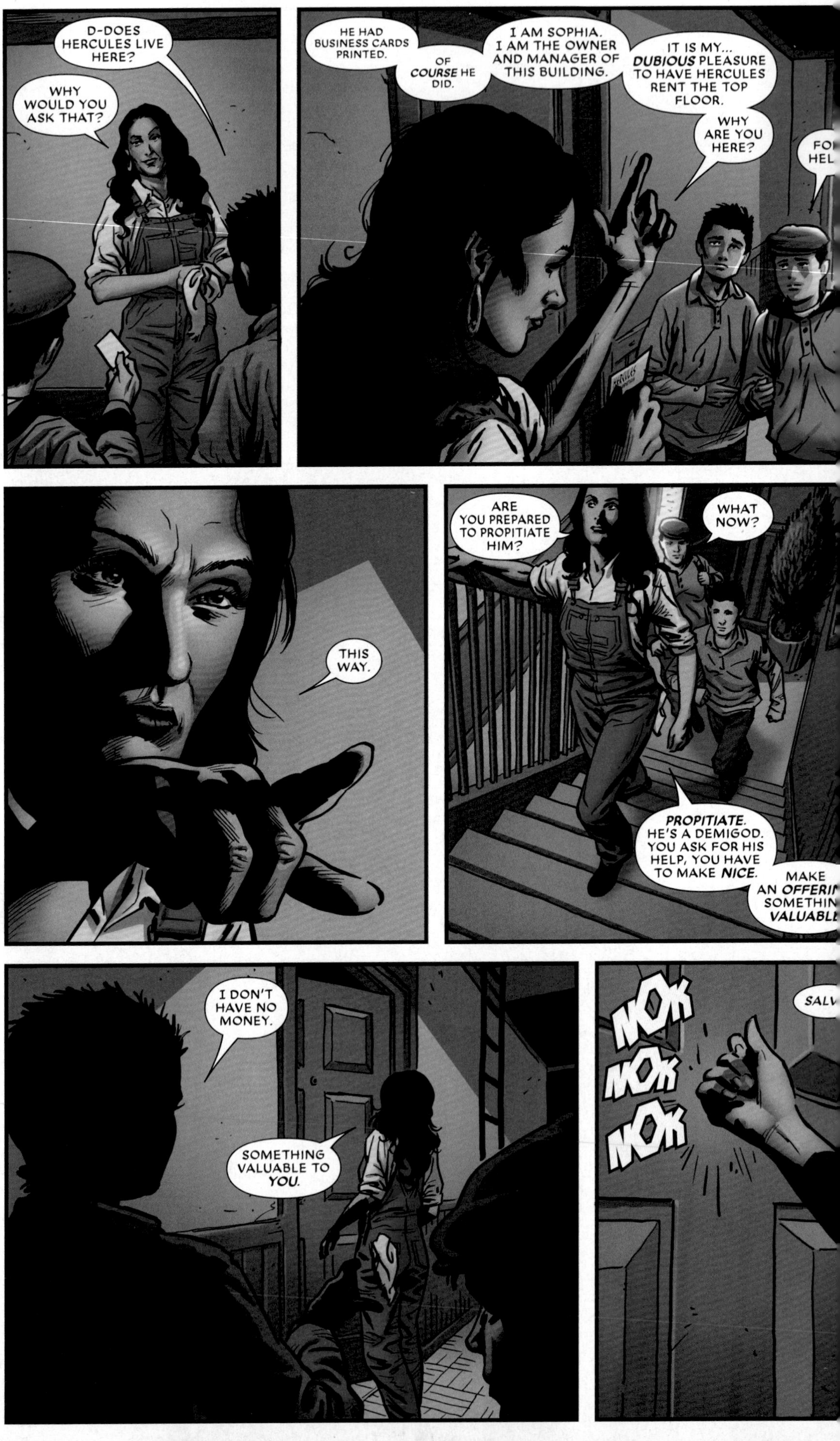
D-DOES HERCULES LIVE HERE?
WHY WOULD YOU ASK THAT?
HE HAD BUSINESS CARDS PRINTED.
OF *COURSE* HE DID.
I AM SOPHIA. I AM THE OWNER AND MANAGER OF THIS BUILDING.
IT IS MY... *DUBIOUS* PLEASURE TO HAVE HERCULES RENT THE TOP FLOOR.
WHY ARE YOU HERE?
THIS WAY.
ARE YOU PREPARED TO PROPITIATE HIM?
WHAT NOW?
PROPITIATE. HE'S A DEMIGOD. YOU ASK FOR HIS HELP, YOU HAVE TO MAKE *NICE*.
MAKE AN
I DON'T HAVE NO MONEY.
SOMETHING VALUABLE TO *YOU*.
NOK NOK NOK

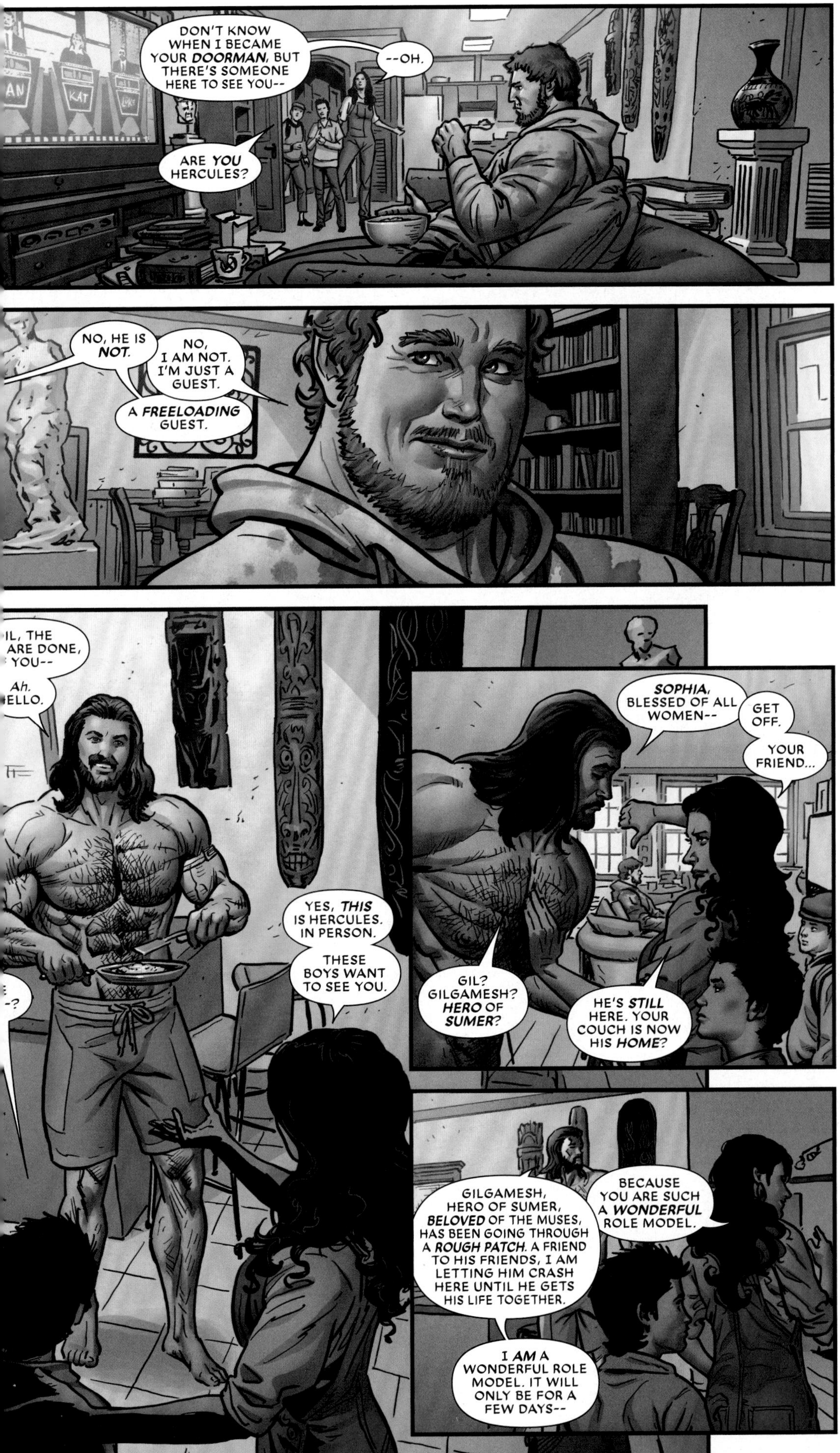

DON'T KNOW WHEN I BECAME YOUR DOORMAN, BUT THERE'S SOMEONE HERE TO SEE YOU--
--OH.
ARE YOU HERCULES?
NO, HE IS NOT.
NO, I AM NOT. I'M JUST A GUEST.
A FREELOADING GUEST.
IL, THE ARE DONE, YOU--
Ah. ELLO.
YES, THIS IS HERCULES. IN PERSON.
THESE BOYS WANT TO SEE YOU.
SOPHIA, BLESSED OF ALL WOMEN--
GET OFF.
YOUR FRIEND...
GIL? GILGAMESH? HERO OF SUMER?
HE'S STILL HERE. YOUR COUCH IS NOW HIS HOME?
GILGAMESH, HERO OF SUMER, BELOVED OF THE MUSES, HAS BEEN GOING THROUGH A ROUGH PATCH. A FRIEND TO HIS FRIENDS, I AM LETTING HIM CRASH HERE UNTIL HE GETS HIS LIFE TOGETHER.
BECAUSE YOU ARE SUCH A WONDERFUL ROLE MODEL.
I AM A WONDERFUL ROLE MODEL. IT WILL ONLY BE FOR A FEW DAYS--

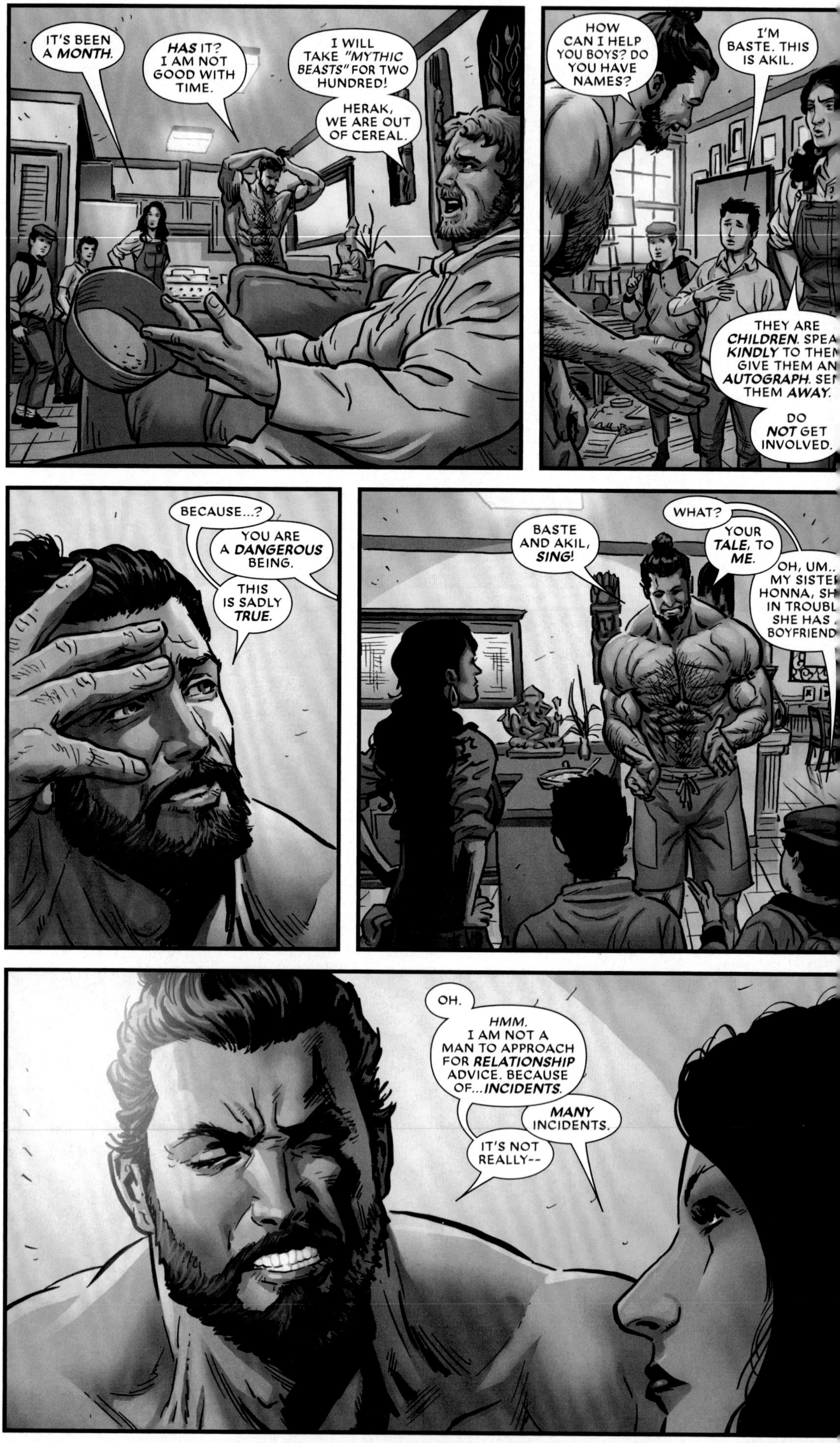
IT'S BEEN A *MONTH*.
HAS IT? I AM NOT GOOD WITH TIME.
I WILL TAKE *"MYTHIC BEASTS"* FOR TWO HUNDRED!
HERAK, WE ARE OUT OF CEREAL.
HOW CAN I HELP YOU BOYS? DO YOU HAVE NAMES?
I'M BASTE. THIS IS AKIL.
THEY ARE *CHILDREN*. SPEA *KINDLY* TO THEM GIVE THEM AN *AUTOGRAPH*. SEN THEM *AWAY*.
DO *NOT* GET INVOLVED.
BECAUSE...?
YOU ARE A *DANGEROUS* BEING.
THIS IS SADLY *TRUE*.
BASTE AND AKIL, *SING*!
WHAT?
YOUR *TALE*, TO *ME*.
OH, UM... MY SISTER HONNA, SH IN TROUBL SHE HAS A BOYFRIEND
OH.
HMM. I AM NOT A MAN TO APPROACH FOR *RELATIONSHIP* ADVICE. BECAUSE OF...*INCIDENTS*.
MANY INCIDENTS.
IT'S NOT REALLY--

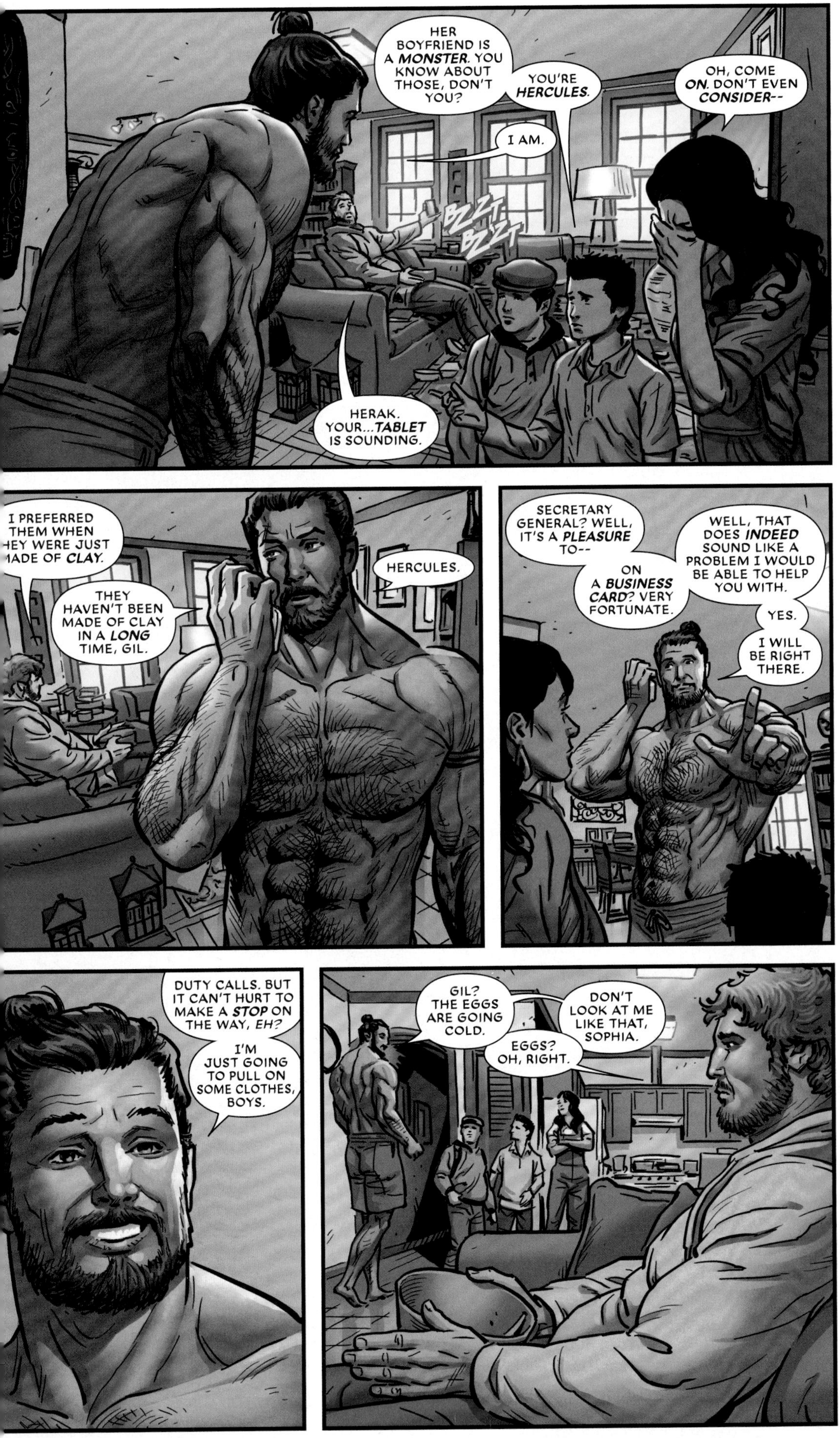
HER BOYFRIEND IS A MONSTER. YOU KNOW ABOUT THOSE, DON'T YOU?
YOU'RE HERCULES.
I AM.
OH, COME ON. DON'T EVEN CONSIDER--
BZZT BZZT
HERAK. YOUR...TABLET IS SOUNDING.
I PREFERRED THEM WHEN HEY WERE JUST ADE OF CLAY.
THEY HAVEN'T BEEN MADE OF CLAY IN A LONG TIME, GIL.
HERCULES.
SECRETARY GENERAL? WELL, IT'S A PLEASURE TO--
ON A BUSINESS CARD? VERY FORTUNATE.
WELL, THAT DOES INDEED SOUND LIKE A PROBLEM I WOULD BE ABLE TO HELP YOU WITH.
YES.
I WILL BE RIGHT THERE.
DUTY CALLS. BUT IT CAN'T HURT TO MAKE A STOP ON THE WAY, EH?
I'M JUST GOING TO PULL ON SOME CLOTHES, BOYS.
GIL? THE EGGS ARE GOING COLD.
DON'T LOOK AT ME LIKE THAT, SOPHIA.
EGGS? OH, RIGHT.

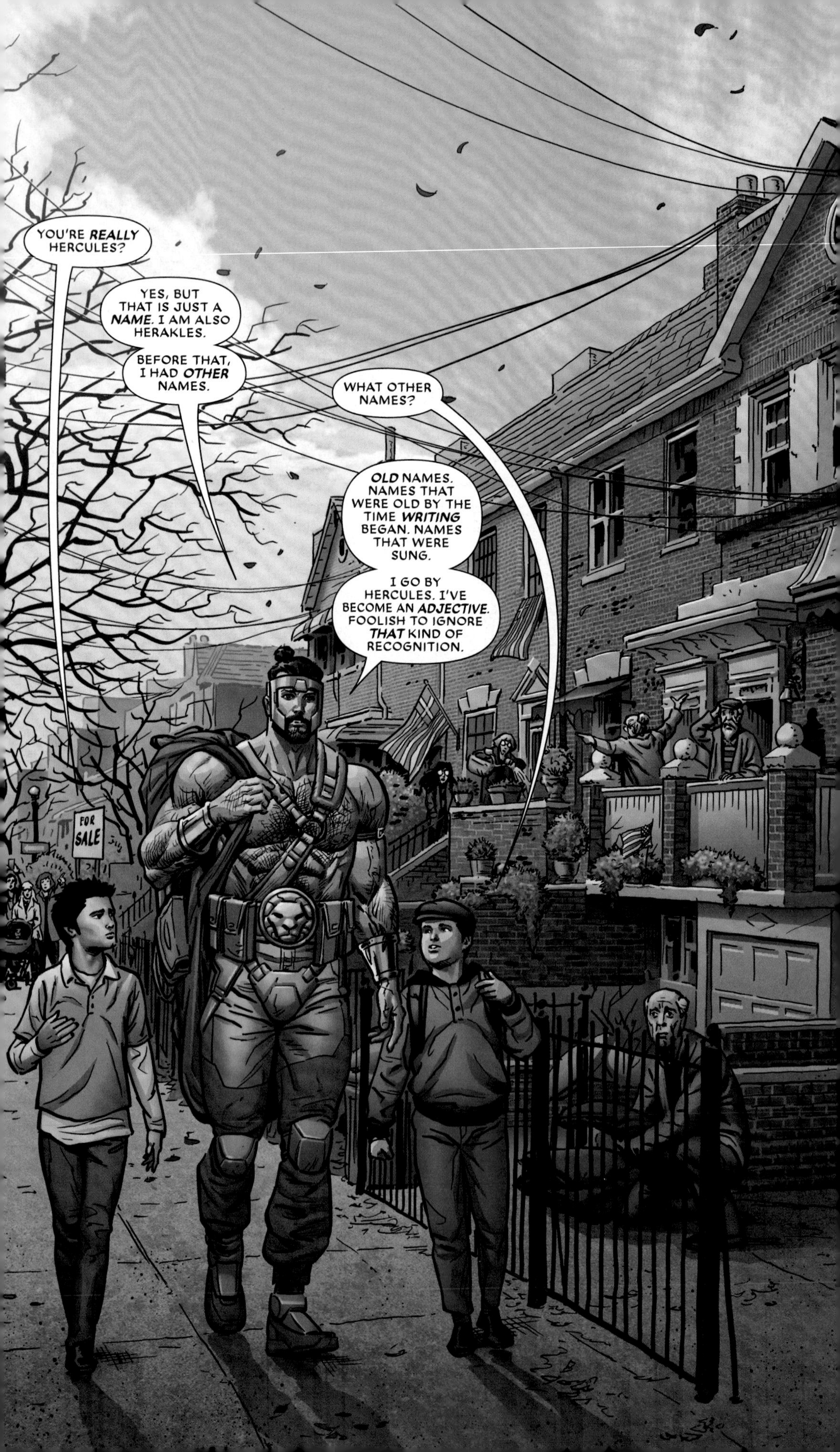

YOU'RE *REALLY* HERCULES?
YES, BUT THAT IS JUST A *NAME*. I AM ALSO HERAKLES.
BEFORE THAT, I HAD *OTHER* NAMES.
WHAT OTHER NAMES?
OLD NAMES. NAMES THAT WERE OLD BY THE TIME *WRITING* BEGAN. NAMES THAT WERE SUNG.
I GO BY HERCULES. I'VE BECOME AN *ADJECTIVE*. FOOLISH TO IGNORE *THAT* KIND OF RECOGNITION.
FOR SALE

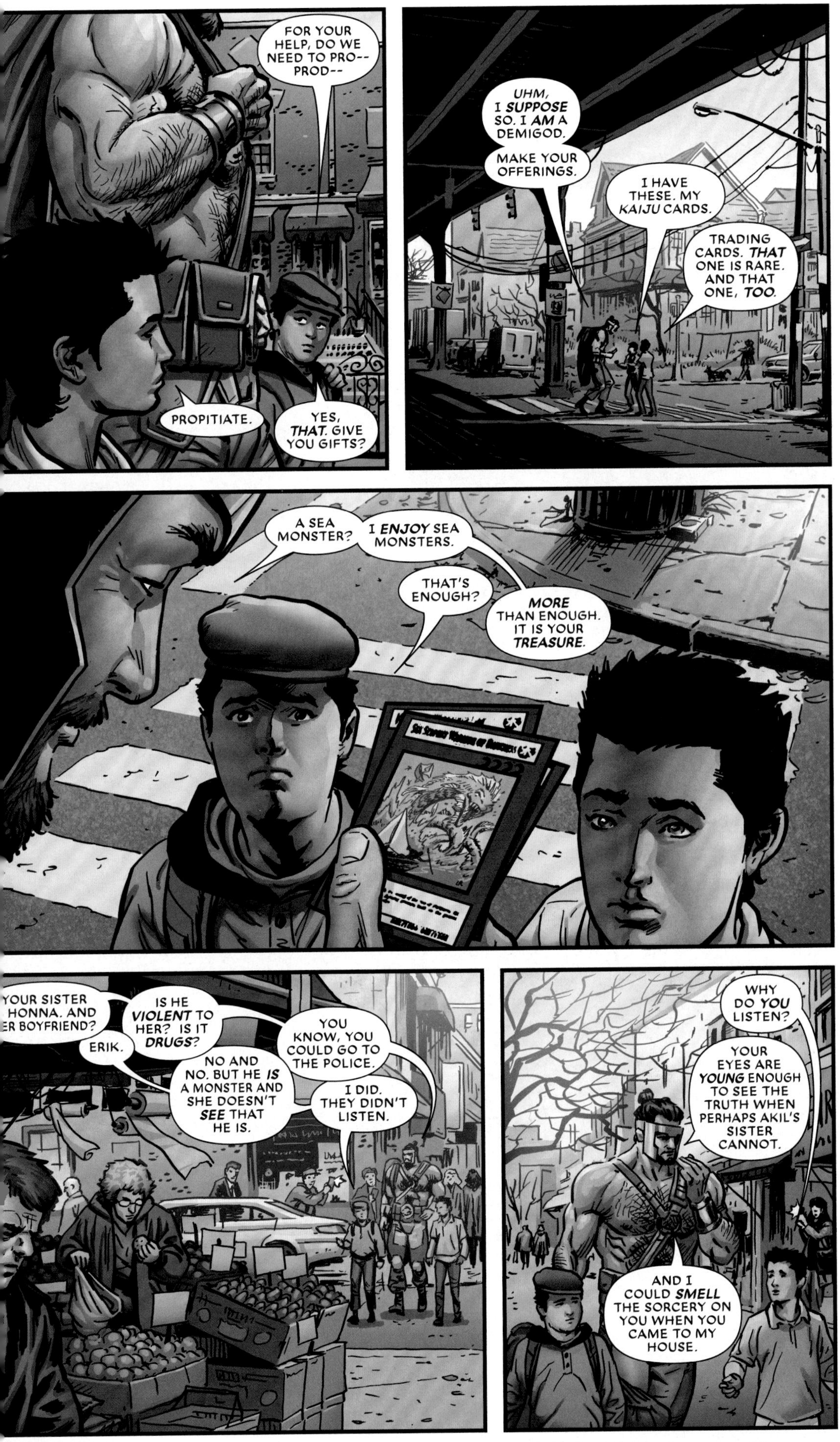
FOR YOUR HELP, DO WE NEED TO PRO-- PROD--
PROPITIATE.
YES, THAT. GIVE YOU GIFTS?
UHM, I SUPPOSE SO. I AM A DEMIGOD.
MAKE YOUR OFFERINGS.
I HAVE THESE. MY KAIJU CARDS.
TRADING CARDS. THAT ONE IS RARE. AND THAT ONE, TOO.
A SEA MONSTER?
I ENJOY SEA MONSTERS.
THAT'S ENOUGH?
MORE THAN ENOUGH. IT IS YOUR TREASURE.
YOUR SISTER HONNA. AND ER BOYFRIEND?
ERIK.
IS HE VIOLENT TO HER? IS IT DRUGS?
NO AND NO. BUT HE IS A MONSTER AND SHE DOESN'T SEE THAT HE IS.
YOU KNOW, YOU COULD GO TO THE POLICE.
I DID. THEY DIDN'T LISTEN.
WHY DO YOU LISTEN?
YOUR EYES ARE YOUNG ENOUGH TO SEE THE TRUTH WHEN PERHAPS AKIL'S SISTER CANNOT.
AND I COULD SMELL THE SORCERY ON YOU WHEN YOU CAME TO MY HOUSE.

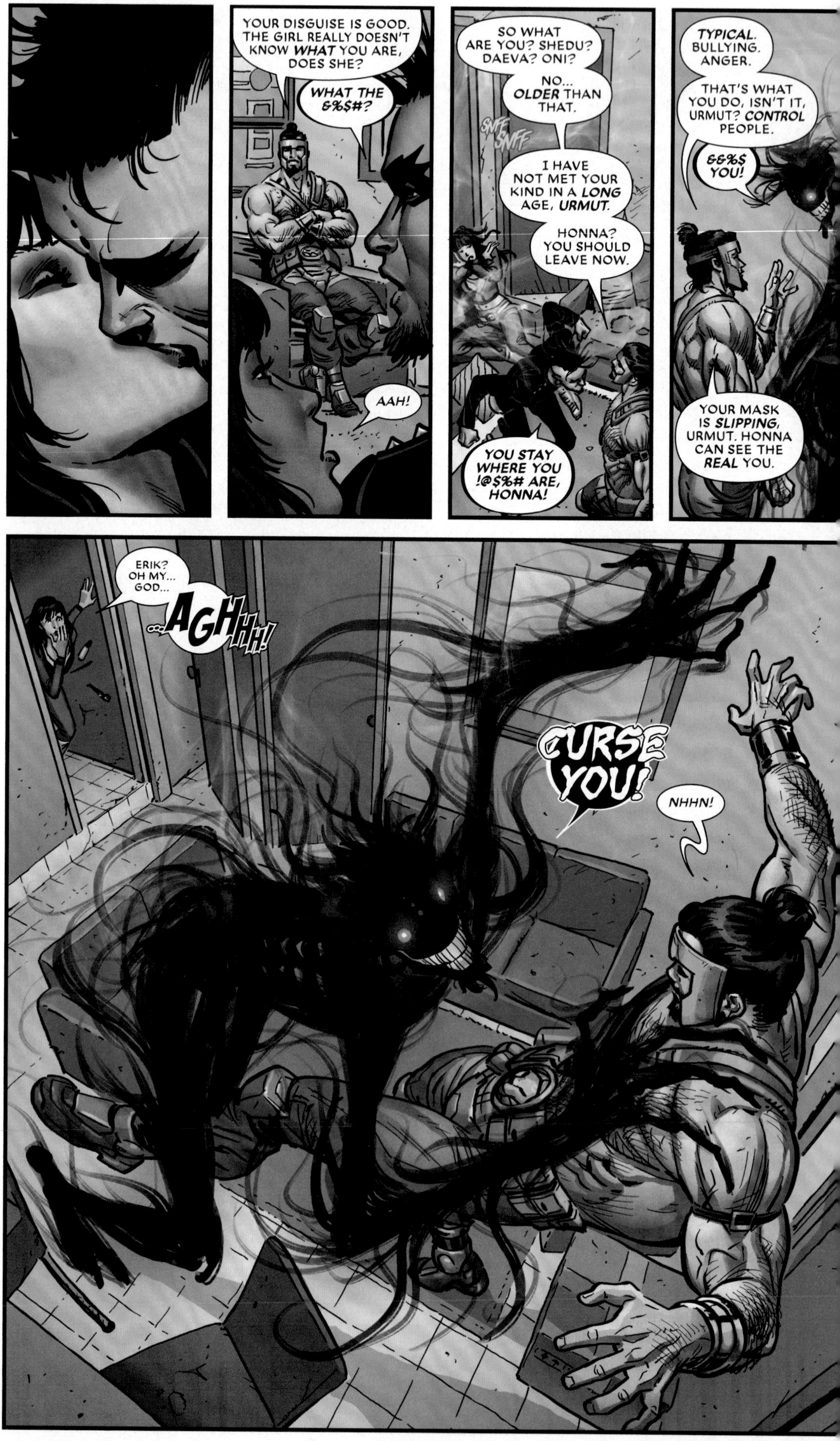
YOUR DISGUISE IS GOOD. THE GIRL REALLY DOESN'T KNOW WHAT YOU ARE, DOES SHE?
WHAT THE &%$#?
AAH!
SO WHAT ARE YOU? SHEDU? DAEVA? ONI?
NO... OLDER THAN THAT.
SNFF SNFF
I HAVE NOT MET YOUR KIND IN A LONG AGE, URMUT.
HONNA? YOU SHOULD LEAVE NOW.
YOU STAY WHERE YOU !@$%# ARE, HONNA!
TYPICAL. BULLYING. ANGER.
THAT'S WHAT YOU DO, ISN'T IT, URMUT? CONTROL PEOPLE.
&&%$ YOU!
YOUR MASK IS SLIPPING, URMUT. HONNA CAN SEE THE REAL YOU.
ERIK? OH MY... GOD...
...AGHHH!
CURSE YOU!
NHHN!

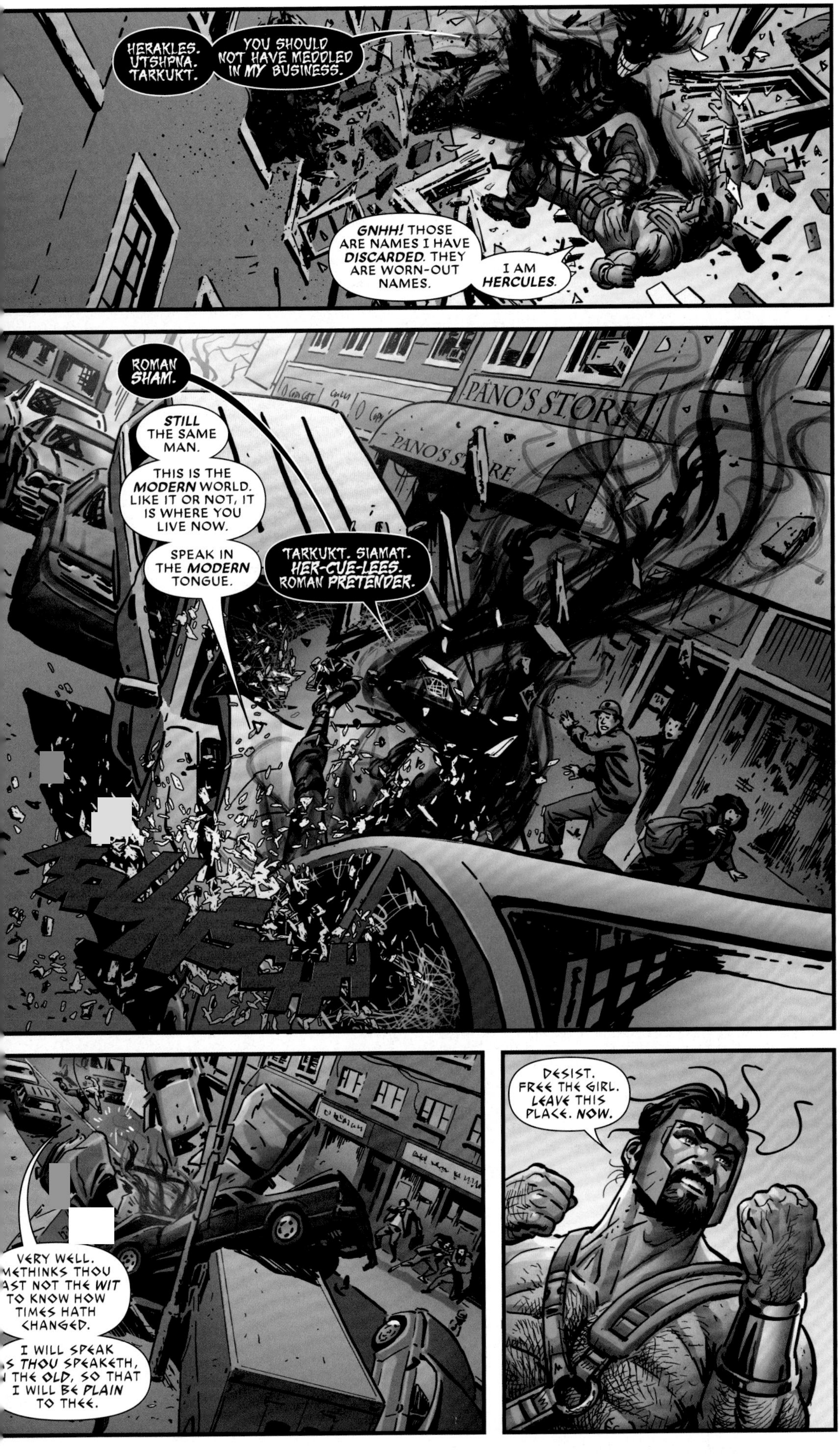

HERAKLES. UTSHPNA. TARKUKT.
YOU SHOULD NOT HAVE MEDDLED IN *MY* BUSINESS.
GNHH! THOSE ARE NAMES I HAVE ***DISCARDED.*** THEY ARE WORN-OUT NAMES.
I AM ***HERCULES.***
ROMAN ***SHAM.***
STILL THE SAME MAN.
THIS IS THE ***MODERN*** WORLD. LIKE IT OR NOT, IT IS WHERE YOU LIVE NOW.
SPEAK IN THE ***MODERN*** TONGUE.
PANO'S STORE
TARKUKT. SIAMAT. ***HER-CUE-LEES.*** ROMAN ***PRETENDER.***
VERY WELL. METHINKS THOU AST NOT THE *WIT* TO KNOW HOW TIMES HATH CHANGED.
I WILL SPEAK S *THOU* SPEAKETH, THE *OLD*, SO THAT I WILL BE *PLAIN* TO THEE.
DESIST. FREE THE GIRL. *LEAVE* THIS PLACE. *NOW.*

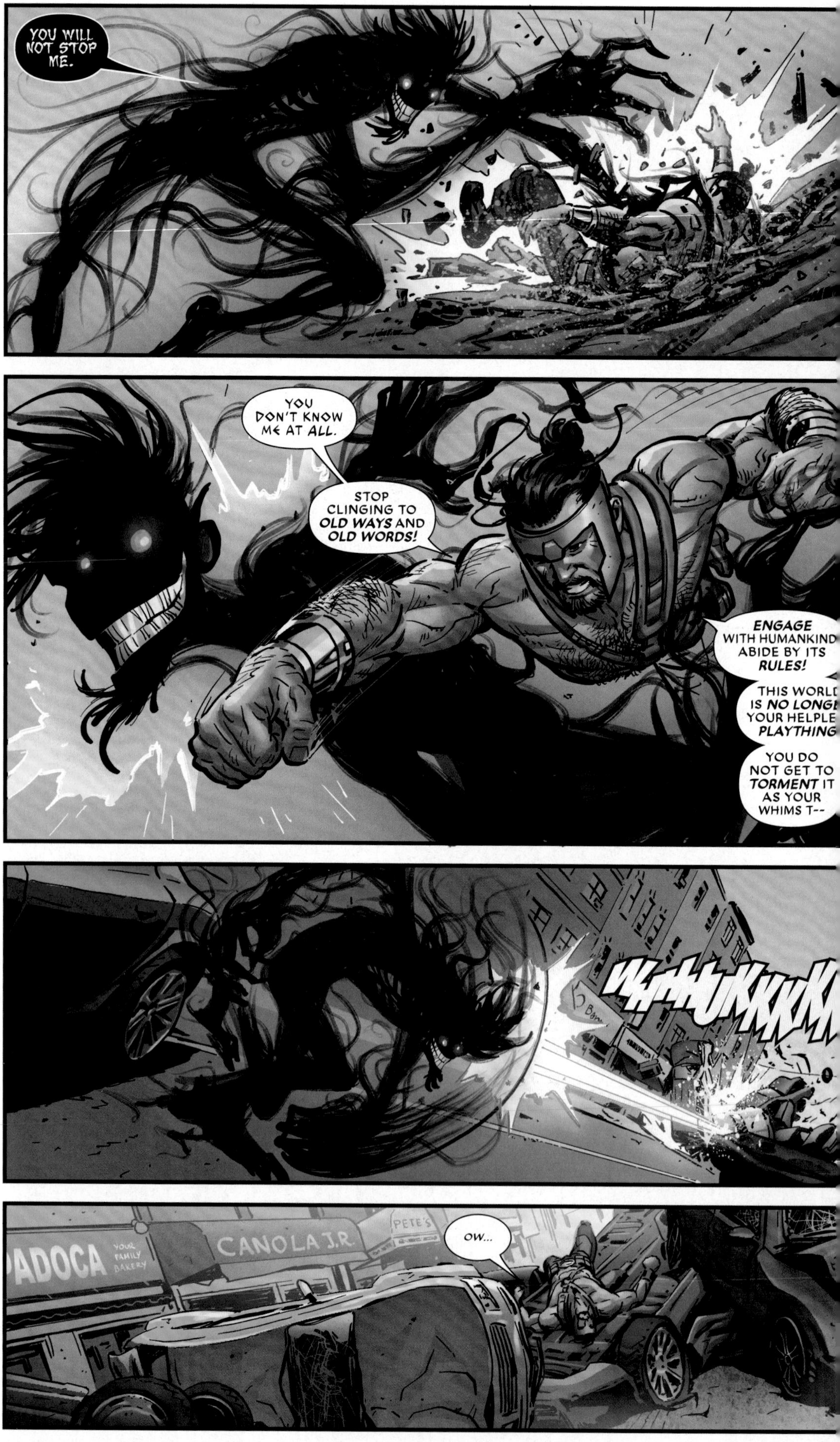
YOU WILL NOT STOP ME.
YOU DON'T KNOW ME AT ALL.
STOP CLINGING TO OLD WAYS AND OLD WORDS!
ENGAGE WITH HUMANKIND
ABIDE BY ITS RULES!
THIS WORLD IS NO LONG YOUR HELPLE PLAYTHING
YOU DO NOT GET TO TORMENT IT AS YOUR WHIMS T--
WHHUKKKM
PADOCA YOUR FAMILY BAKERY
CANOLA J.R.
PETE'S
OW...

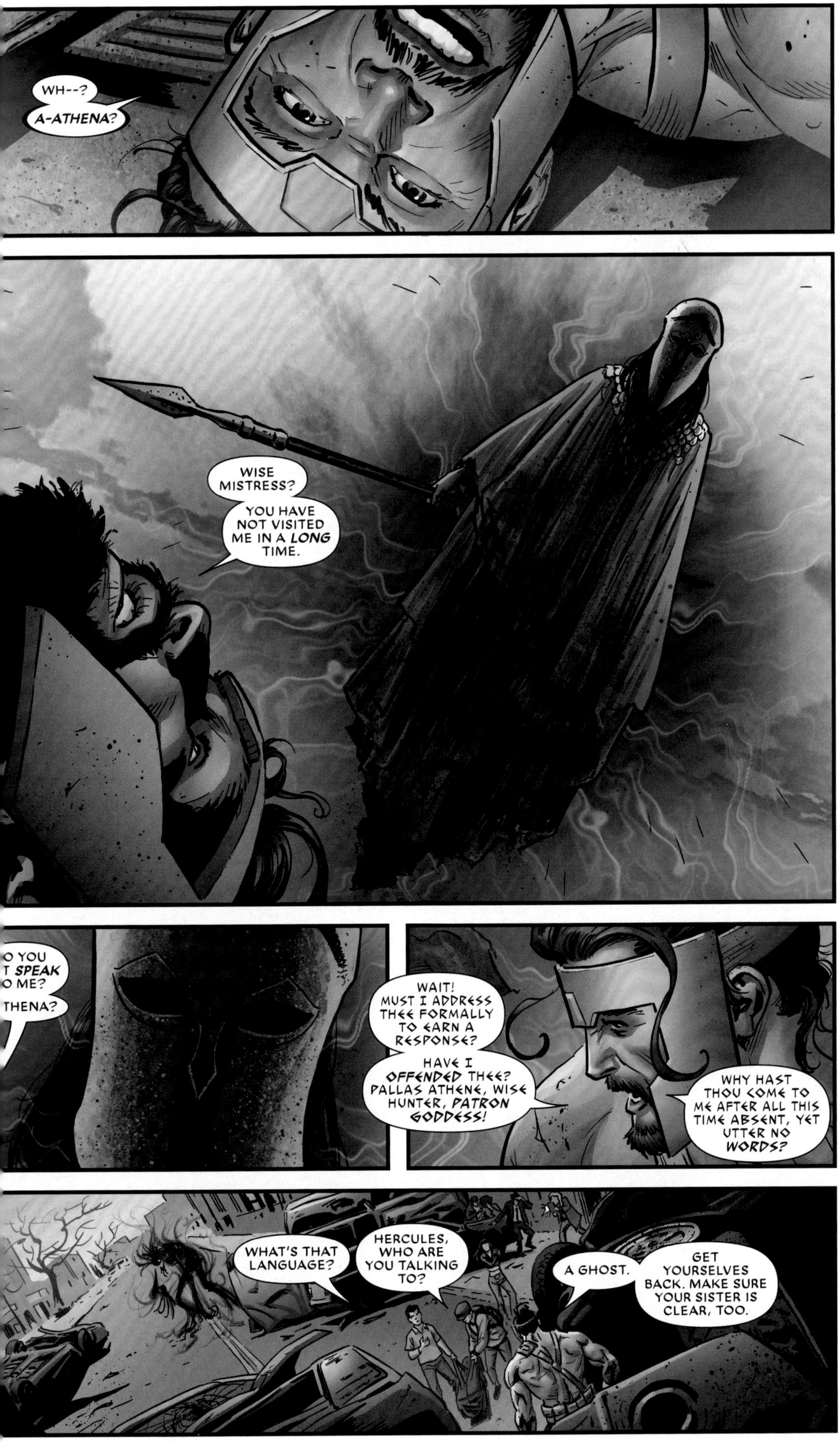
WH--?
A-ATHENA?
WISE MISTRESS?
YOU HAVE NOT VISITED ME IN A *LONG* TIME.
O YOU
T *SPEAK*
O ME?
THENA?
WAIT! MUST I ADDRESS THEE FORMALLY TO EARN A RESPONSE?
HAVE I *OFFENDED* THEE? PALLAS ATHENE, WISE HUNTER, *PATRON GODDESS!*
WHY HAST THOU COME TO ME AFTER ALL THIS TIME ABSENT, YET UTTER NO *WORDS?*
WHAT'S THAT LANGUAGE?
HERCULES, WHO ARE YOU TALKING TO?
A GHOST.
GET YOURSELVES BACK. MAKE SURE YOUR SISTER IS CLEAR, TOO.

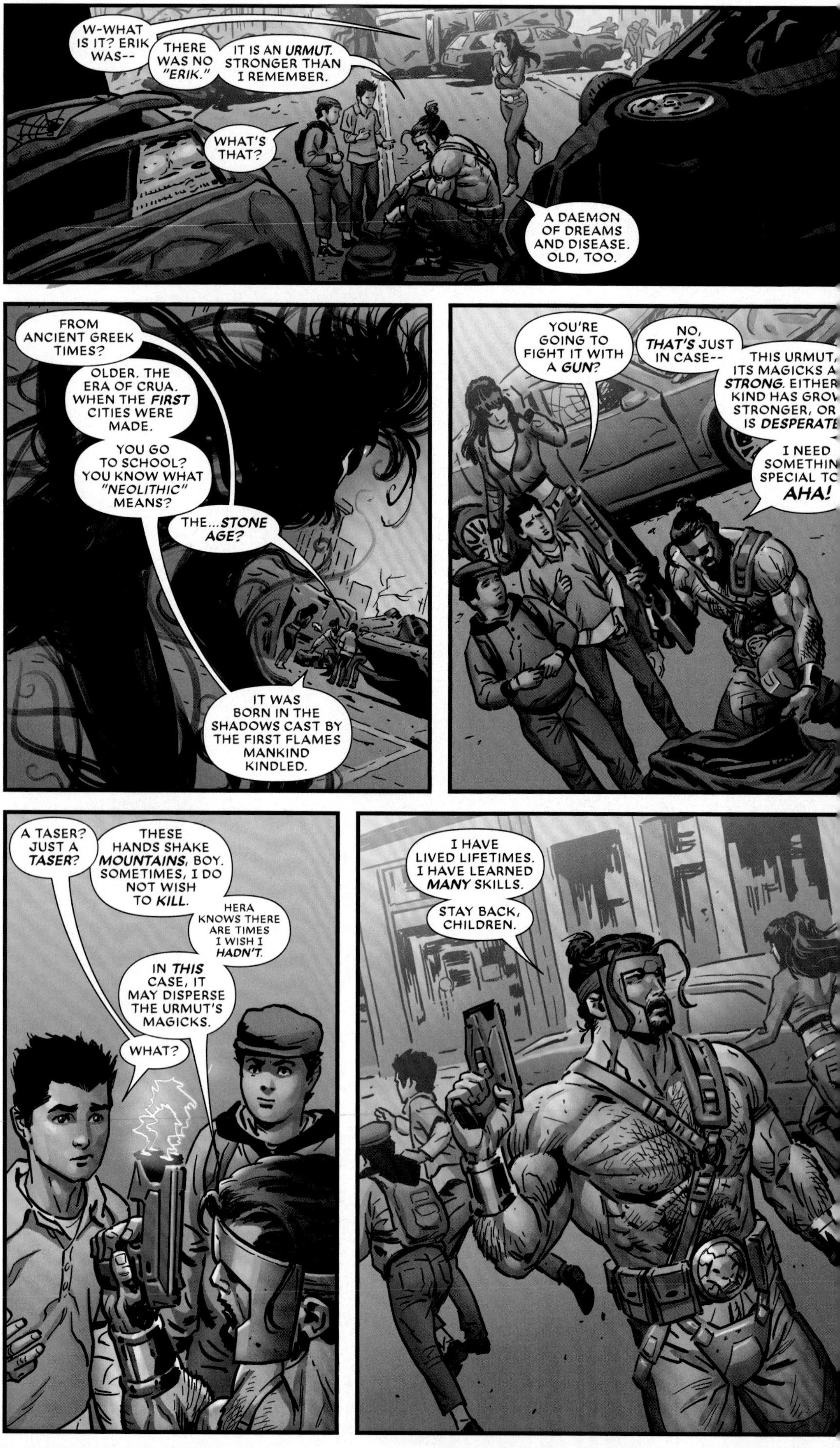
W-WHAT IS IT? ERIK WAS--
THERE WAS NO "ERIK."
IT IS AN *URMUT.* STRONGER THAN I REMEMBER.
WHAT'S THAT?
A DAEMON OF DREAMS AND DISEASE. OLD, TOO.
FROM ANCIENT GREEK TIMES?
OLDER. THE ERA OF CRUA. WHEN THE *FIRST* CITIES WERE MADE.
YOU GO TO SCHOOL? YOU KNOW WHAT *"NEOLITHIC"* MEANS?
THE... *STONE AGE?*
IT WAS BORN IN THE SHADOWS CAST BY THE FIRST FLAMES MANKIND KINDLED.
YOU'RE GOING TO FIGHT IT WITH A *GUN*?
NO, *THAT'S* JUST IN CASE--
A TASER? JUST A *TASER*?
THESE HANDS SHAKE *MOUNTAINS*, BOY. SOMETIMES, I DO NOT WISH TO *KILL*.
HERA KNOWS THERE ARE TIMES I WISH I *HADN'T*.
IN *THIS* CASE, IT MAY DISPERSE THE URMUT'S MAGICKS.
WHAT?
I HAVE LIVED LIFETIMES. I HAVE LEARNED *MANY* SKILLS.
STAY BACK, CHILDREN.

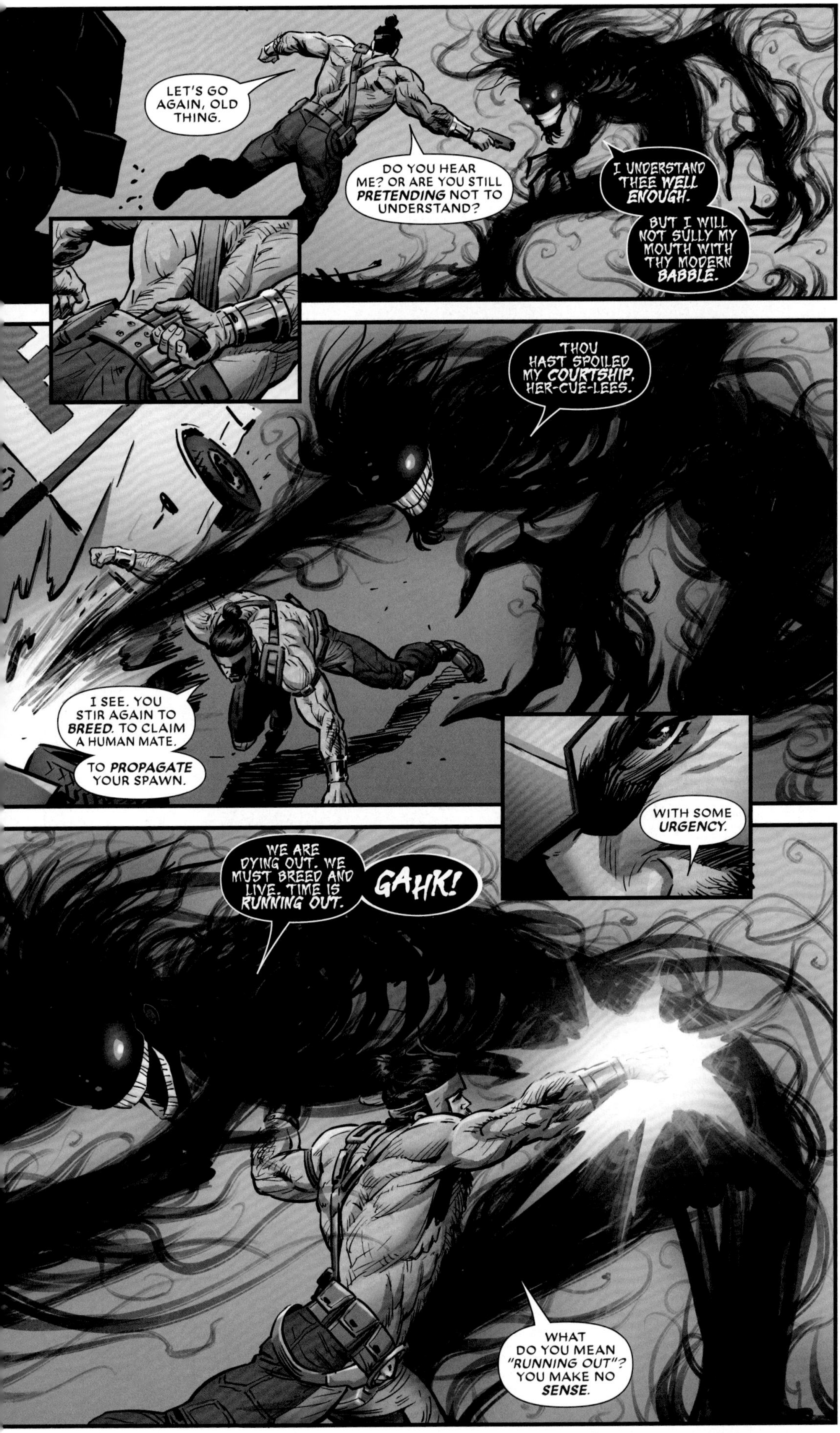
LET'S GO AGAIN, OLD THING.
DO YOU HEAR ME? OR ARE YOU STILL *PRETENDING* NOT TO UNDERSTAND?
I UNDERSTAND THEE *WELL ENOUGH.*
BUT I WILL NOT SULLY MY MOUTH WITH THY MODERN *BABBLE.*
THOU HAST SPOILED MY *COURTSHIP,* HER-CUE-LEES.
I SEE. YOU STIR AGAIN TO *BREED.* TO CLAIM A HUMAN MATE.
TO *PROPAGATE* YOUR SPAWN.
WITH SOME *URGENCY.*
WE ARE DYING OUT. WE MUST BREED AND LIVE. TIME IS *RUNNING OUT.*
GAHK!
WHAT DO YOU MEAN *"RUNNING OUT"*? YOU MAKE NO *SENSE.*

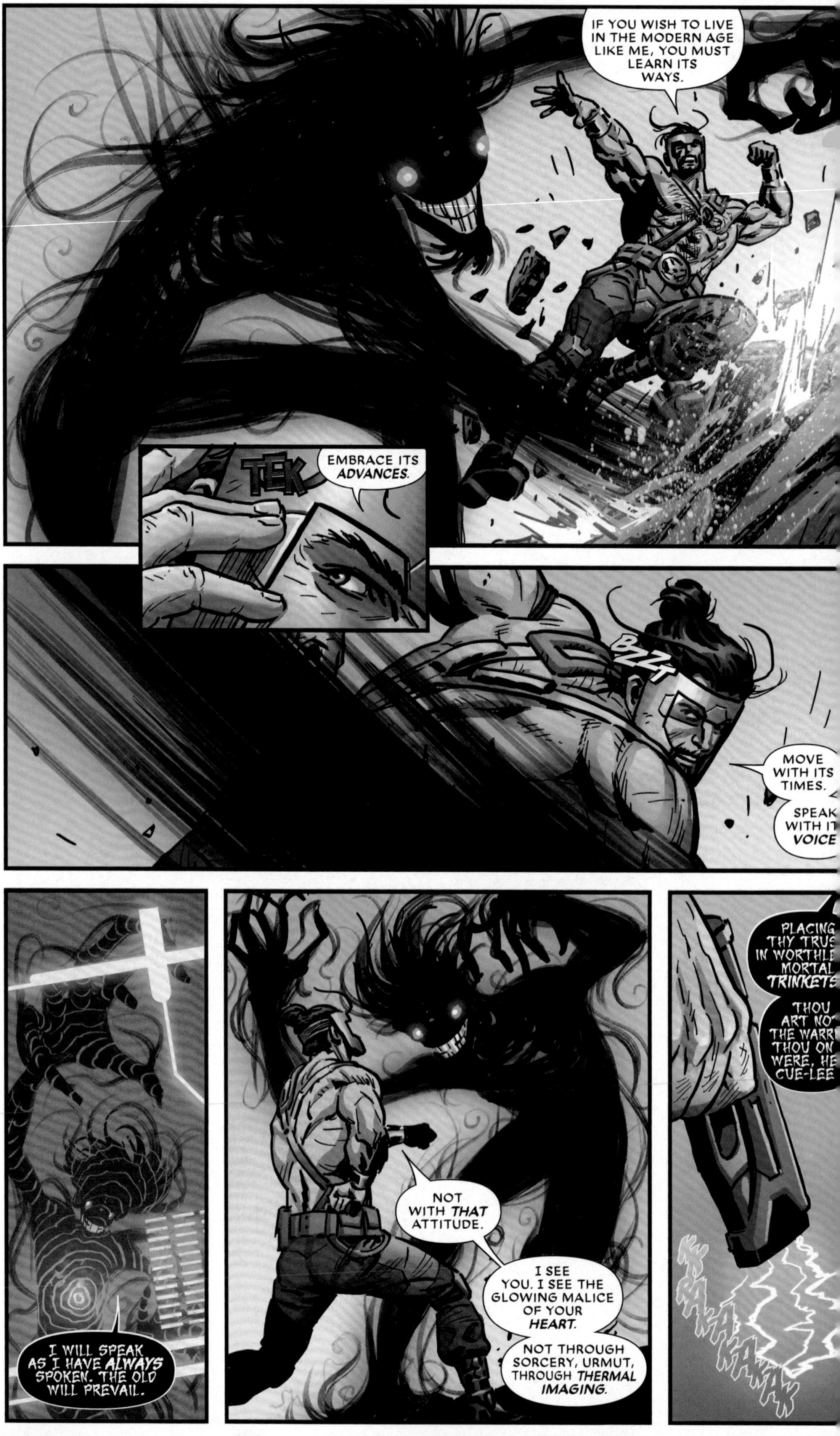
IF YOU WISH TO LIVE IN THE MODERN AGE LIKE ME, YOU MUST LEARN ITS WAYS.
TEK
EMBRACE ITS *ADVANCES*.
BZZT
MOVE WITH ITS TIMES.
SPEAK WITH IT *VOICE*
I WILL SPEAK AS I HAVE *ALWAYS* SPOKEN. THE OLD WILL PREVAIL.
NOT WITH *THAT* ATTITUDE.
I SEE YOU. I SEE THE GLOWING MALICE OF YOUR *HEART*.
NOT THROUGH SORCERY, URMUT, THROUGH *THERMAL IMAGING*.
PLACING THY TRUS IN WORTHLE MORTAL *TRINKETS*
THOU ART NO THE WARR THOU ON WERE, HE CUE-LEE

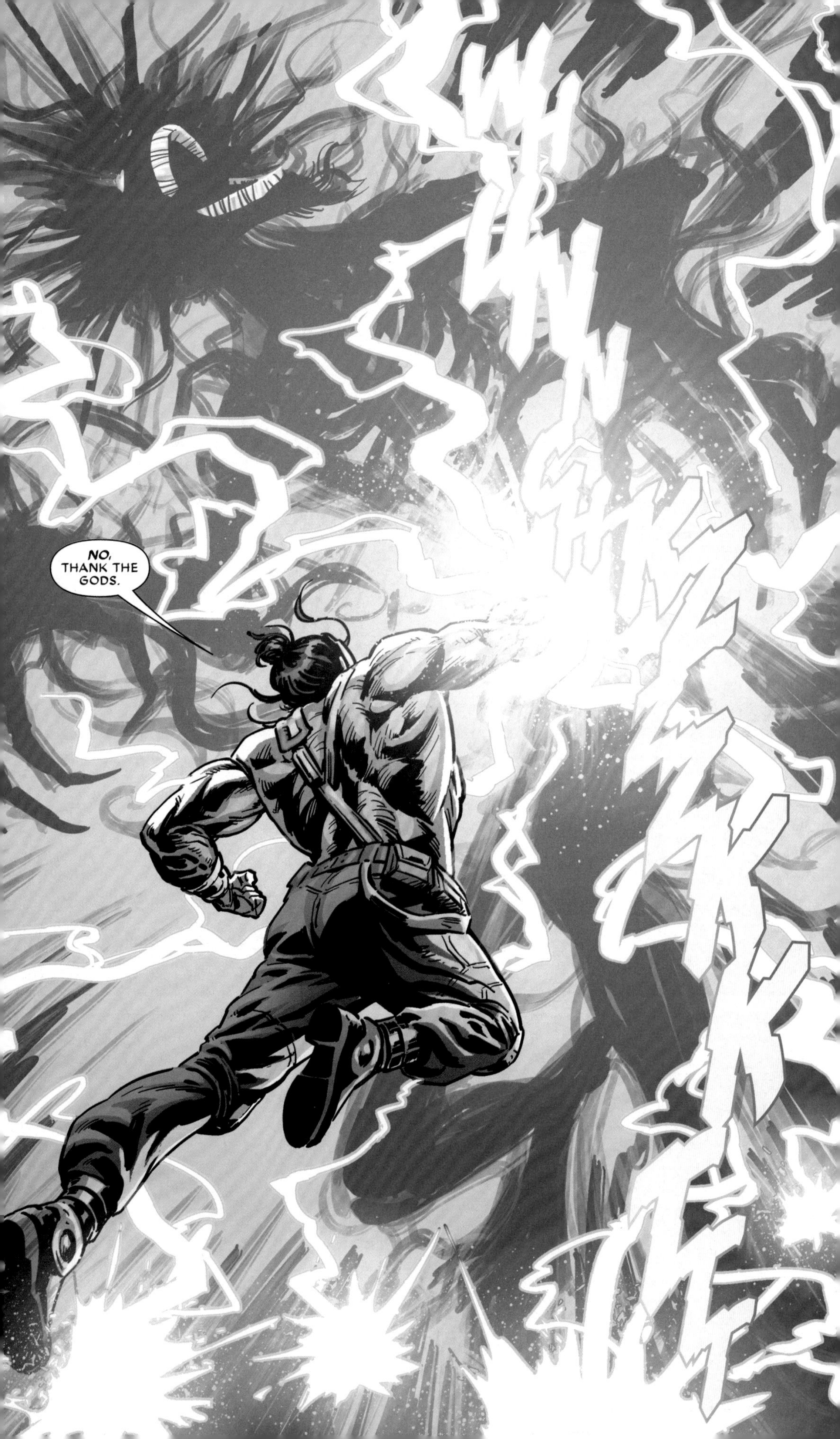
NO, THANK THE GODS.

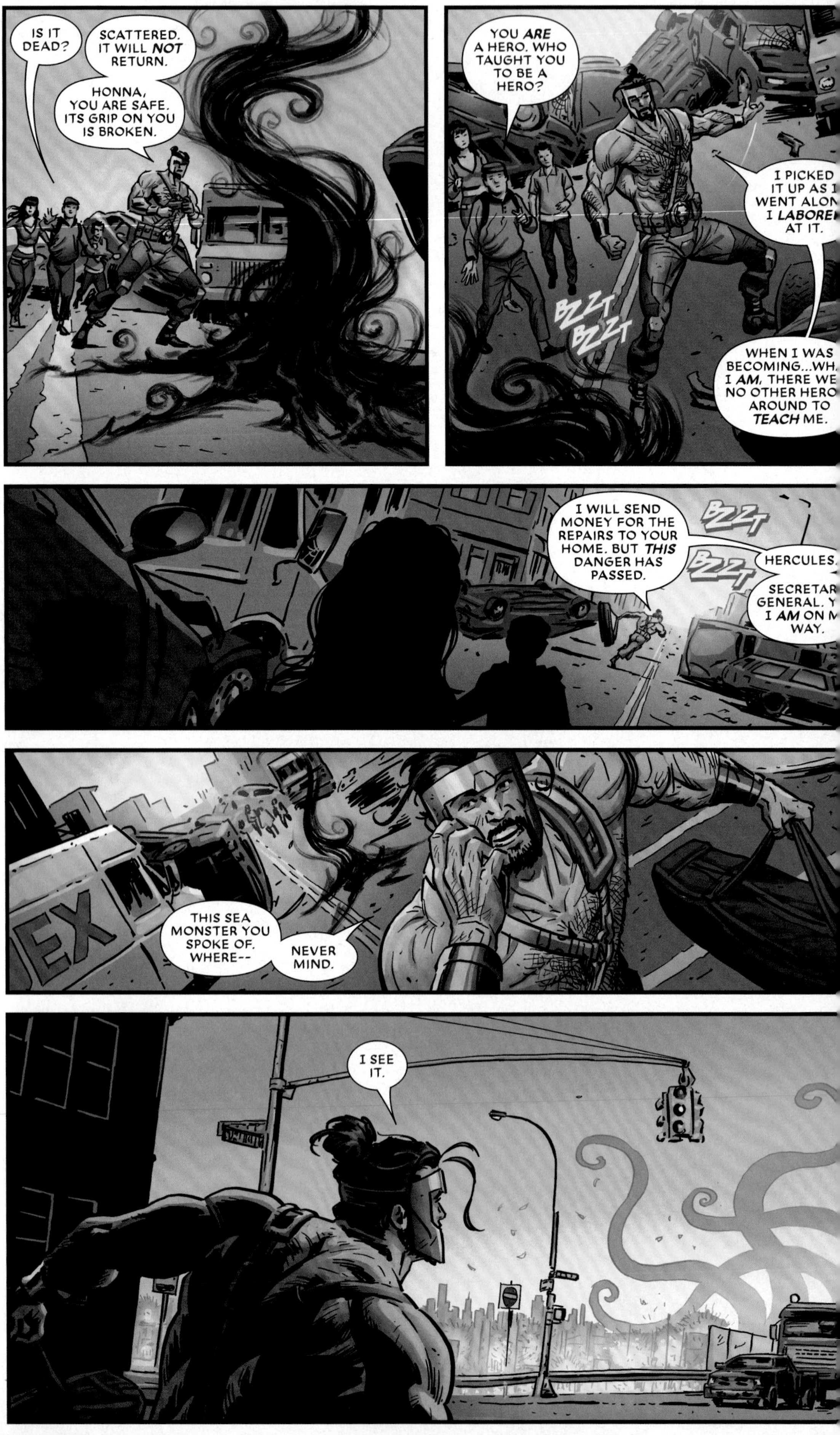
IS IT DEAD?
SCATTERED. IT WILL *NOT* RETURN.
HONNA, YOU ARE SAFE. ITS GRIP ON YOU IS BROKEN.
YOU *ARE* A HERO. WHO TAUGHT YOU TO BE A HERO?
BZZT
BZZT
I PICKED IT UP AS I WENT ALON I *LABORE* AT IT.
WHEN I WAS BECOMING...WH I *AM*, THERE WE NO OTHER HERO AROUND TO *TEACH* ME.
I WILL SEND MONEY FOR THE REPAIRS TO YOUR HOME. BUT *THIS* DANGER HAS PASSED.
BZZT
BZZT
HERCULES.
SECRETAR GENERAL. Y I *AM* ON M WAY.
EX
THIS SEA MONSTER YOU SPOKE OF. WHERE--
NEVER MIND.
I SEE IT.

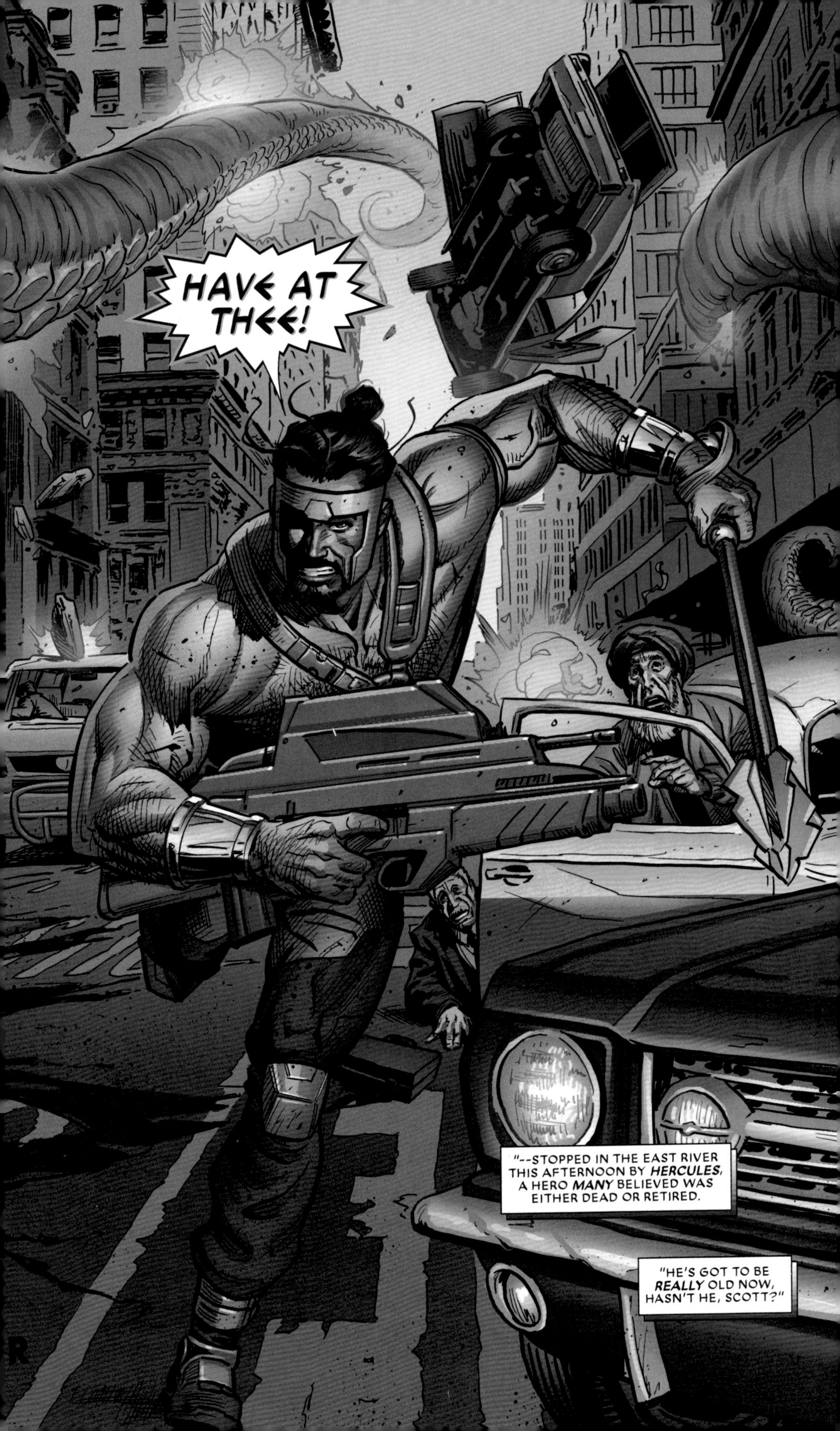
HAVE AT THEE!
"--STOPPED IN THE EAST RIVER THIS AFTERNOON BY *HERCULES*, A HERO *MANY* BELIEVED WAS EITHER DEAD OR RETIRED.
"HE'S GOT TO BE *REALLY* OLD NOW, HASN'T HE, SCOTT?"

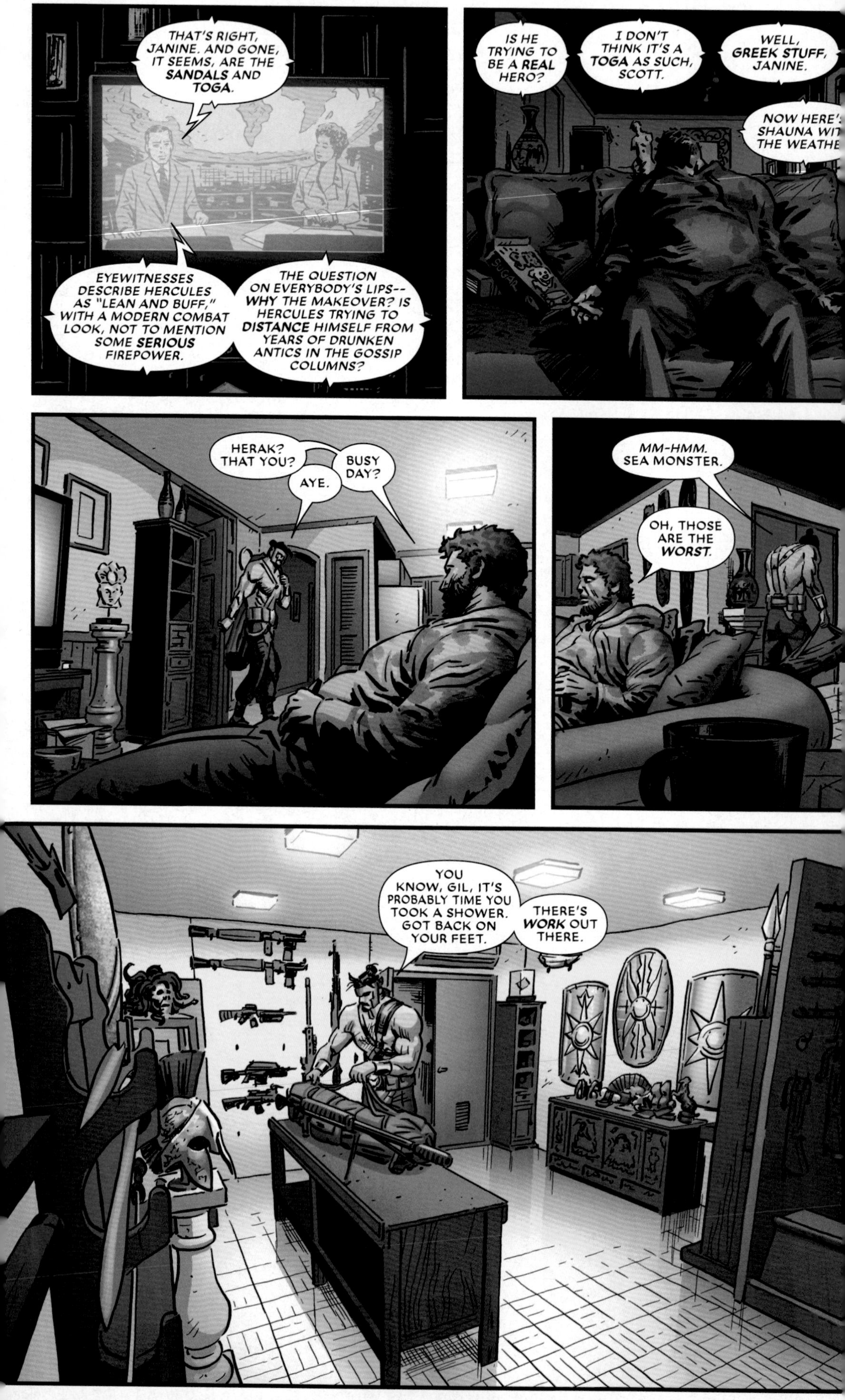
THAT'S RIGHT, JANINE. AND GONE, IT SEEMS, ARE THE **SANDALS** AND **TOGA**.
EYEWITNESSES DESCRIBE HERCULES AS "LEAN AND BUFF," WITH A MODERN COMBAT LOOK, NOT TO MENTION SOME **SERIOUS** FIREPOWER.
THE QUESTION ON EVERYBODY'S LIPS-- **WHY** THE MAKEOVER? IS HERCULES TRYING TO **DISTANCE** HIMSELF FROM YEARS OF DRUNKEN ANTICS IN THE GOSSIP COLUMNS?
IS HE TRYING TO BE A **REAL** HERO?
I DON'T THINK IT'S A **TOGA** AS SUCH, SCOTT.
WELL, **GREEK STUFF**, JANINE.
NOW HERE'S SHAUNA WIT THE WEATHE
SUGAR
HERAK? THAT YOU?
AYE.
BUSY DAY?
MM-HMM. SEA MONSTER.
OH, THOSE ARE THE ***WORST***.
YOU KNOW, GIL, IT'S PROBABLY TIME YOU TOOK A SHOWER. GOT BACK ON YOUR FEET.
THERE'S ***WORK*** OUT THERE.

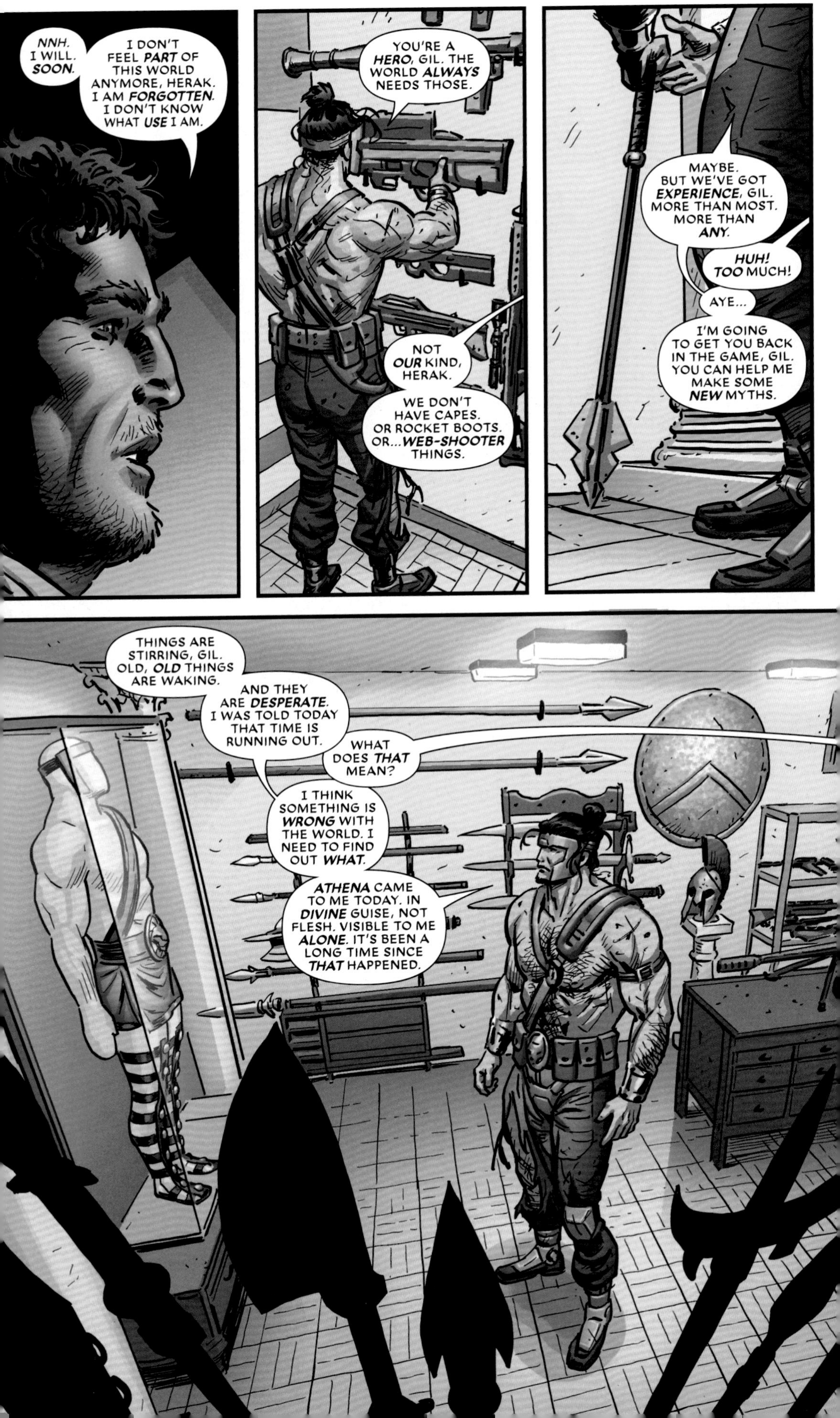
NNH. I WILL. SOON.
I DON'T FEEL PART OF THIS WORLD ANYMORE, HERAK. I AM FORGOTTEN. I DON'T KNOW WHAT USE I AM.
YOU'RE A HERO, GIL. THE WORLD ALWAYS NEEDS THOSE.
NOT OUR KIND, HERAK.
WE DON'T HAVE CAPES. OR ROCKET BOOTS. OR...WEB-SHOOTER THINGS.
MAYBE. BUT WE'VE GOT EXPERIENCE, GIL. MORE THAN MOST. MORE THAN ANY.
HUH! TOO MUCH!
AYE...
I'M GOING TO GET YOU BACK IN THE GAME, GIL. YOU CAN HELP ME MAKE SOME NEW MYTHS.
THINGS ARE STIRRING, GIL. OLD, OLD THINGS ARE WAKING.
AND THEY ARE DESPERATE. I WAS TOLD TODAY THAT TIME IS RUNNING OUT.
WHAT DOES THAT MEAN?
I THINK SOMETHING IS WRONG WITH THE WORLD. I NEED TO FIND OUT WHAT.
ATHENA CAME TO ME TODAY. IN DIVINE GUISE, NOT FLESH. VISIBLE TO ME ALONE. IT'S BEEN A LONG TIME SINCE THAT HAPPENED.

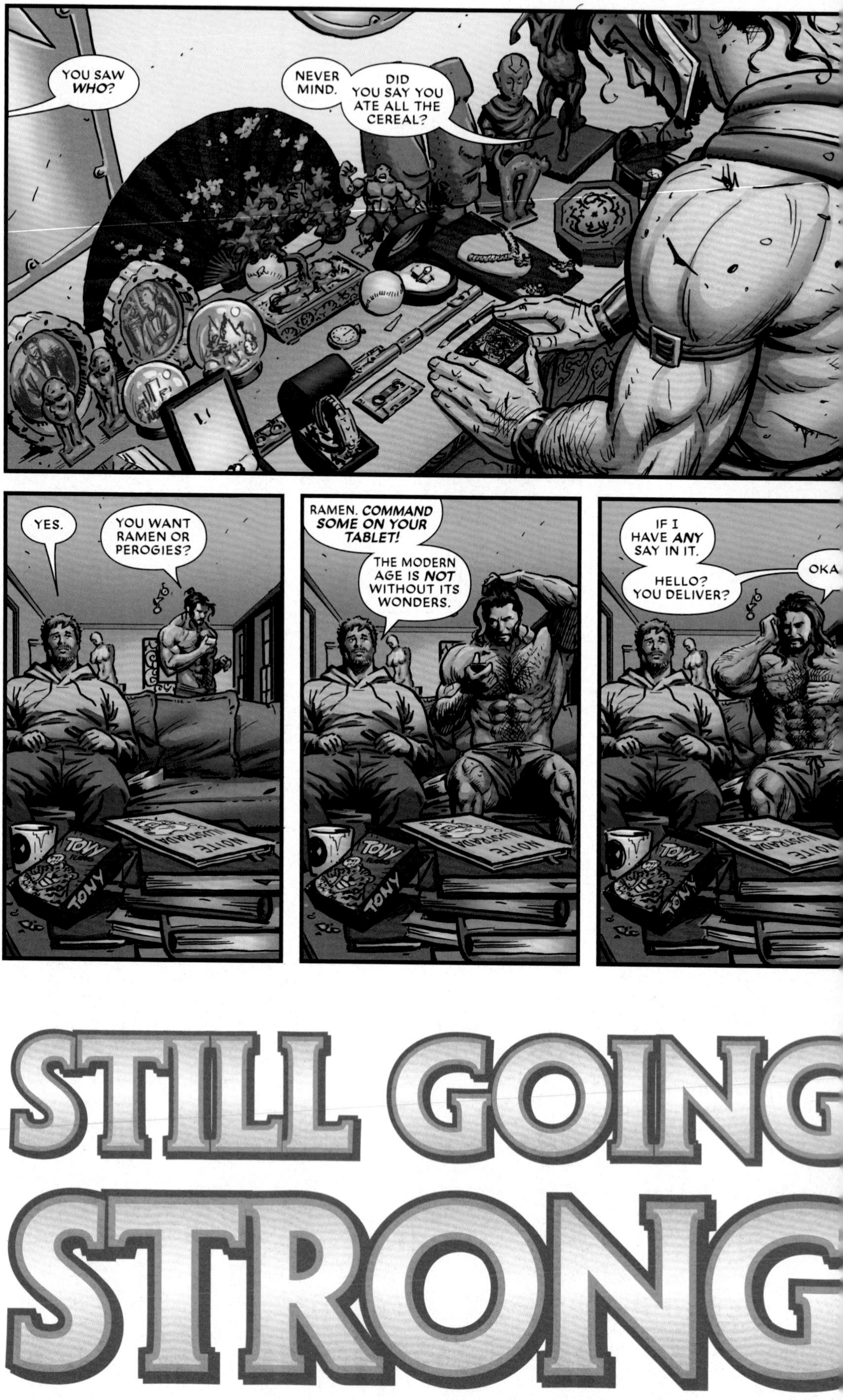
YOU SAW *WHO*?
NEVER MIND.
DID YOU SAY YOU ATE ALL THE CEREAL?
YES.
YOU WANT RAMEN OR PEROGIES?
RAMEN. *COMMAND SOME ON YOUR TABLET!*
THE MODERN AGE IS *NOT* WITHOUT ITS WONDERS.
IF I HAVE *ANY* SAY IN IT.
HELLO? YOU DELIVER?
OKA

STILL GOING STRONG

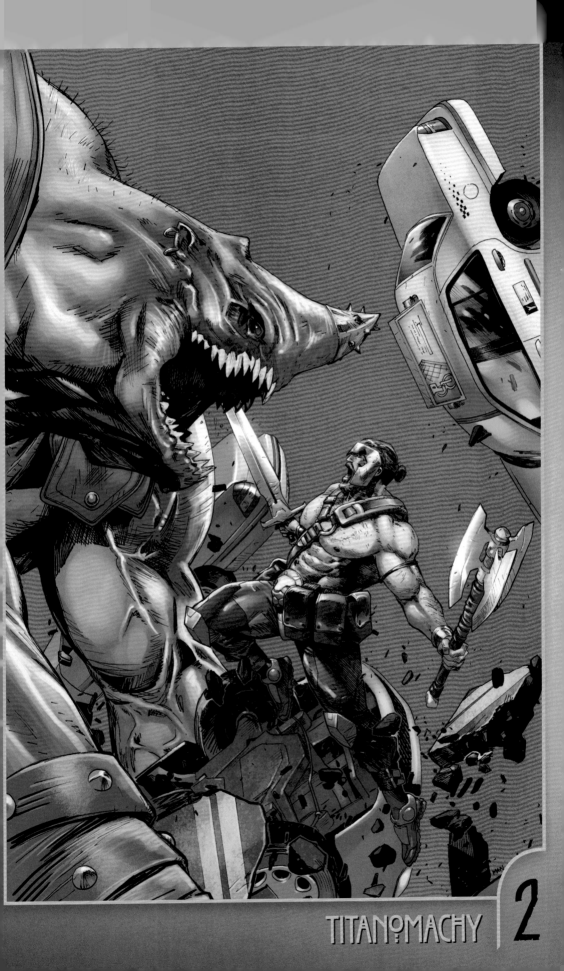

TITANOMACHY 2

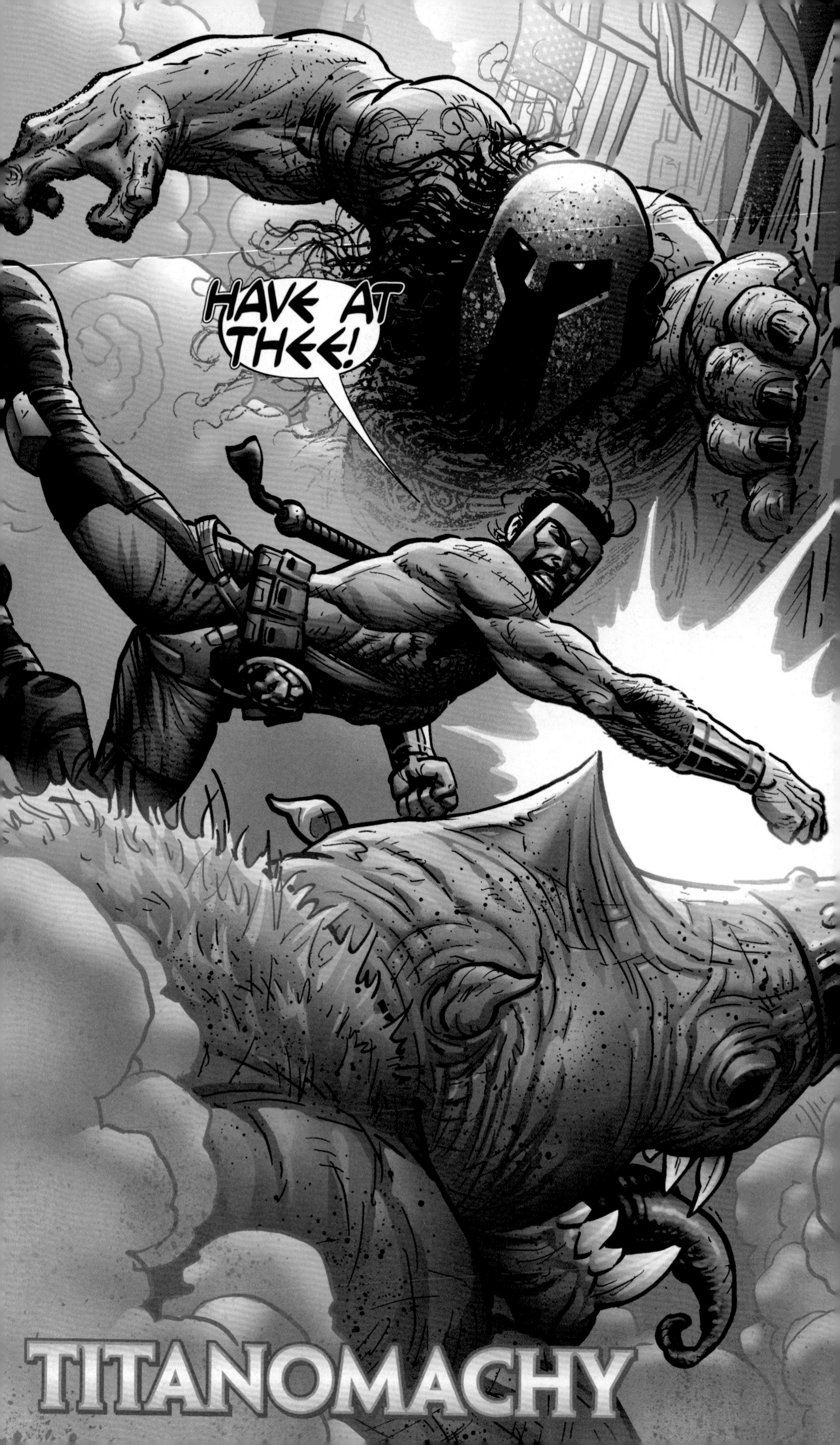
HAVE AT THEE!
TITANOMACHY

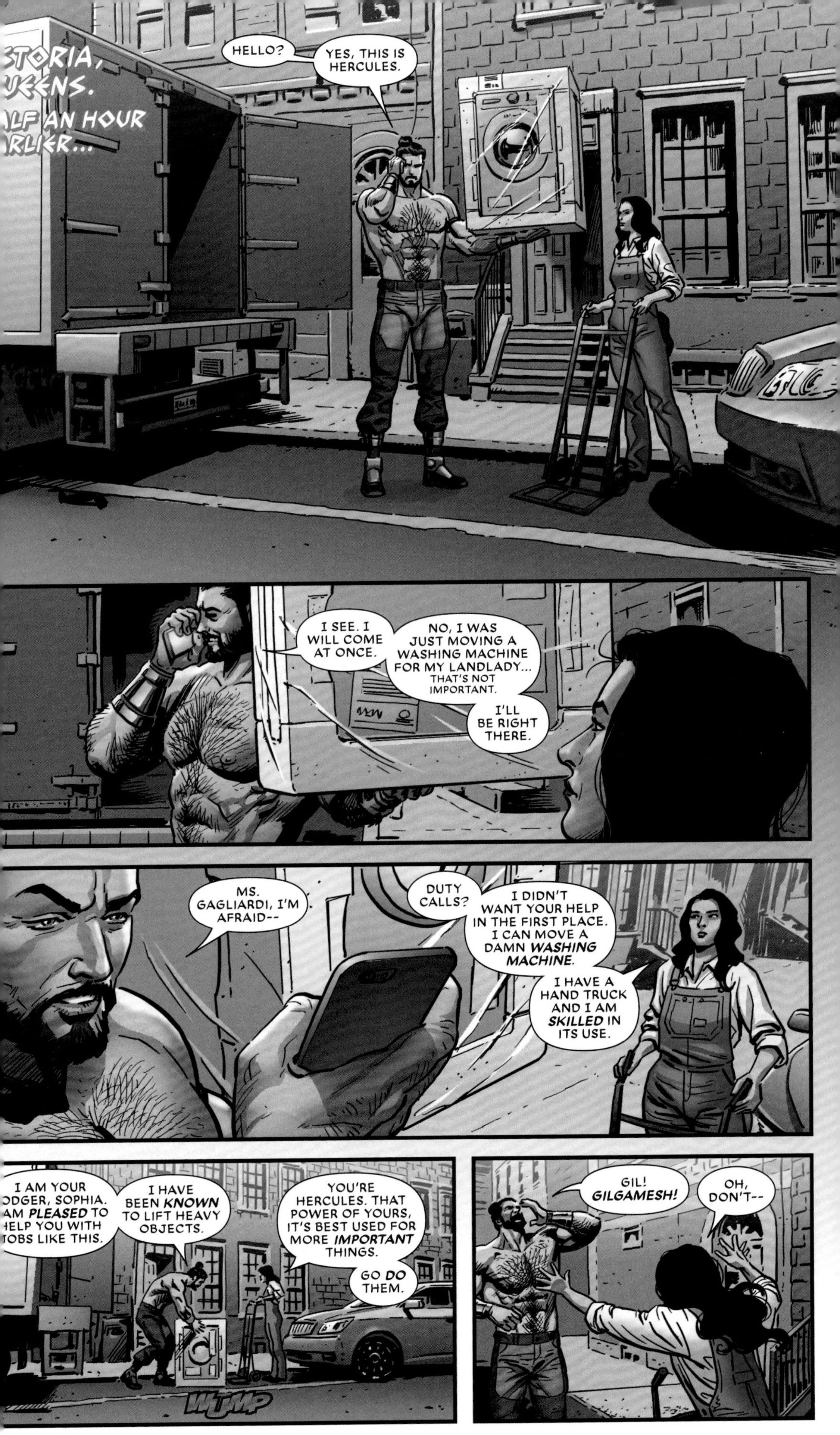

STORIA, UEENS. ALF AN HOUR RLIER...
HELLO?
YES, THIS IS HERCULES.
I SEE. I WILL COME AT ONCE.
NO, I WAS JUST MOVING A WASHING MACHINE FOR MY LANDLADY... THAT'S NOT IMPORTANT.
I'LL BE RIGHT THERE.
MS. GAGLIARDI, I'M AFRAID--
DUTY CALLS?
I DIDN'T WANT YOUR HELP IN THE FIRST PLACE. I CAN MOVE A DAMN *WASHING MACHINE*.
I HAVE A HAND TRUCK AND I AM *SKILLED* IN ITS USE.
I AM YOUR ODGER, SOPHIA. AM *PLEASED* TO HELP YOU WITH JOBS LIKE THIS.
I HAVE BEEN *KNOWN* TO LIFT HEAVY OBJECTS.
YOU'RE HERCULES. THAT POWER OF YOURS, IT'S BEST USED FOR MORE *IMPORTANT* THINGS.
GO *DO* THEM.
WUMP
GIL! *GILGAMESH!*
OH, DON'T--

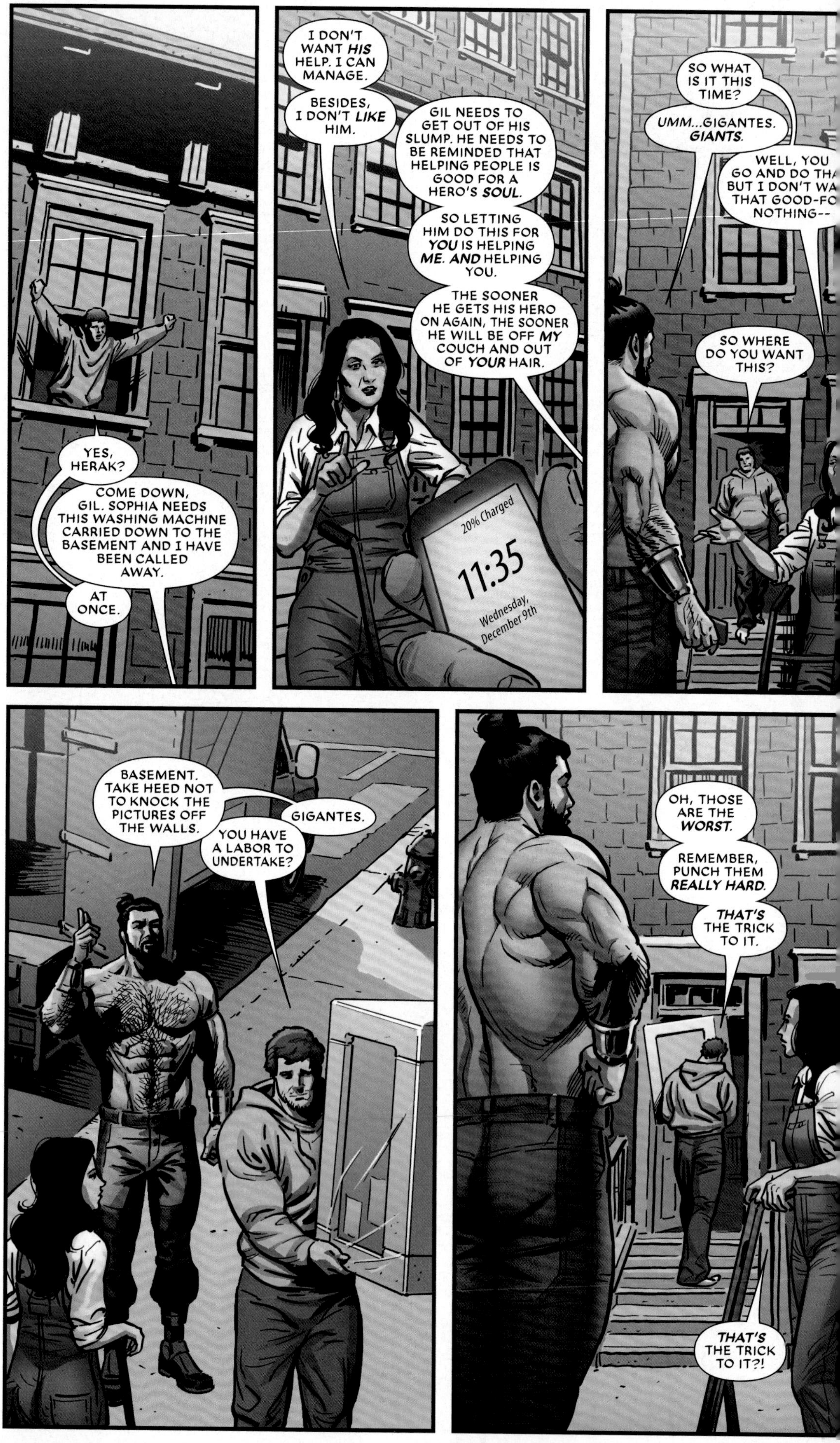
YES, HERAK?
COME DOWN, GIL. SOPHIA NEEDS THIS WASHING MACHINE CARRIED DOWN TO THE BASEMENT AND I HAVE BEEN CALLED AWAY.
AT ONCE.
I DON'T WANT HIS HELP. I CAN MANAGE.
BESIDES, I DON'T LIKE HIM.
GIL NEEDS TO GET OUT OF HIS SLUMP. HE NEEDS TO BE REMINDED THAT HELPING PEOPLE IS GOOD FOR A HERO'S SOUL.
SO LETTING HIM DO THIS FOR YOU IS HELPING ME. AND HELPING YOU.
THE SOONER HE GETS HIS HERO ON AGAIN, THE SOONER HE WILL BE OFF MY COUCH AND OUT OF YOUR HAIR.
20% Charged
11:35
Wednesday, December 9th
SO WHAT IS IT THIS TIME?
UMM...GIGANTES. GIANTS.
WELL, YOU GO AND DO THA BUT I DON'T WA THAT GOOD-FO NOTHING--
SO WHERE DO YOU WANT THIS?
BASEMENT. TAKE HEED NOT TO KNOCK THE PICTURES OFF THE WALLS.
GIGANTES.
YOU HAVE A LABOR TO UNDERTAKE?
OH, THOSE ARE THE WORST.
REMEMBER, PUNCH THEM REALLY HARD.
THAT'S THE TRICK TO IT.
THAT'S THE TRICK TO IT?!

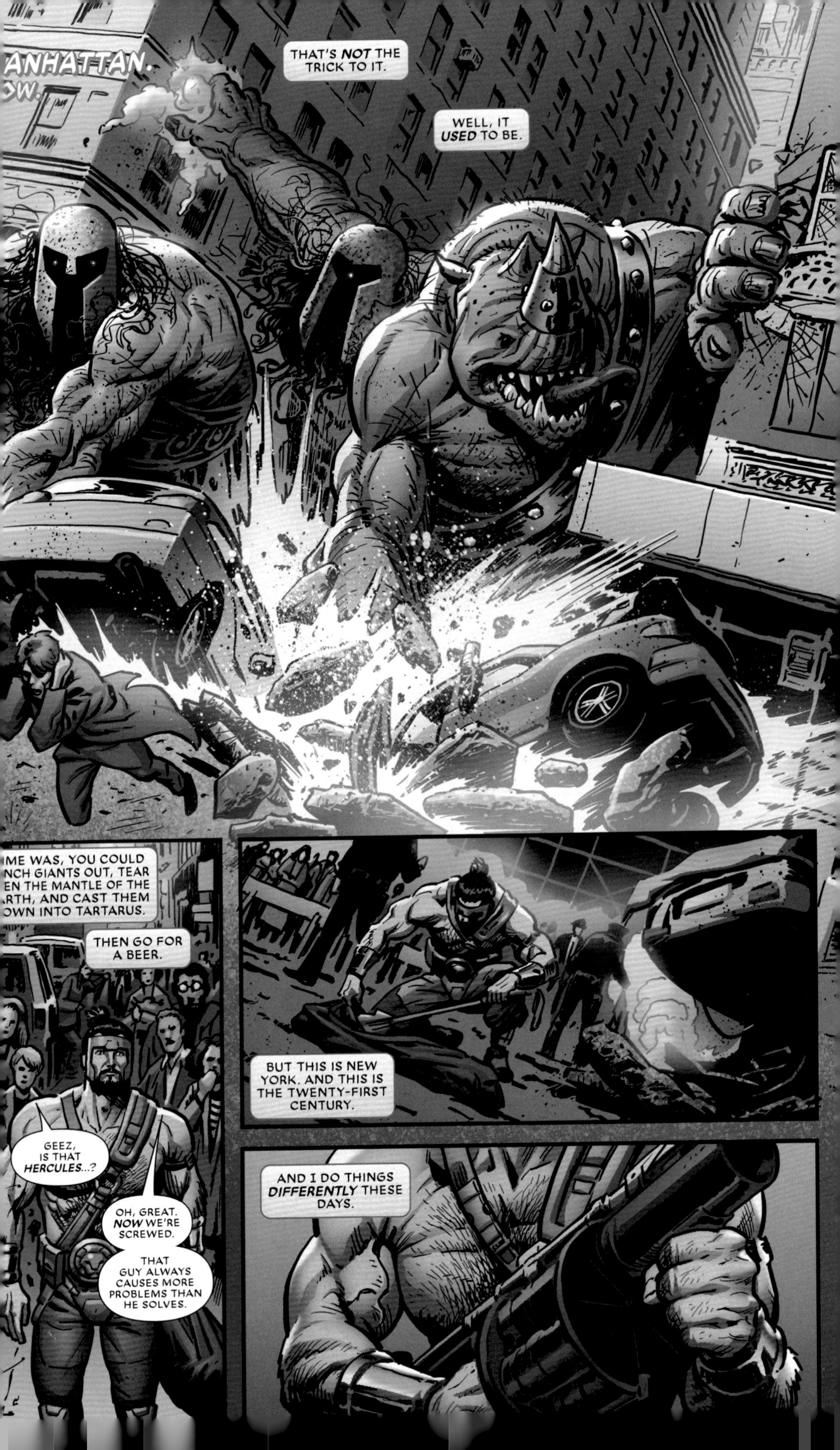

ANHATTAN.
OW.
THAT'S NOT THE TRICK TO IT.
WELL, IT USED TO BE.
IME WAS, YOU COULD NCH GIANTS OUT, TEAR EN THE MANTLE OF THE RTH, AND CAST THEM OWN INTO TARTARUS.
THEN GO FOR A BEER.
GEEZ, IS THAT HERCULES...?
OH, GREAT. NOW WE'RE SCREWED.
THAT GUY ALWAYS CAUSES MORE PROBLEMS THAN HE SOLVES.
BUT THIS IS NEW YORK. AND THIS IS THE TWENTY-FIRST CENTURY.
AND I DO THINGS DIFFERENTLY THESE DAYS.

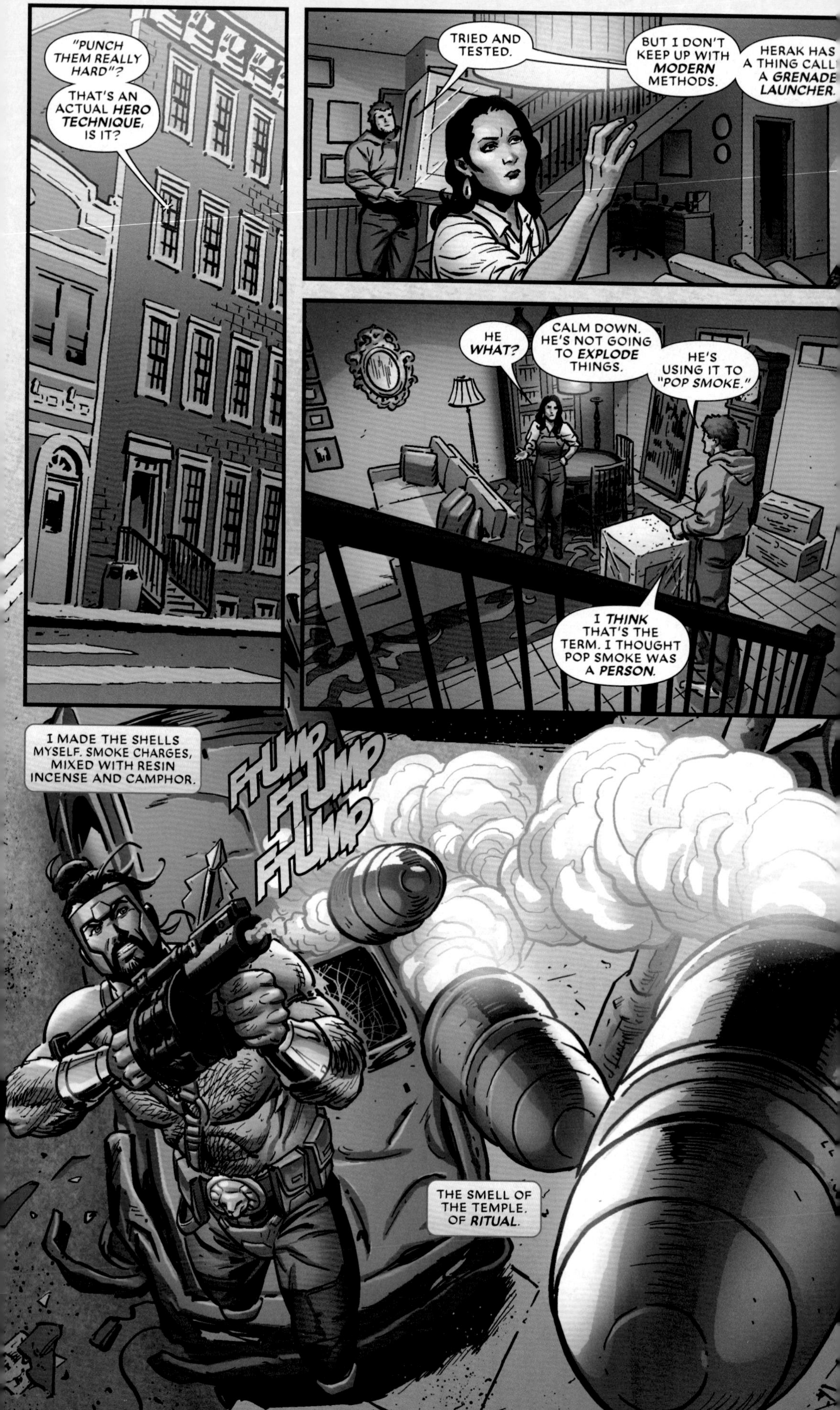
"PUNCH THEM REALLY HARD"?
THAT'S AN ACTUAL HERO TECHNIQUE, IS IT?
TRIED AND TESTED.
BUT I DON'T KEEP UP WITH MODERN METHODS.
HERAK HAS A THING CALL A GRENADE LAUNCHER.
HE WHAT?
CALM DOWN. HE'S NOT GOING TO EXPLODE THINGS.
HE'S USING IT TO "POP SMOKE."
I THINK THAT'S THE TERM. I THOUGHT POP SMOKE WAS A PERSON.
I MADE THE SHELLS MYSELF. SMOKE CHARGES, MIXED WITH RESIN INCENSE AND CAMPHOR.
FTUMP FTUMP FTUMP FTUMP
THE SMELL OF THE TEMPLE. OF RITUAL.

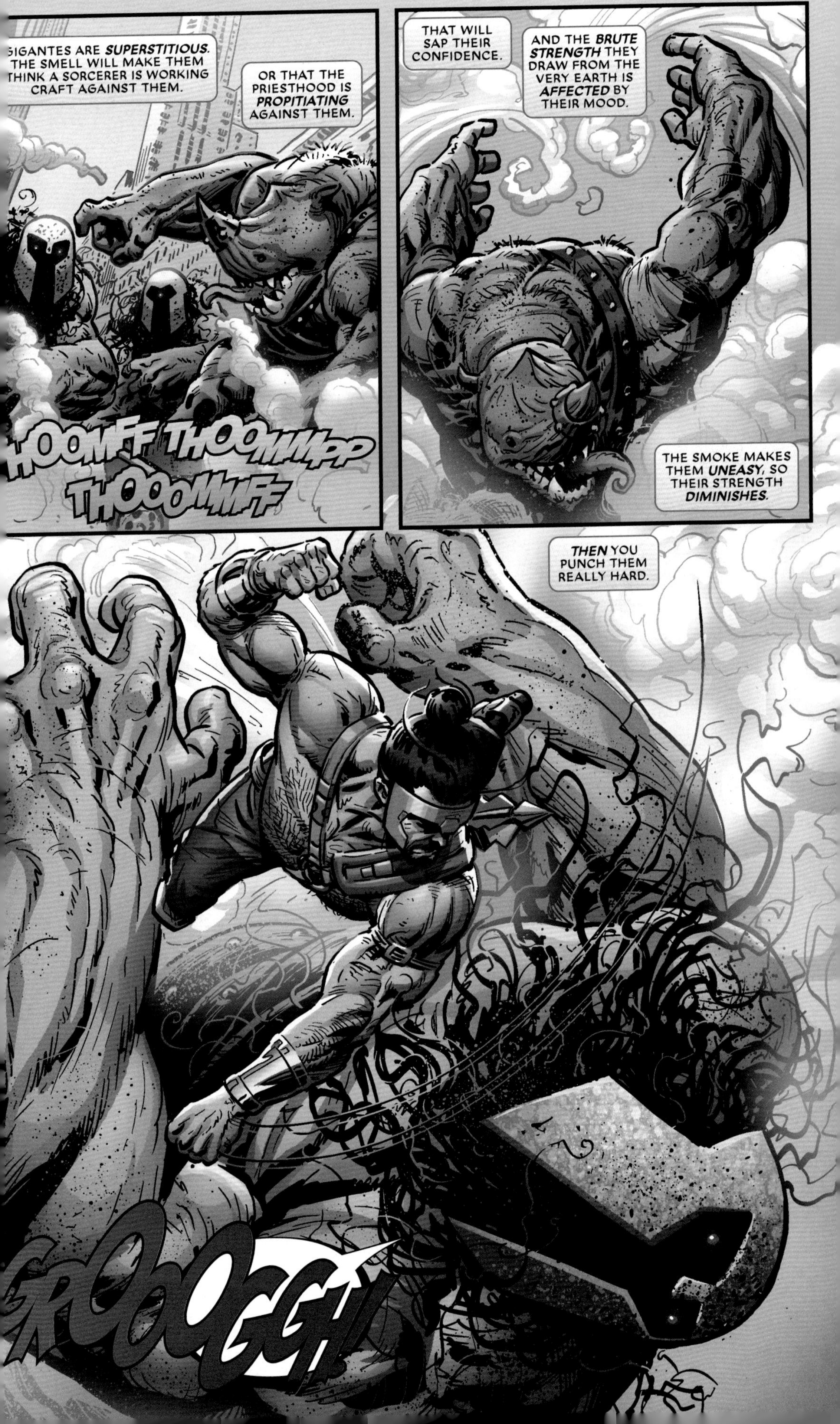
GIGANTES ARE SUPERSTITIOUS. THE SMELL WILL MAKE THEM THINK A SORCERER IS WORKING CRAFT AGAINST THEM.
OR THAT THE PRIESTHOOD IS PROPITIATING AGAINST THEM.
THOOMFF THOOMMPP
THOOOMMFF
THAT WILL SAP THEIR CONFIDENCE.
AND THE BRUTE STRENGTH THEY DRAW FROM THE VERY EARTH IS AFFECTED BY THEIR MOOD.
THE SMOKE MAKES THEM UNEASY, SO THEIR STRENGTH DIMINISHES.
THEN YOU PUNCH THEM REALLY HARD.
GROOGGH!

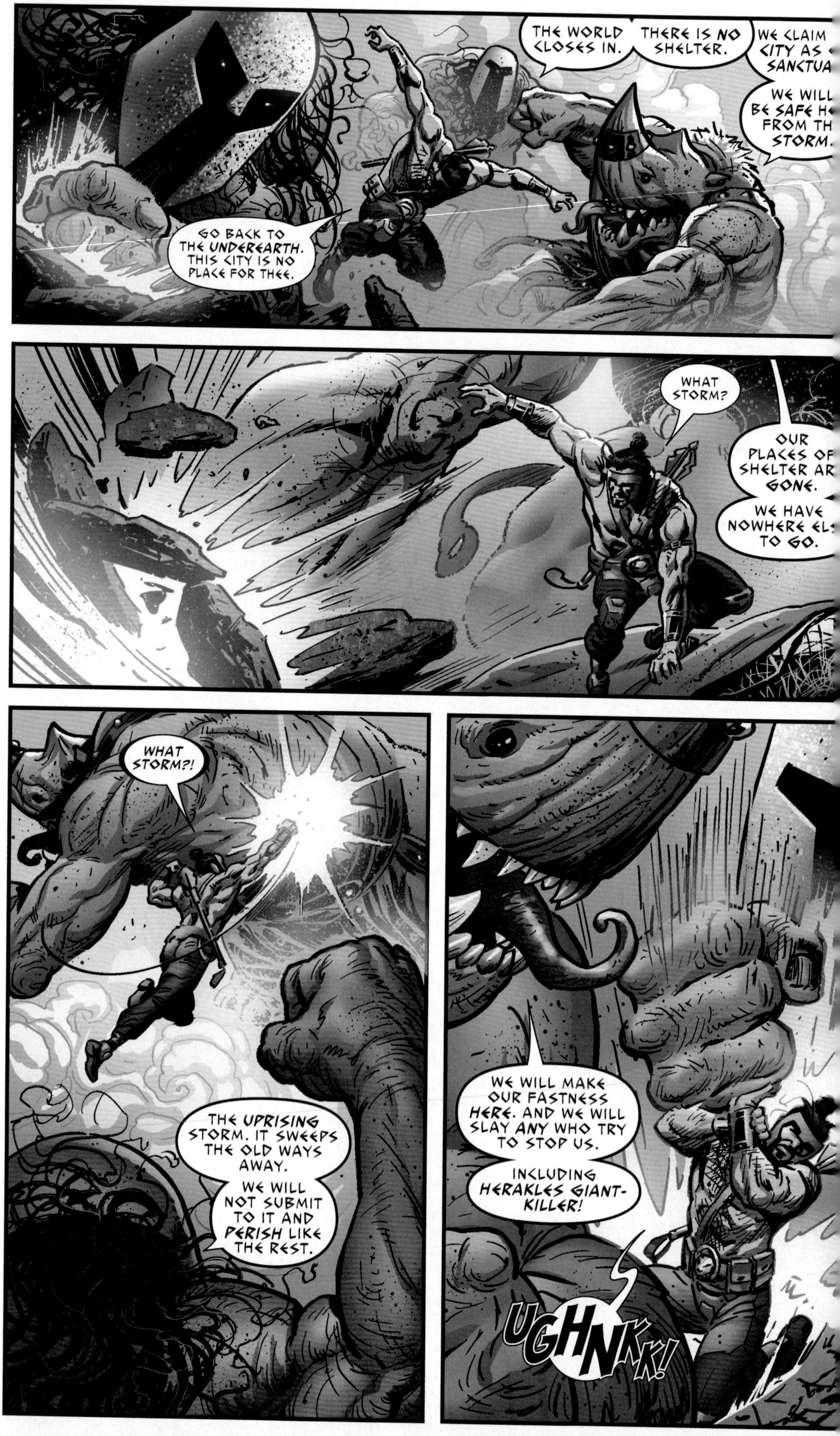
THE WORLD CLOSES IN.
THERE IS NO SHELTER.
WE CLAIM CITY AS SANCTUA
WE WILL BE SAFE H FROM TH STORM.
GO BACK TO THE UNDEREARTH. THIS CITY IS NO PLACE FOR THEE.
WHAT STORM?
OUR PLACES OF SHELTER AR GONE.
WE HAVE NOWHERE EL TO GO.
WHAT STORM?!
THE UPRISING STORM. IT SWEEPS THE OLD WAYS AWAY.
WE WILL NOT SUBMIT TO IT AND PERISH LIKE THE REST.
WE WILL MAKE OUR FASTNESS HERE. AND WE WILL SLAY ANY WHO TRY TO STOP US.
INCLUDING HERAKLES GIANT-KILLER!
UGHNKK!

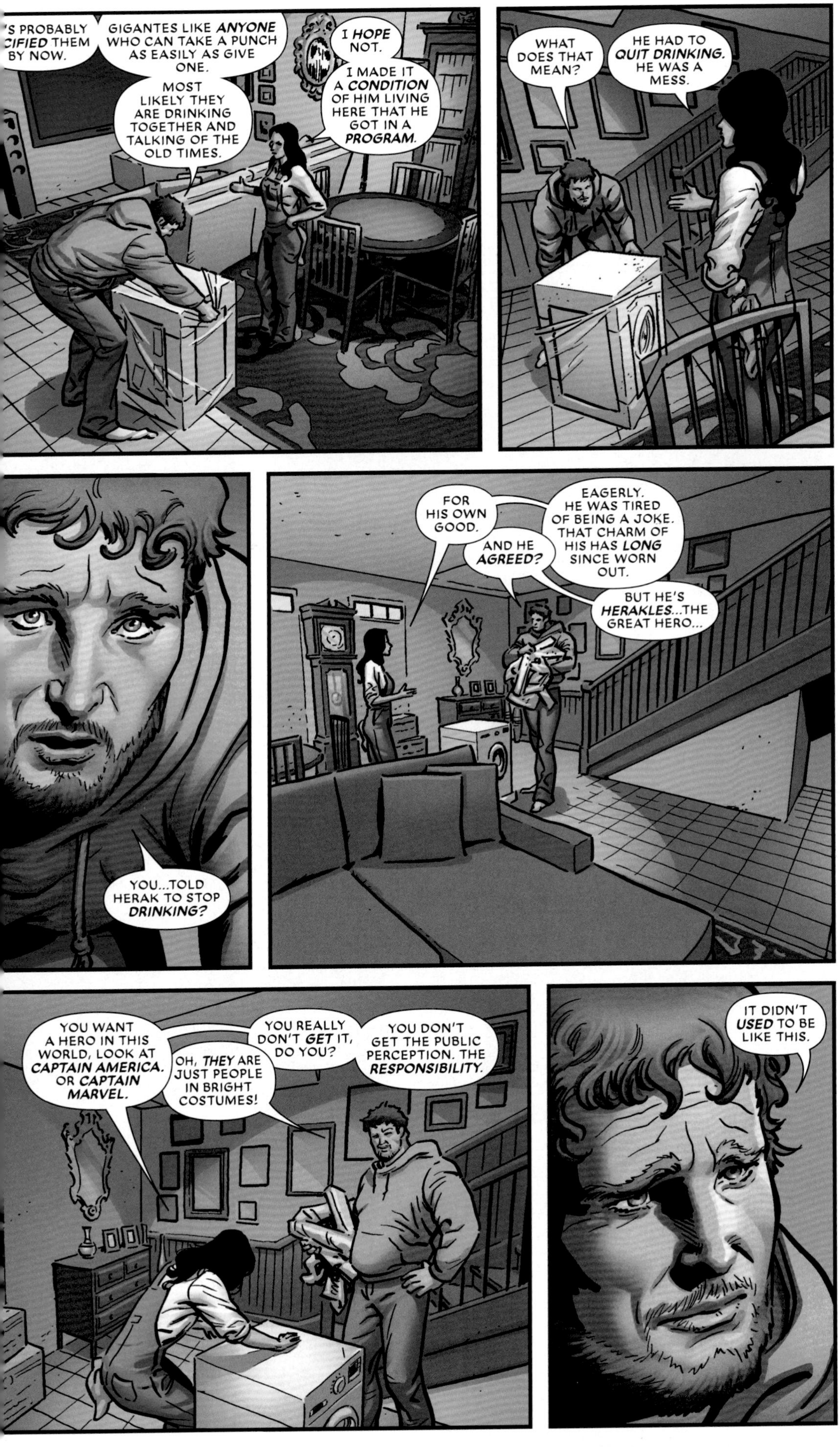

'S PROBABLY
CIFIED THEM BY NOW.
GIGANTES LIKE ANYONE WHO CAN TAKE A PUNCH AS EASILY AS GIVE ONE.
MOST LIKELY THEY ARE DRINKING TOGETHER AND TALKING OF THE OLD TIMES.
I HOPE NOT.
I MADE IT A CONDITION OF HIM LIVING HERE THAT HE GOT IN A PROGRAM.
WHAT DOES THAT MEAN?
HE HAD TO QUIT DRINKING. HE WAS A MESS.
YOU...TOLD HERAK TO STOP DRINKING?
FOR HIS OWN GOOD.
AND HE AGREED?
EAGERLY. HE WAS TIRED OF BEING A JOKE. THAT CHARM OF HIS HAS LONG SINCE WORN OUT.
BUT HE'S HERAKLES...THE GREAT HERO...
YOU WANT A HERO IN THIS WORLD, LOOK AT CAPTAIN AMERICA. OR CAPTAIN MARVEL.
OH, THEY ARE JUST PEOPLE IN BRIGHT COSTUMES!
YOU REALLY DON'T GET IT, DO YOU?
YOU DON'T GET THE PUBLIC PERCEPTION. THE RESPONSIBILITY.
IT DIDN'T USED TO BE LIKE THIS.

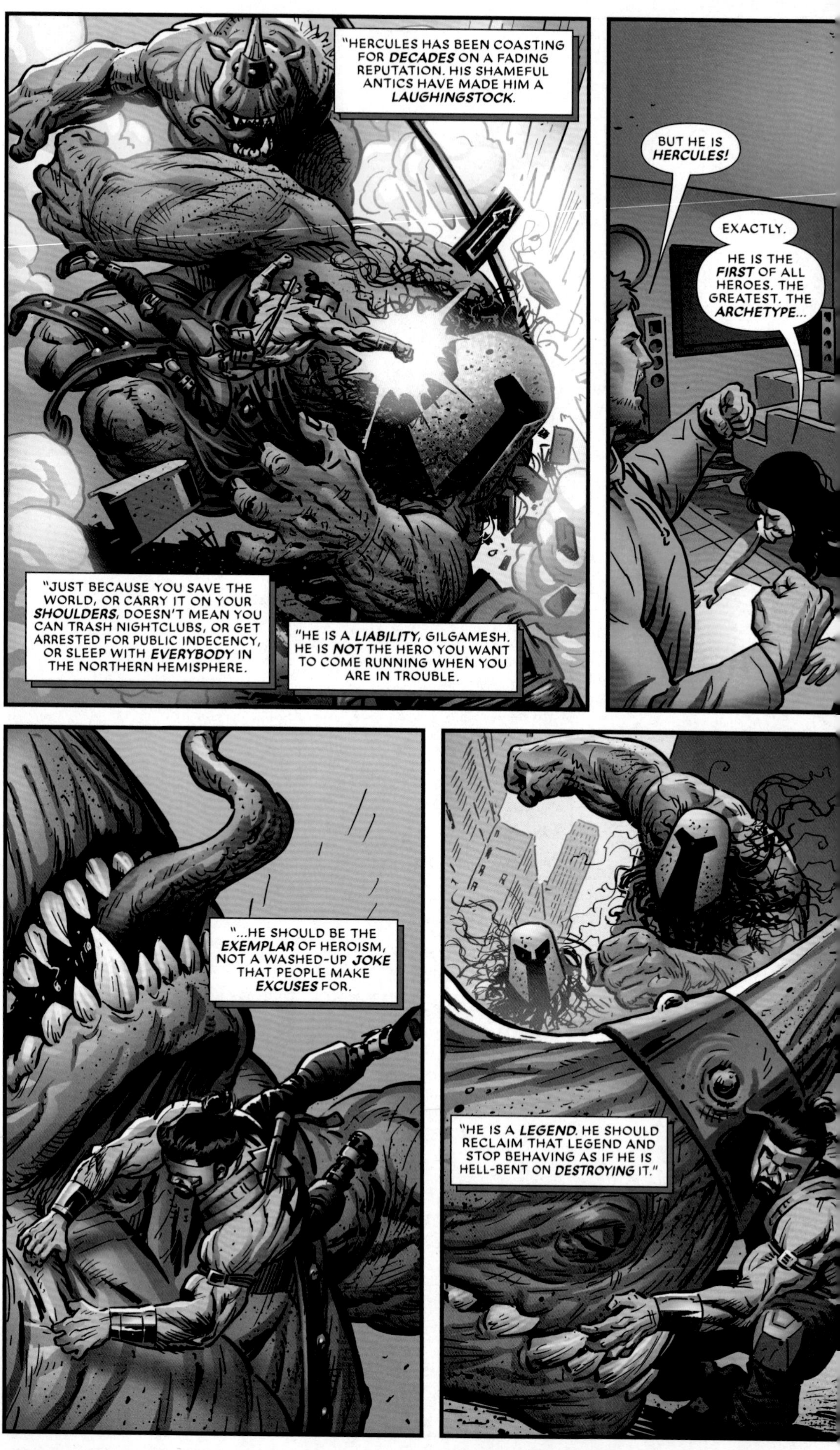
"HERCULES HAS BEEN COASTING FOR DECADES ON A FADING REPUTATION. HIS SHAMEFUL ANTICS HAVE MADE HIM A LAUGHINGSTOCK.
"JUST BECAUSE YOU SAVE THE WORLD, OR CARRY IT ON YOUR SHOULDERS, DOESN'T MEAN YOU CAN TRASH NIGHTCLUBS, OR GET ARRESTED FOR PUBLIC INDECENCY, OR SLEEP WITH EVERYBODY IN THE NORTHERN HEMISPHERE.
"HE IS A LIABILITY, GILGAMESH. HE IS NOT THE HERO YOU WANT TO COME RUNNING WHEN YOU ARE IN TROUBLE.
BUT HE IS HERCULES!
EXACTLY.
HE IS THE FIRST OF ALL HEROES. THE GREATEST. THE ARCHETYPE...
"...HE SHOULD BE THE EXEMPLAR OF HEROISM, NOT A WASHED-UP JOKE THAT PEOPLE MAKE EXCUSES FOR.
"HE IS A LEGEND. HE SHOULD RECLAIM THAT LEGEND AND STOP BEHAVING AS IF HE IS HELL-BENT ON DESTROYING IT."

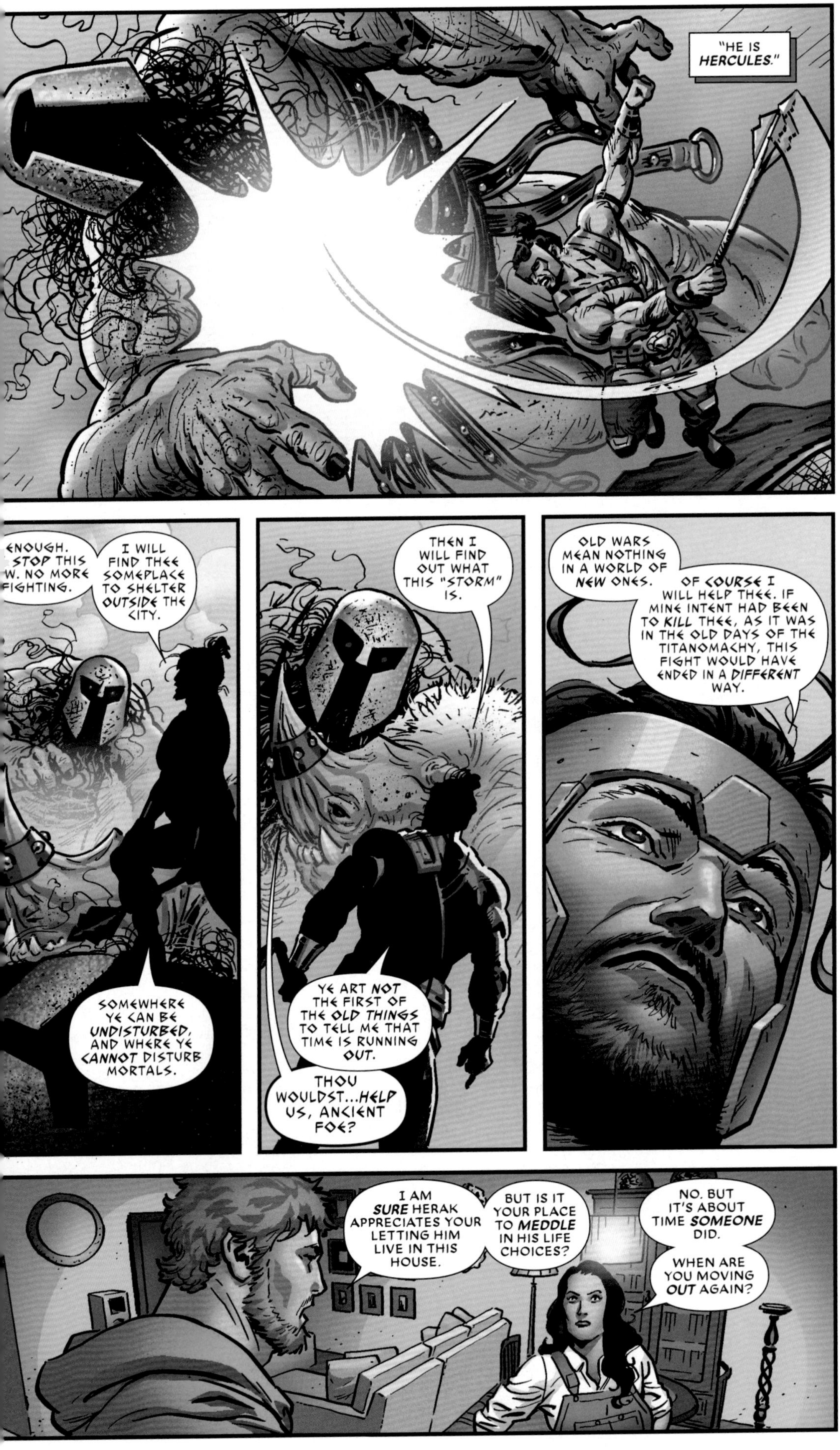
"HE IS HERCULES."
ENOUGH. STOP THIS W. NO MORE FIGHTING.
I WILL FIND THEE SOMEPLACE TO SHELTER OUTSIDE THE CITY.
SOMEWHERE YE CAN BE UNDISTURBED, AND WHERE YE CANNOT DISTURB MORTALS.
THEN I WILL FIND OUT WHAT THIS "STORM" IS.
YE ART NOT THE FIRST OF THE OLD THINGS TO TELL ME THAT TIME IS RUNNING OUT.
THOU WOULDST...HELP US, ANCIENT FOE?
OLD WARS MEAN NOTHING IN A WORLD OF NEW ONES.
OF COURSE I WILL HELP THEE. IF MINE INTENT HAD BEEN TO KILL THEE, AS IT WAS IN THE OLD DAYS OF THE TITANOMACHY, THIS FIGHT WOULD HAVE ENDED IN A DIFFERENT WAY.
I AM SURE HERAK APPRECIATES YOUR LETTING HIM LIVE IN THIS HOUSE.
BUT IS IT YOUR PLACE TO MEDDLE IN HIS LIFE CHOICES?
NO. BUT IT'S ABOUT TIME SOMEONE DID.
WHEN ARE YOU MOVING OUT AGAIN?

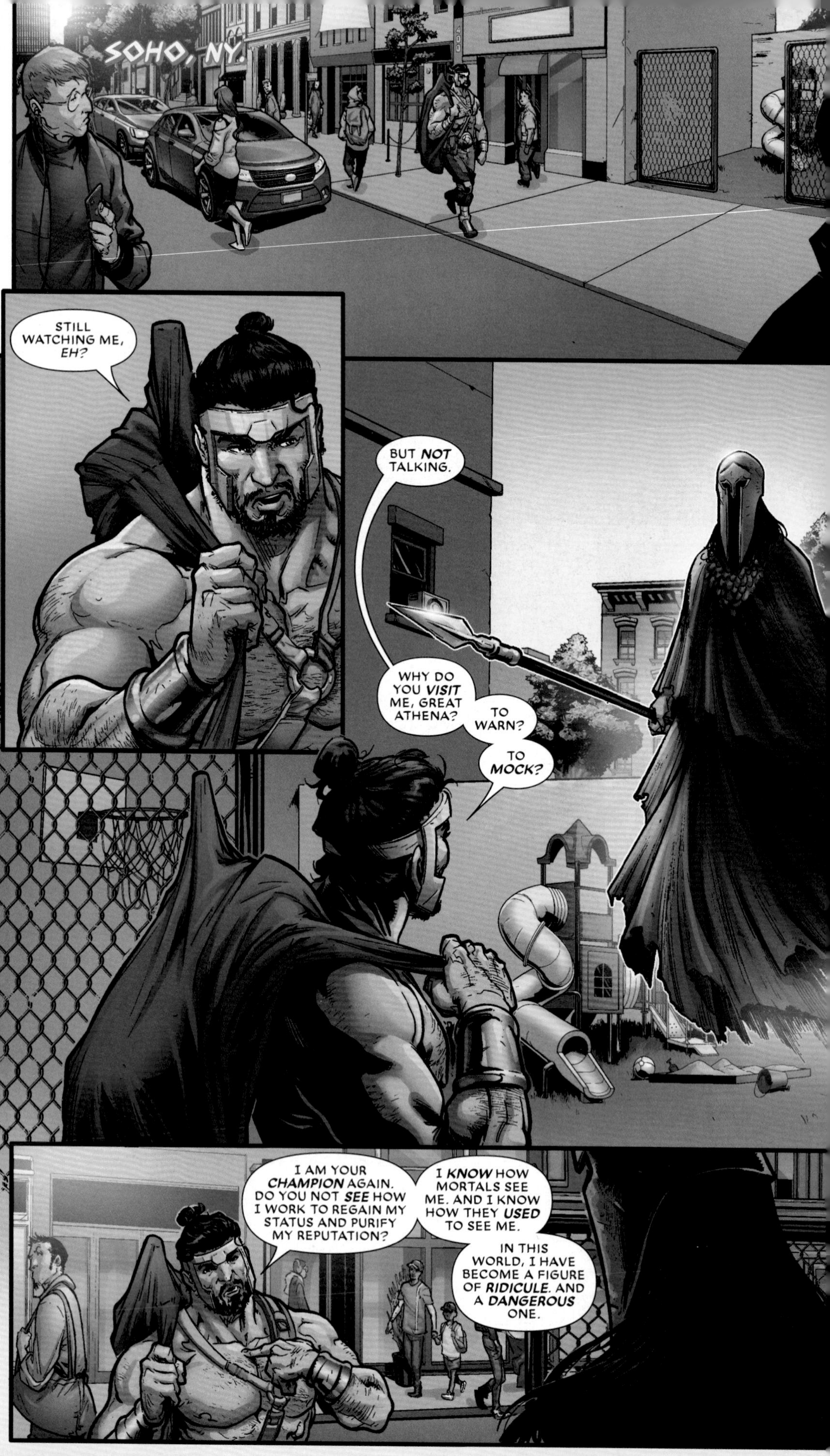
SOHO, NY.
STILL WATCHING ME, *EH?*
BUT **NOT** TALKING.
WHY DO YOU **VISIT** ME, GREAT ATHENA?
TO WARN?
TO **MOCK?**
I AM YOUR **CHAMPION** AGAIN. DO YOU NOT **SEE** HOW I WORK TO REGAIN MY STATUS AND PURIFY MY REPUTATION?
I **KNOW** HOW MORTALS SEE ME. AND I KNOW HOW THEY **USED** TO SEE ME.
IN THIS WORLD, I HAVE BECOME A FIGURE OF **RIDICULE**. AND A **DANGEROUS** ONE.

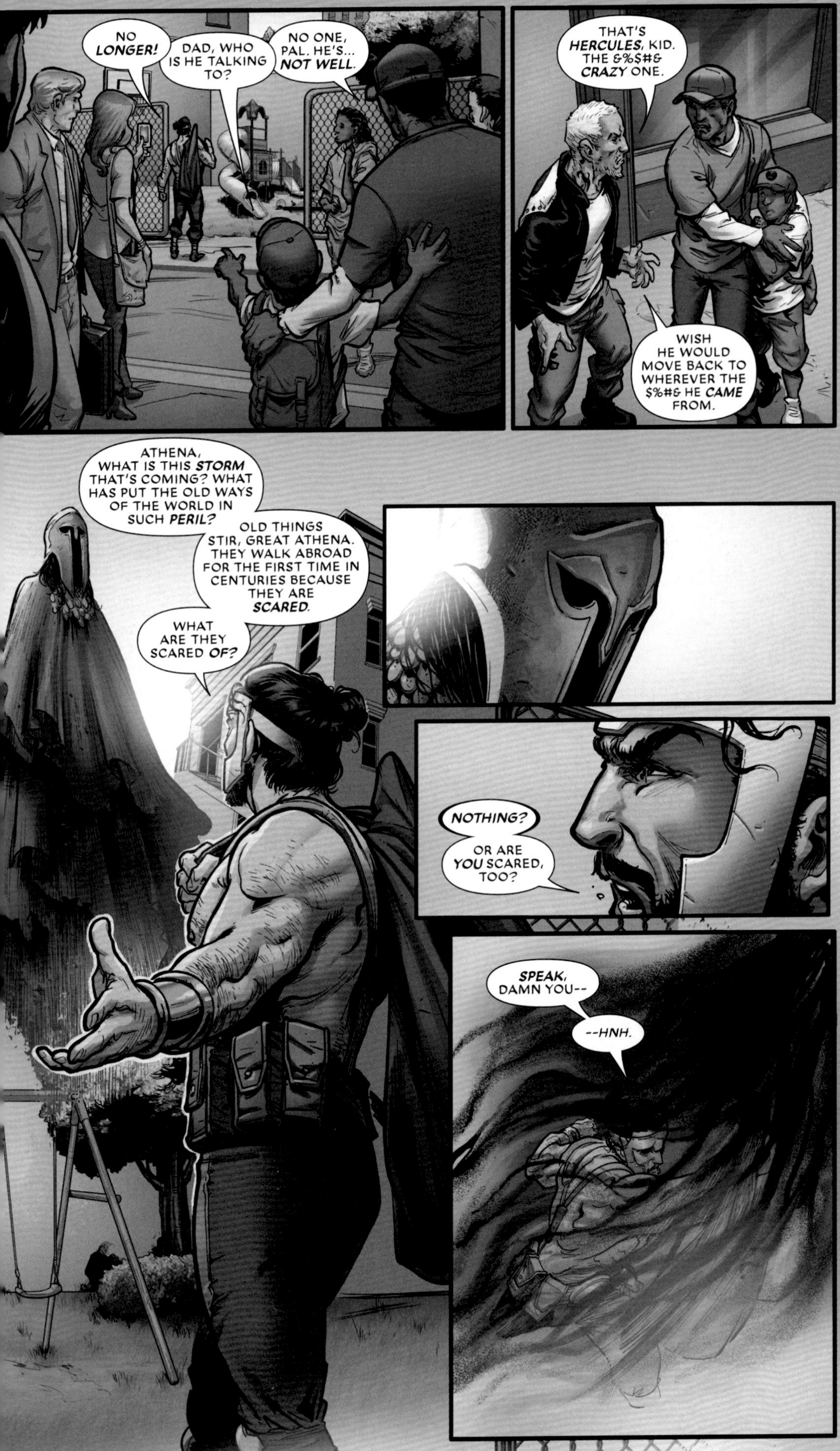

NO LONGER!
DAD, WHO IS HE TALKING TO?
NO ONE, PAL. HE'S... NOT WELL.
THAT'S HERCULES, KID. THE &%$#& CRAZY ONE.
WISH HE WOULD MOVE BACK TO WHEREVER THE $%#& HE CAME FROM.
ATHENA, WHAT IS THIS STORM THAT'S COMING? WHAT HAS PUT THE OLD WAYS OF THE WORLD IN SUCH PERIL?
OLD THINGS STIR, GREAT ATHENA. THEY WALK ABROAD FOR THE FIRST TIME IN CENTURIES BECAUSE THEY ARE SCARED.
WHAT ARE THEY SCARED OF?
NOTHING?
OR ARE YOU SCARED, TOO?
SPEAK, DAMN YOU--
--HNH.

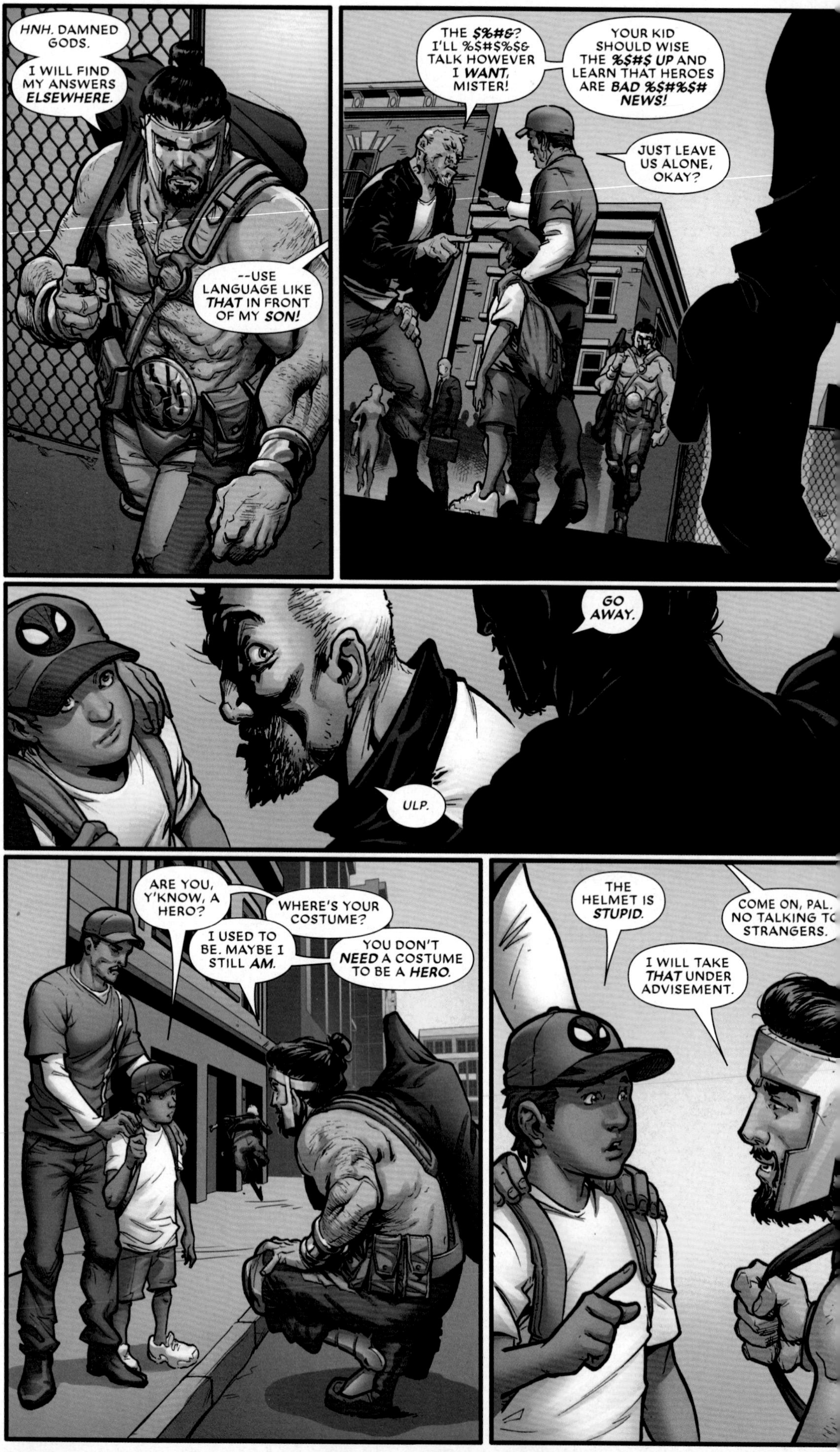

HNH. DAMNED GODS.
I WILL FIND MY ANSWERS ELSEWHERE.
--USE LANGUAGE LIKE THAT IN FRONT OF MY SON!
THE $%#&? I'LL %$#$%$& TALK HOWEVER I WANT, MISTER!
YOUR KID SHOULD WISE THE %$#$ UP AND LEARN THAT HEROES ARE BAD %$#%$# NEWS!
JUST LEAVE US ALONE, OKAY?
GO AWAY.
ULP.
ARE YOU, Y'KNOW, A HERO?
WHERE'S YOUR COSTUME?
I USED TO BE. MAYBE I STILL AM.
YOU DON'T NEED A COSTUME TO BE A HERO.
THE HELMET IS STUPID.
COME ON, PAL. NO TALKING TO STRANGERS.
I WILL TAKE THAT UNDER ADVISEMENT.

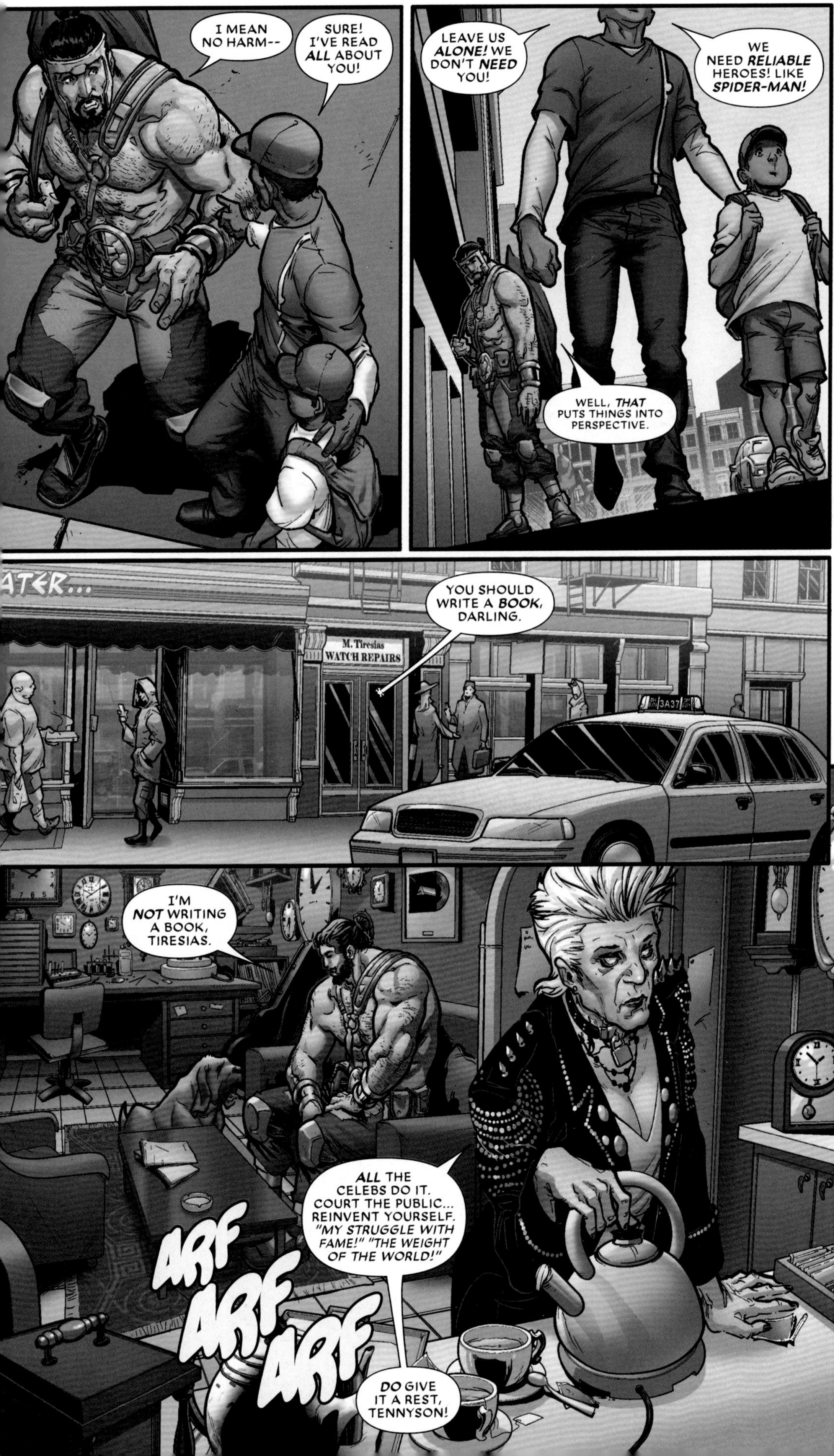

I MEAN NO HARM--
SURE! I'VE READ ALL ABOUT YOU!
LEAVE US ALONE! WE DON'T NEED YOU!
WE NEED RELIABLE HEROES! LIKE SPIDER-MAN!
WELL, THAT PUTS THINGS INTO PERSPECTIVE.
ATER...
YOU SHOULD WRITE A BOOK, DARLING.
M. Tiresias WATCH REPAIRS
3A37
I'M NOT WRITING A BOOK, TIRESIAS.
ALL THE CELEBS DO IT. COURT THE PUBLIC... REINVENT YOURSELF. "MY STRUGGLE WITH FAME!" "THE WEIGHT OF THE WORLD!"
ARF ARF ARF
DO GIVE IT A REST, TENNYSON!

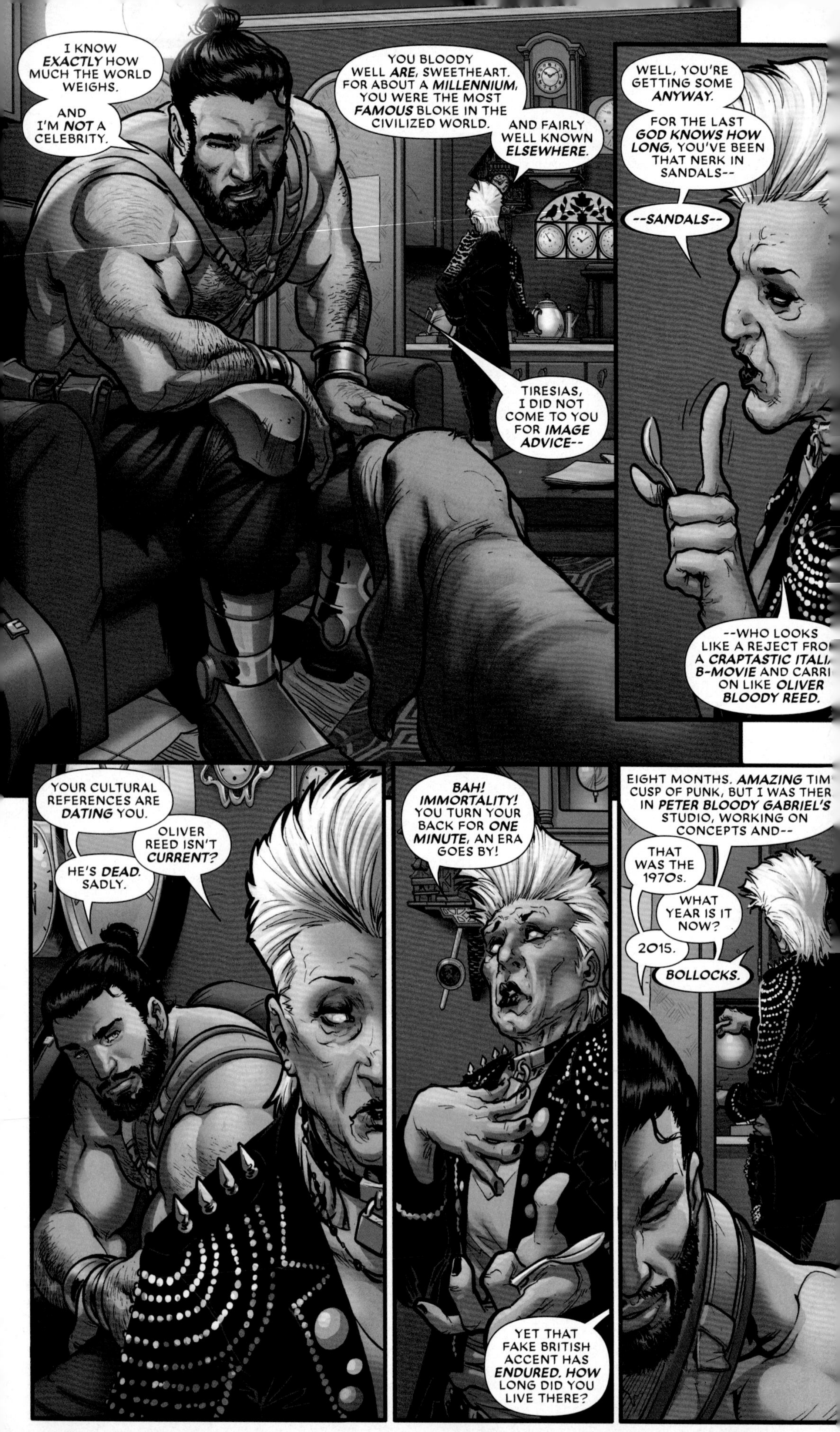
I KNOW EXACTLY HOW MUCH THE WORLD WEIGHS.
AND I'M NOT A CELEBRITY.
YOU BLOODY WELL ARE, SWEETHEART. FOR ABOUT A MILLENNIUM, YOU WERE THE MOST FAMOUS BLOKE IN THE CIVILIZED WORLD.
AND FAIRLY WELL KNOWN ELSEWHERE.
TIRESIAS, I DID NOT COME TO YOU FOR IMAGE ADVICE--
WELL, YOU'RE GETTING SOME ANYWAY.
FOR THE LAST GOD KNOWS HOW LONG, YOU'VE BEEN THAT NERK IN SANDALS--
--SANDALS--
--WHO LOOKS LIKE A REJECT FRO A CRAPTASTIC ITALI B-MOVIE AND CARRI ON LIKE OLIVER BLOODY REED.
YOUR CULTURAL REFERENCES ARE DATING YOU.
OLIVER REED ISN'T CURRENT?
HE'S DEAD. SADLY.
BAH! IMMORTALITY! YOU TURN YOUR BACK FOR ONE MINUTE, AN ERA GOES BY!
YET THAT FAKE BRITISH ACCENT HAS ENDURED. HOW LONG DID YOU LIVE THERE?
EIGHT MONTHS. AMAZING TIM CUSP OF PUNK, BUT I WAS THER IN PETER BLOODY GABRIEL'S STUDIO, WORKING ON CONCEPTS AND--
THAT WAS THE 1970s.
WHAT YEAR IS IT NOW?
2015.
BOLLOCKS.

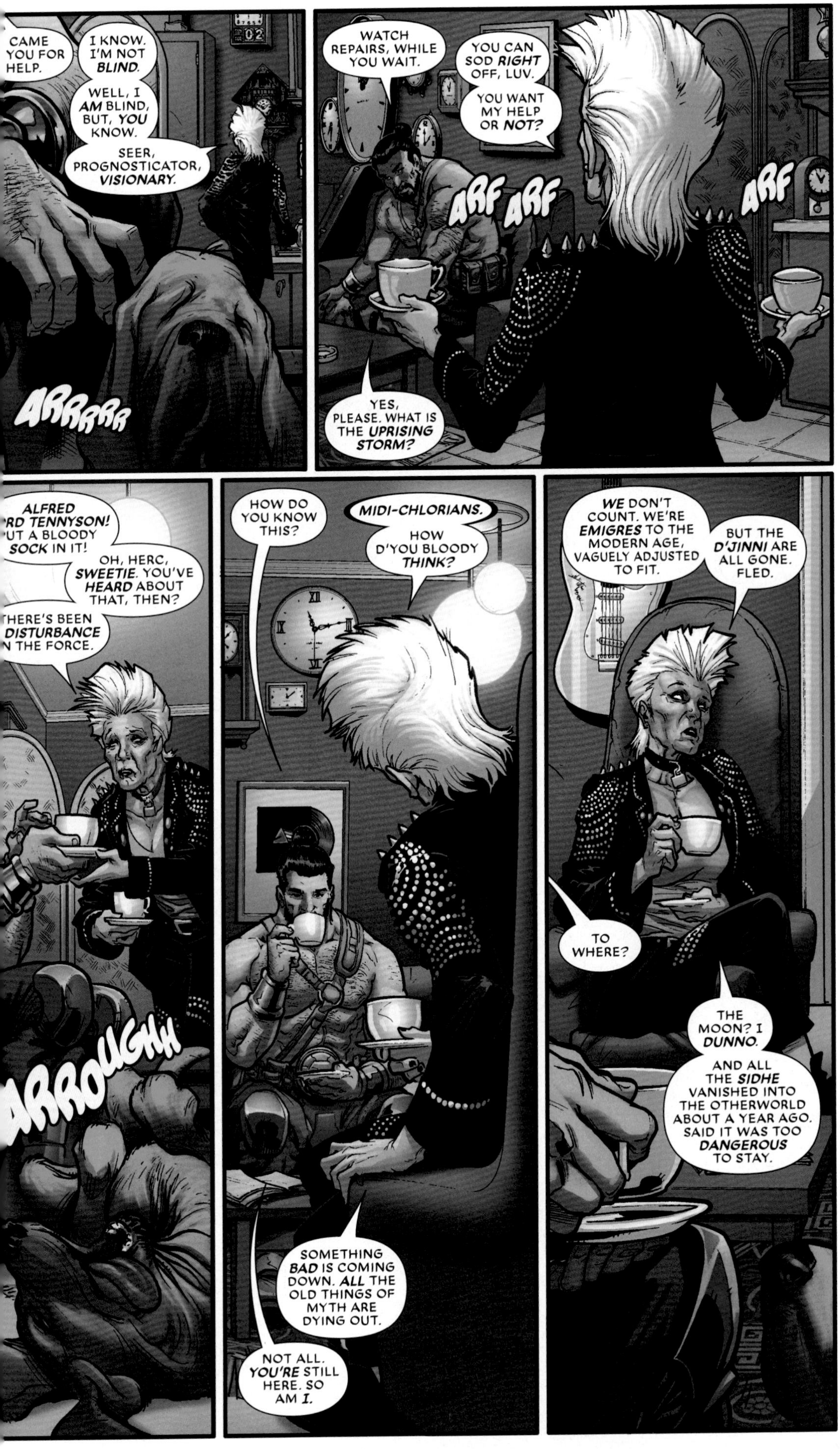
CAME YOU FOR HELP.
I KNOW. I'M NOT BLIND.
WELL, I AM BLIND, BUT, YOU KNOW.
SEER, PROGNOSTICATOR, VISIONARY.
ARRRRRR
WATCH REPAIRS, WHILE YOU WAIT.
YOU CAN SOD RIGHT OFF, LUV.
YOU WANT MY HELP OR NOT?
ARF ARF
ARF
YES, PLEASE. WHAT IS THE UPRISING STORM?
ALFRED
RD TENNYSON!
UT A BLOODY SOCK IN IT!
OH, HERC, SWEETIE. YOU'VE HEARD ABOUT THAT, THEN?
THERE'S BEEN DISTURBANCE N THE FORCE.
ARROUGHH
HOW DO YOU KNOW THIS?
MIDI-CHLORIANS.
HOW D'YOU BLOODY THINK?
SOMETHING BAD IS COMING DOWN. ALL THE OLD THINGS OF MYTH ARE DYING OUT.
NOT ALL. YOU'RE STILL HERE. SO AM I.
WE DON'T COUNT. WE'RE EMIGRES TO THE MODERN AGE, VAGUELY ADJUSTED TO FIT.
BUT THE D'JINNI ARE ALL GONE. FLED.
TO WHERE?
THE MOON? I DUNNO.
AND ALL THE SIDHE VANISHED INTO THE OTHERWORLD ABOUT A YEAR AGO. SAID IT WAS TOO DANGEROUS TO STAY.

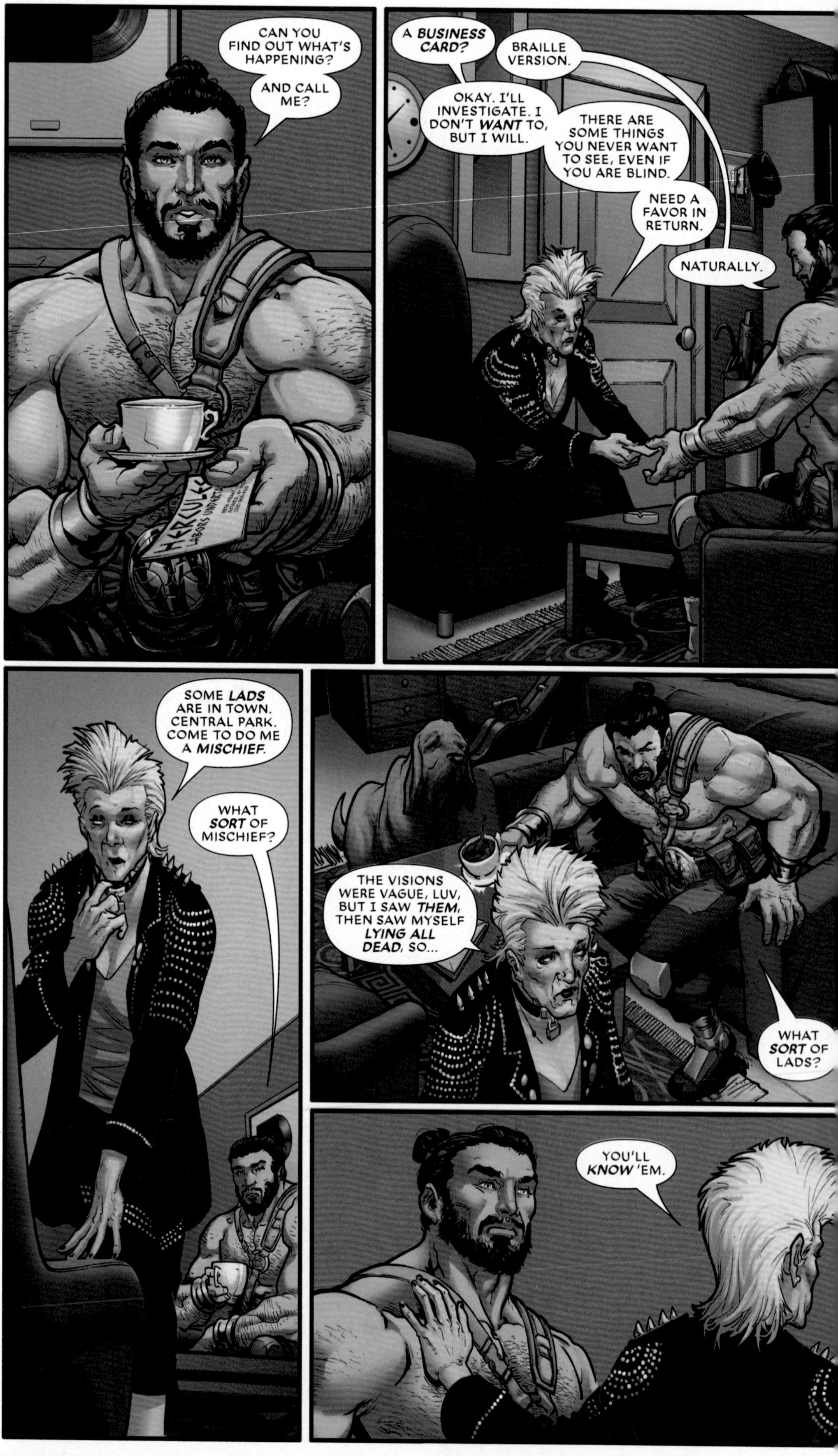
CAN YOU FIND OUT WHAT'S HAPPENING?
AND CALL ME?
A BUSINESS CARD?
BRAILLE VERSION.
OKAY. I'LL INVESTIGATE. I DON'T WANT TO, BUT I WILL.
THERE ARE SOME THINGS YOU NEVER WANT TO SEE, EVEN IF YOU ARE BLIND.
NEED A FAVOR IN RETURN.
NATURALLY.
SOME LADS ARE IN TOWN. CENTRAL PARK. COME TO DO ME A MISCHIEF.
WHAT SORT OF MISCHIEF?
THE VISIONS WERE VAGUE, LUV, BUT I SAW THEM, THEN SAW MYSELF LYING ALL DEAD, SO...
WHAT SORT OF LADS?
YOU'LL KNOW 'EM.

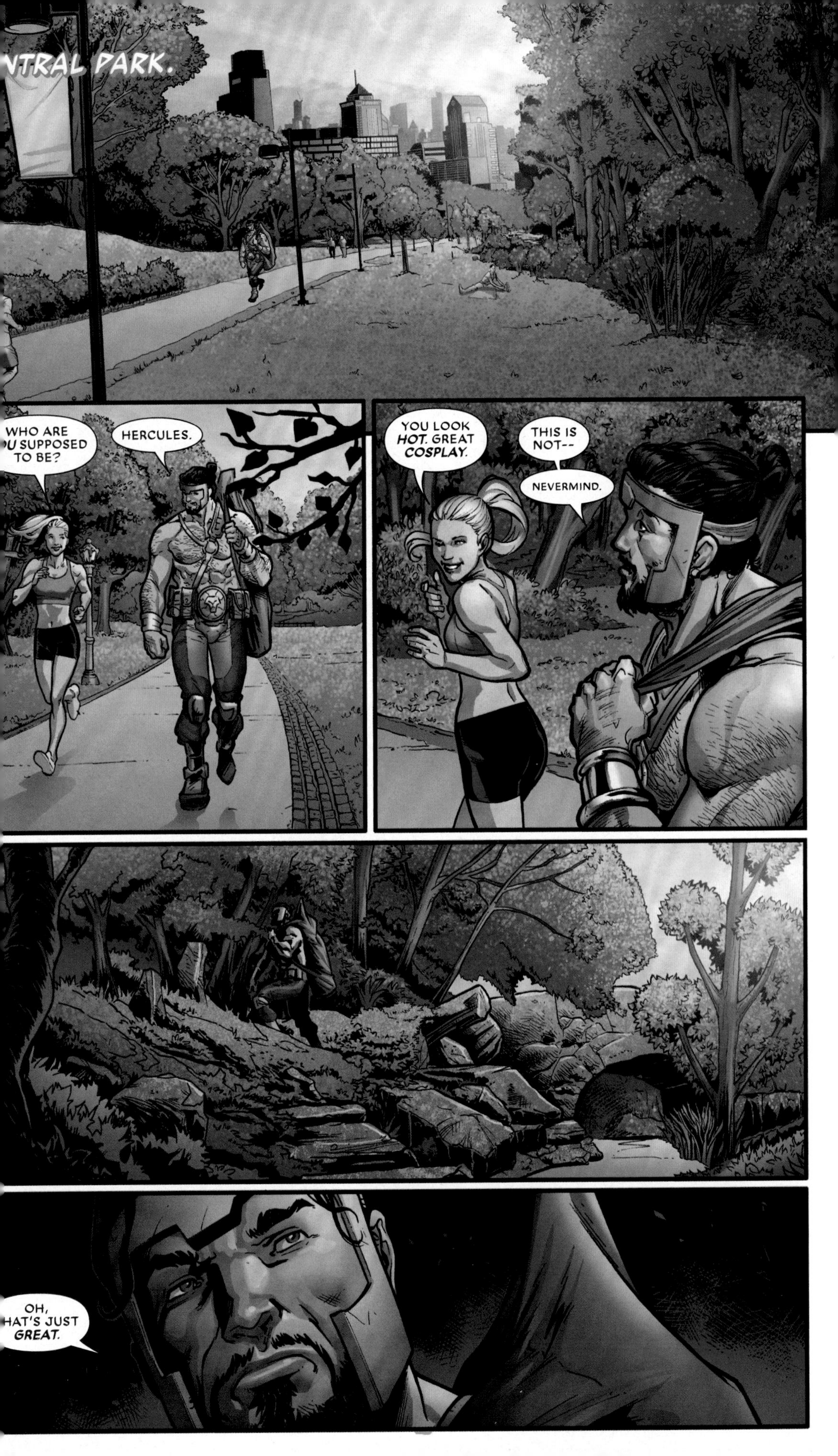
NTRAL PARK.
WHO ARE
U SUPPOSED
TO BE?
HERCULES.
YOU LOOK HOT. GREAT COSPLAY.
THIS IS NOT--
NEVERMIND.
OH,
HAT'S JUST
GREAT.

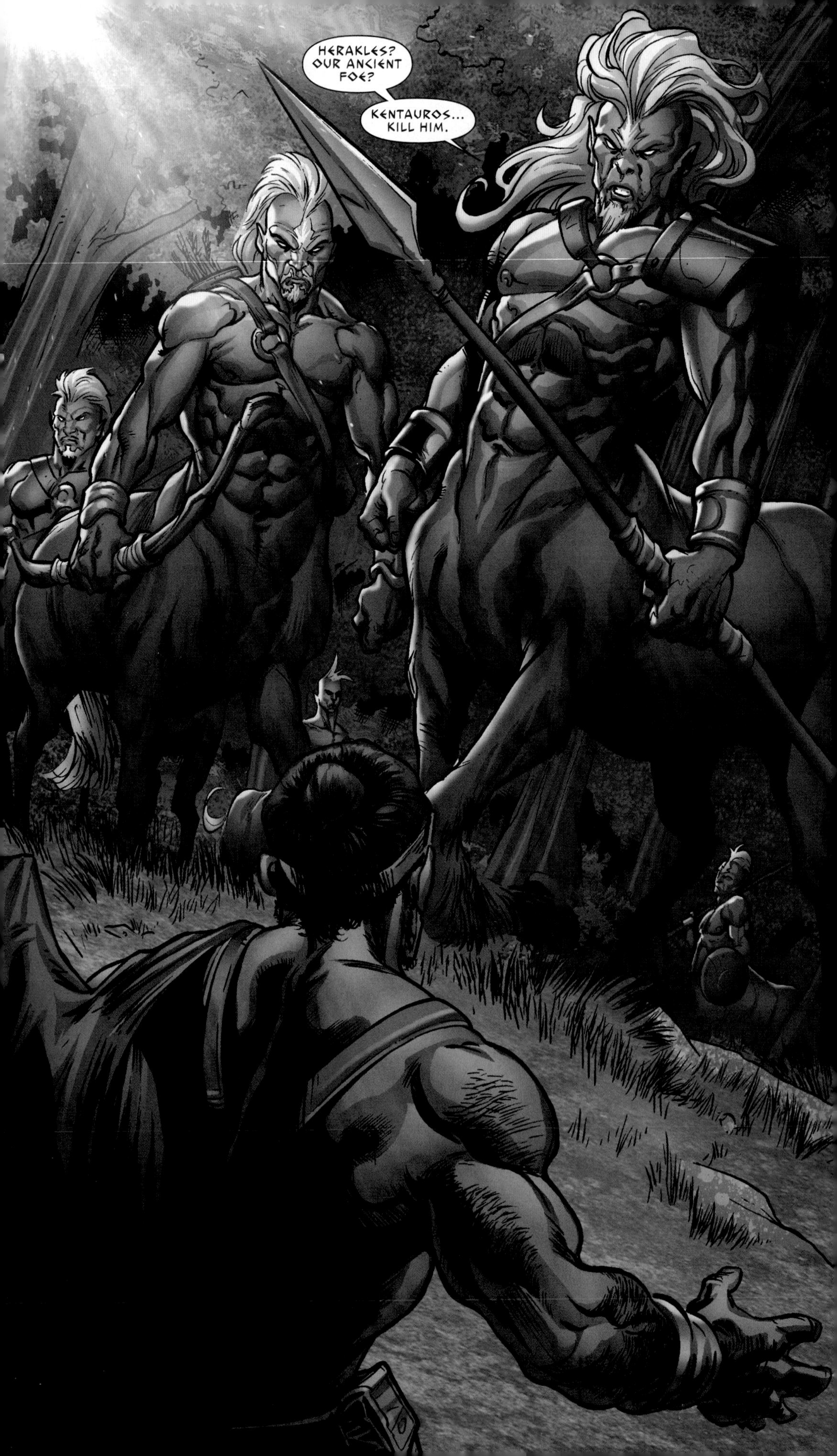
HERAKLES? OUR ANCIENT FOE?
KENTAUROS... KILL HIM.

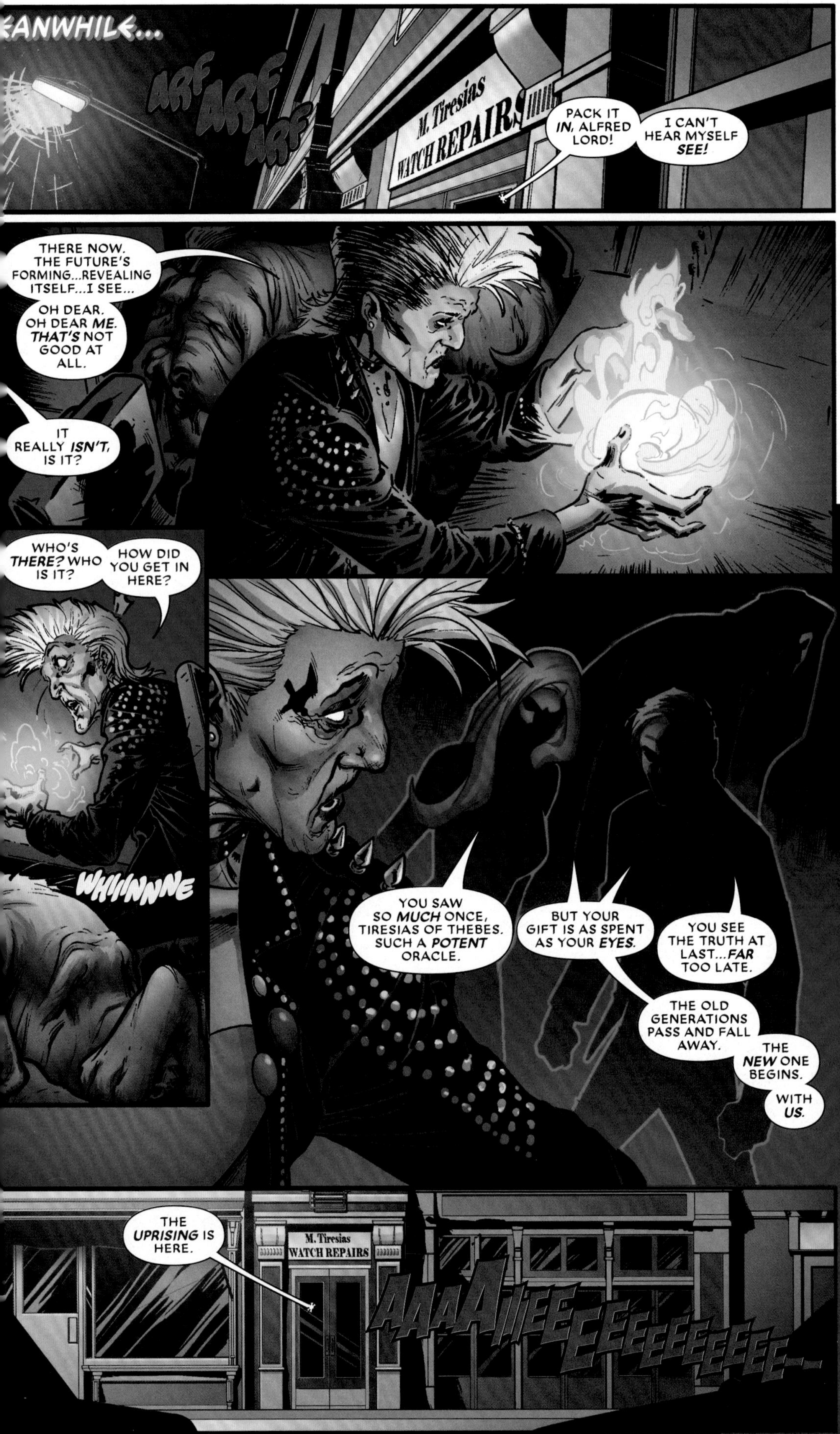

ANWHILE...
ARF ARF ARF
M. Tiresias WATCH REPAIRS
PACK IT IN, ALFRED LORD!
I CAN'T HEAR MYSELF SEE!
THERE NOW. THE FUTURE'S FORMING...REVEALING ITSELF...I SEE...
OH DEAR. OH DEAR ME. THAT'S NOT GOOD AT ALL.
IT REALLY ISN'T, IS IT?
WHO'S THERE? WHO IS IT?
HOW DID YOU GET IN HERE?
WHIIINNNE
YOU SAW SO MUCH ONCE, TIRESIAS OF THEBES. SUCH A POTENT ORACLE.
BUT YOUR GIFT IS AS SPENT AS YOUR EYES.
YOU SEE THE TRUTH AT LAST...FAR TOO LATE.
THE OLD GENERATIONS PASS AND FALL AWAY.
THE NEW ONE BEGINS.
WITH US.
THE UPRISING IS HERE.
M. Tiresias WATCH REPAIRS
AAAAIIIEEEEEEEEEEEEE...

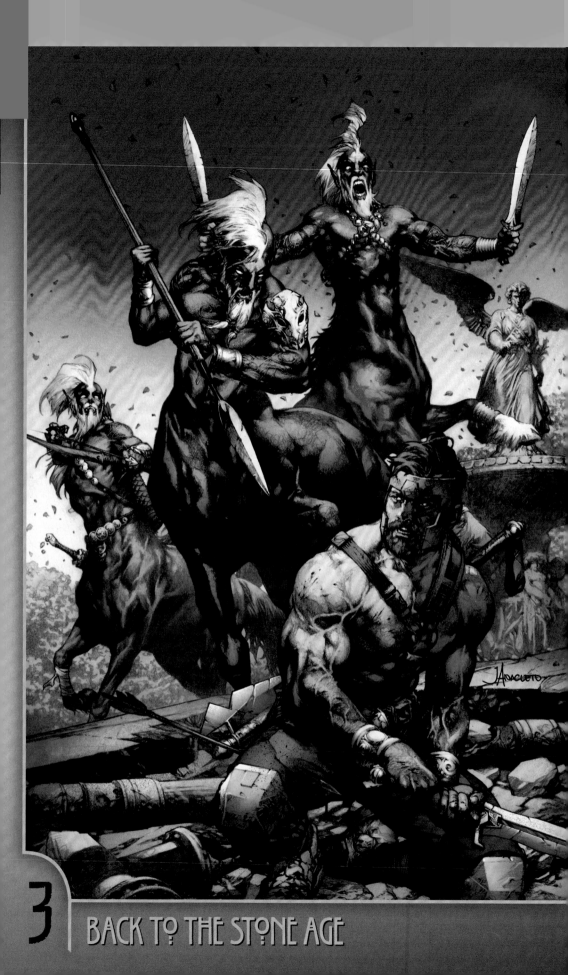

BACK TO THE STONE AGE

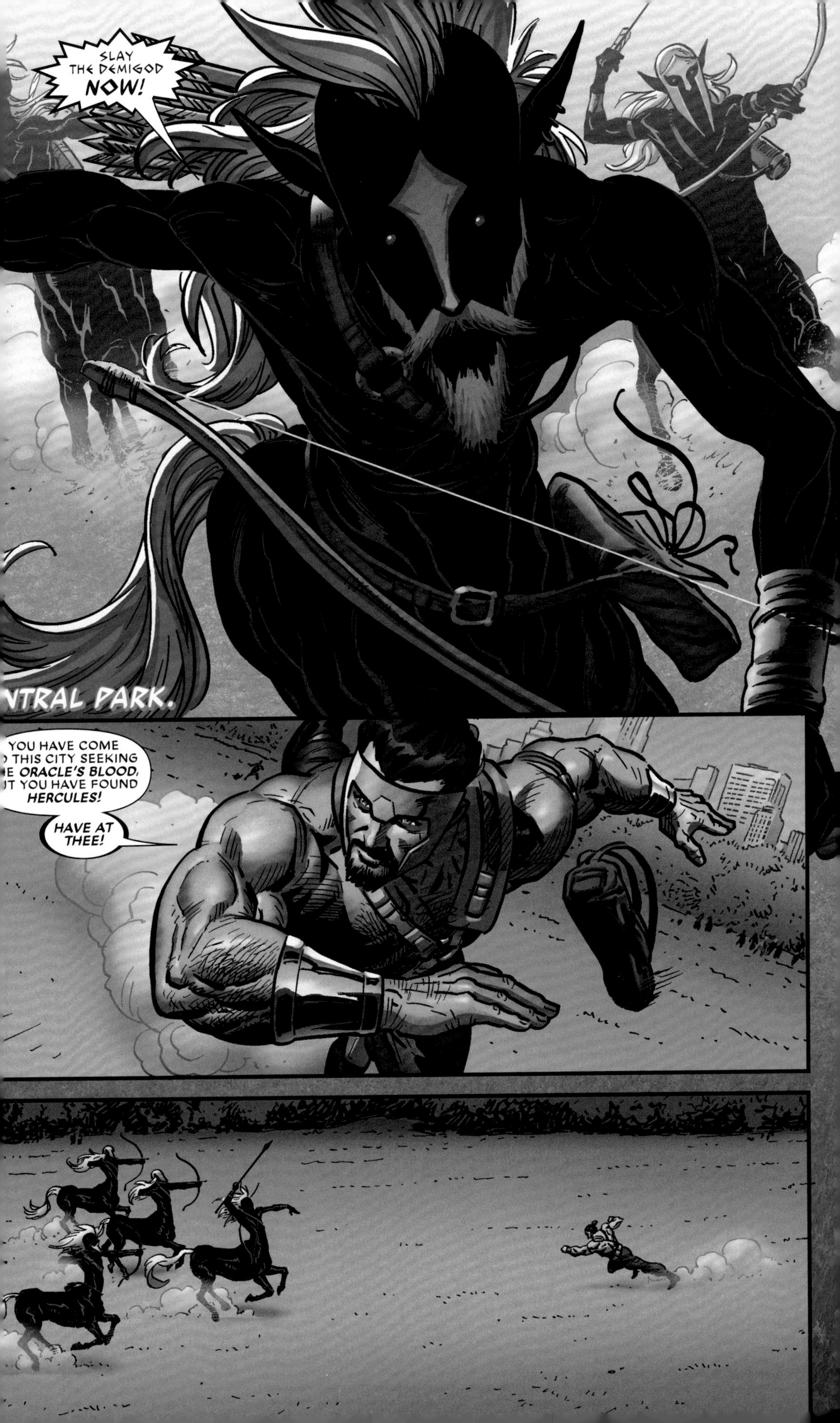
SLAY THE DEMIGOD NOW!
NTRAL PARK.
YOU HAVE COME
) THIS CITY SEEKING
E ORACLE'S BLOOD,
JT YOU HAVE FOUND
HERCULES!
HAVE AT THEE!

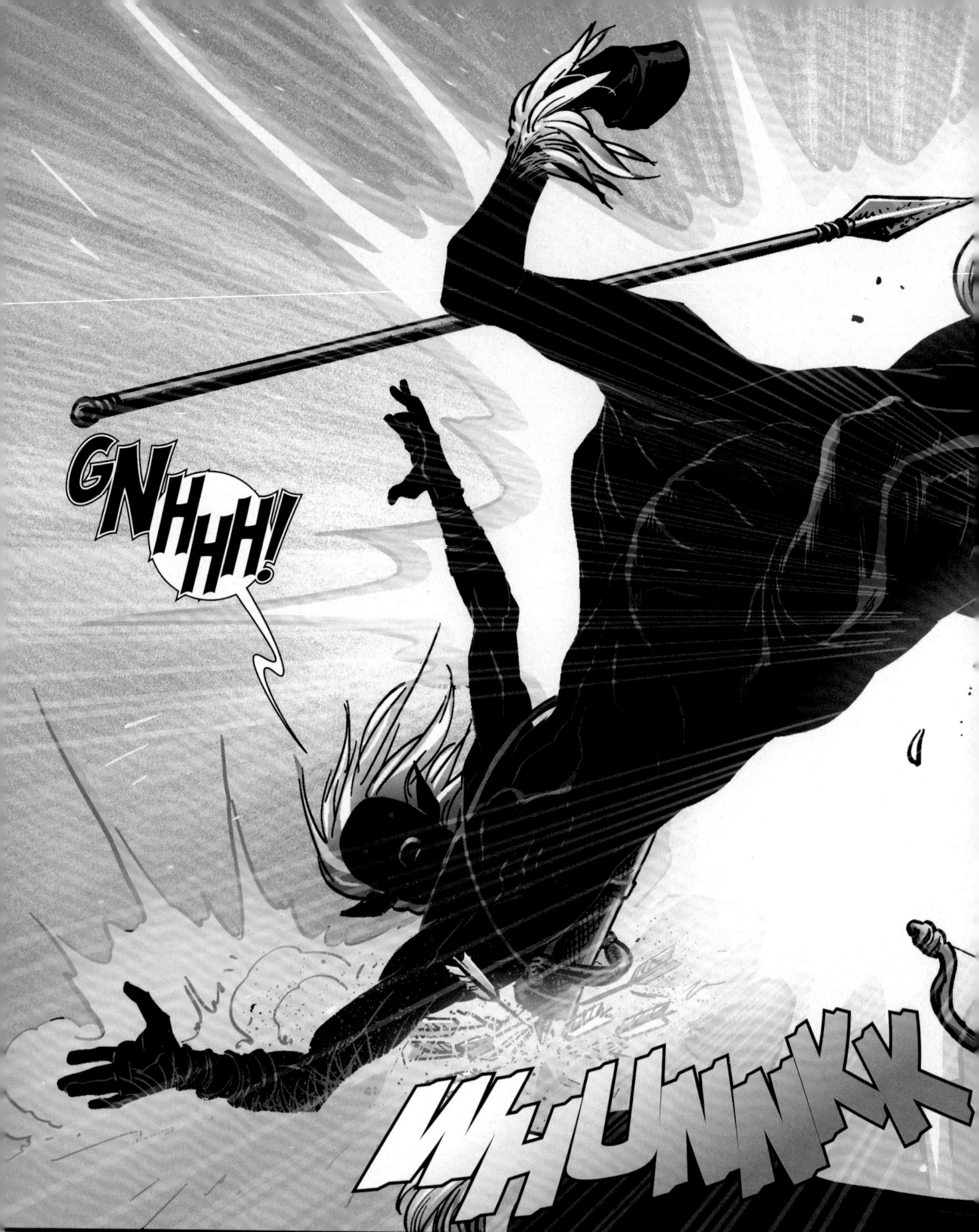
GNHHH!
WHUNKK

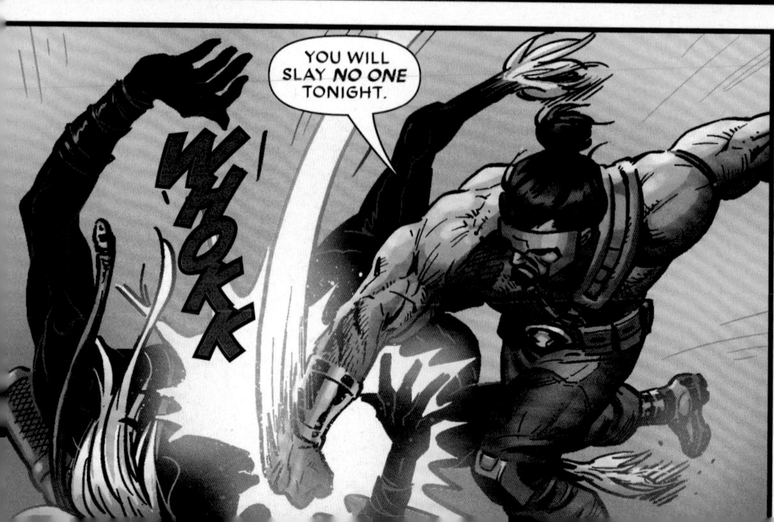
YOU WILL SLAY NO ONE TONIGHT.
WHOKK

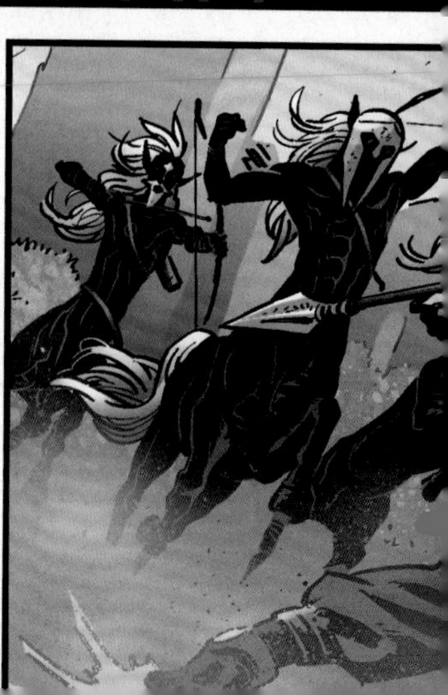

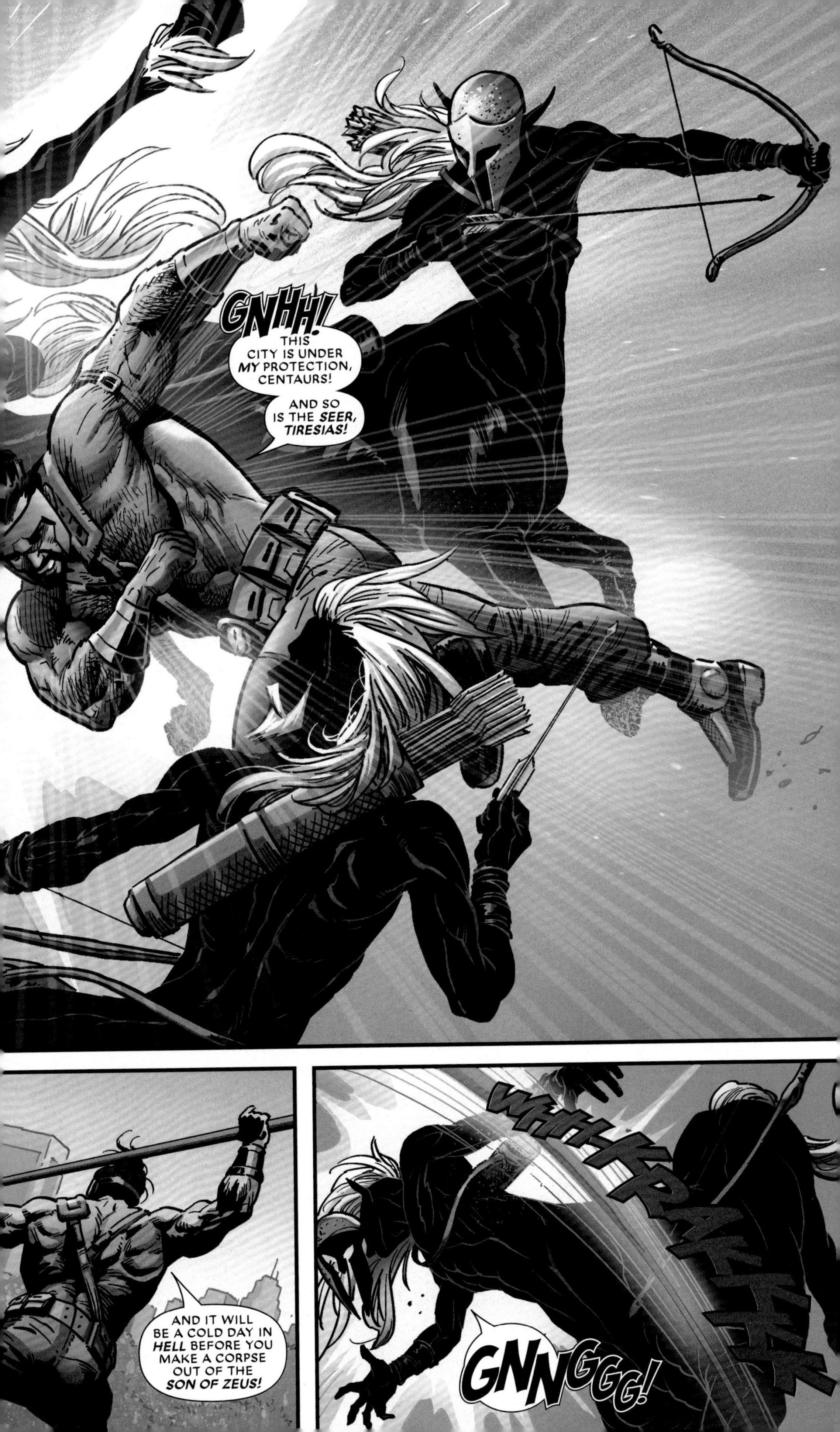
GNHH!
THIS CITY IS UNDER MY PROTECTION, CENTAURS!
AND SO IS THE SEER, TIRESIAS!
AND IT WILL BE A COLD DAY IN HELL BEFORE YOU MAKE A CORPSE OUT OF THE SON OF ZEUS!
WHH-KRAKKK
GNNGGG!

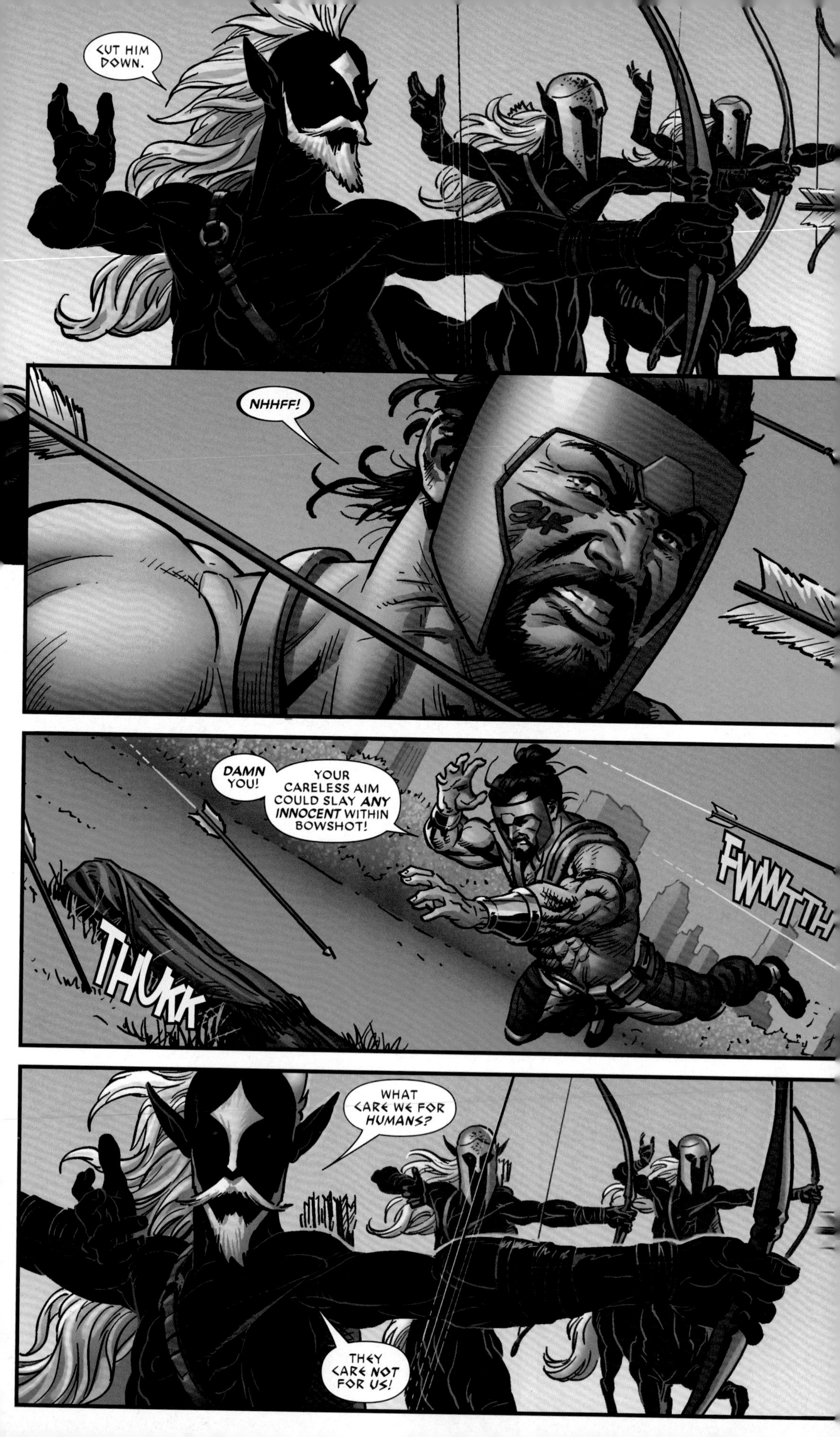
CUT HIM DOWN.
NHHFF!
DAMN YOU!
YOUR CARELESS AIM COULD SLAY ANY INNOCENT WITHIN BOWSHOT!
FWWTTH
THUKK
WHAT CARE WE FOR HUMANS?
THEY CARE NOT FOR US!

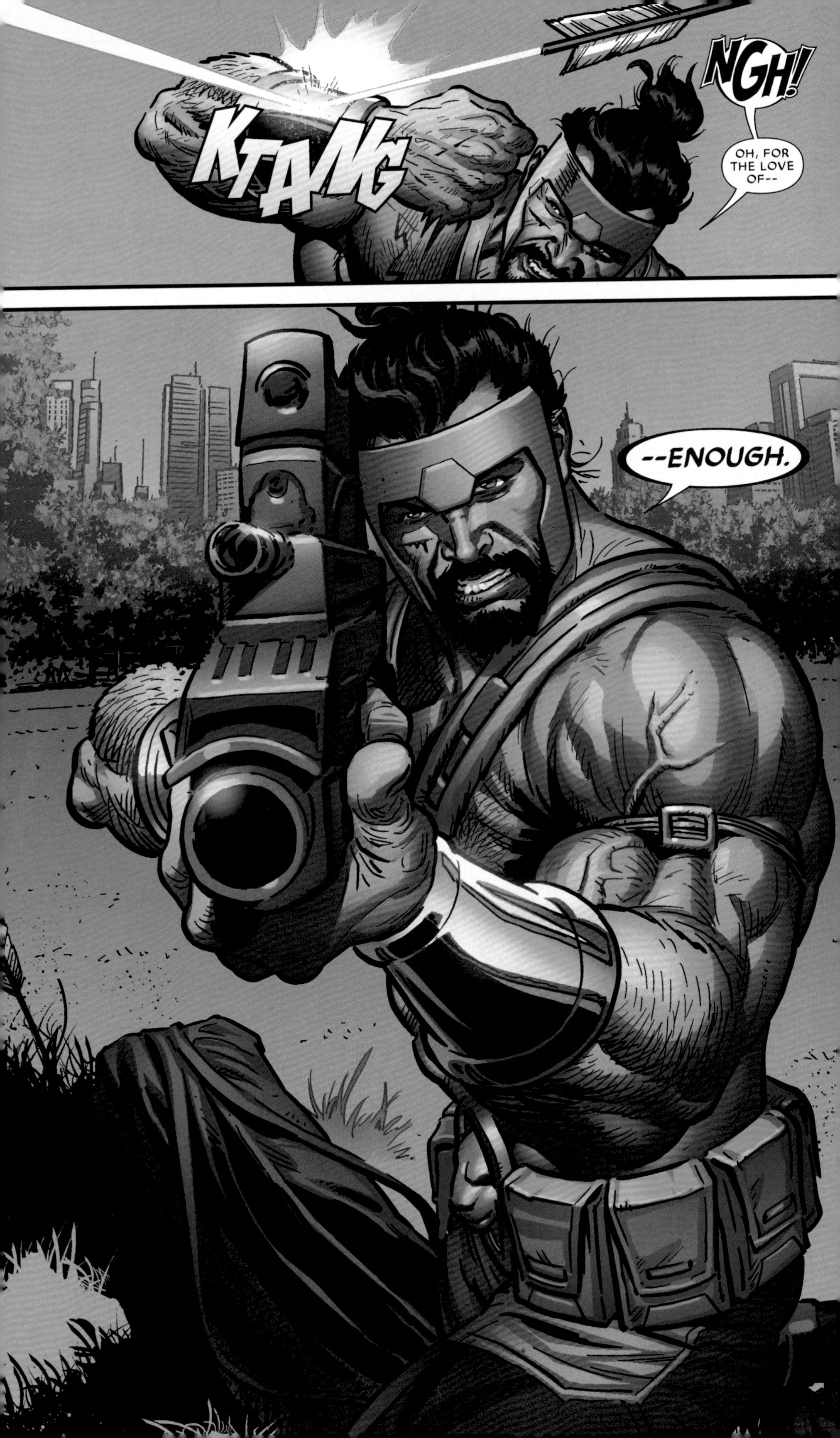
KTANG
NGH!
OH, FOR THE LOVE OF--
--ENOUGH.

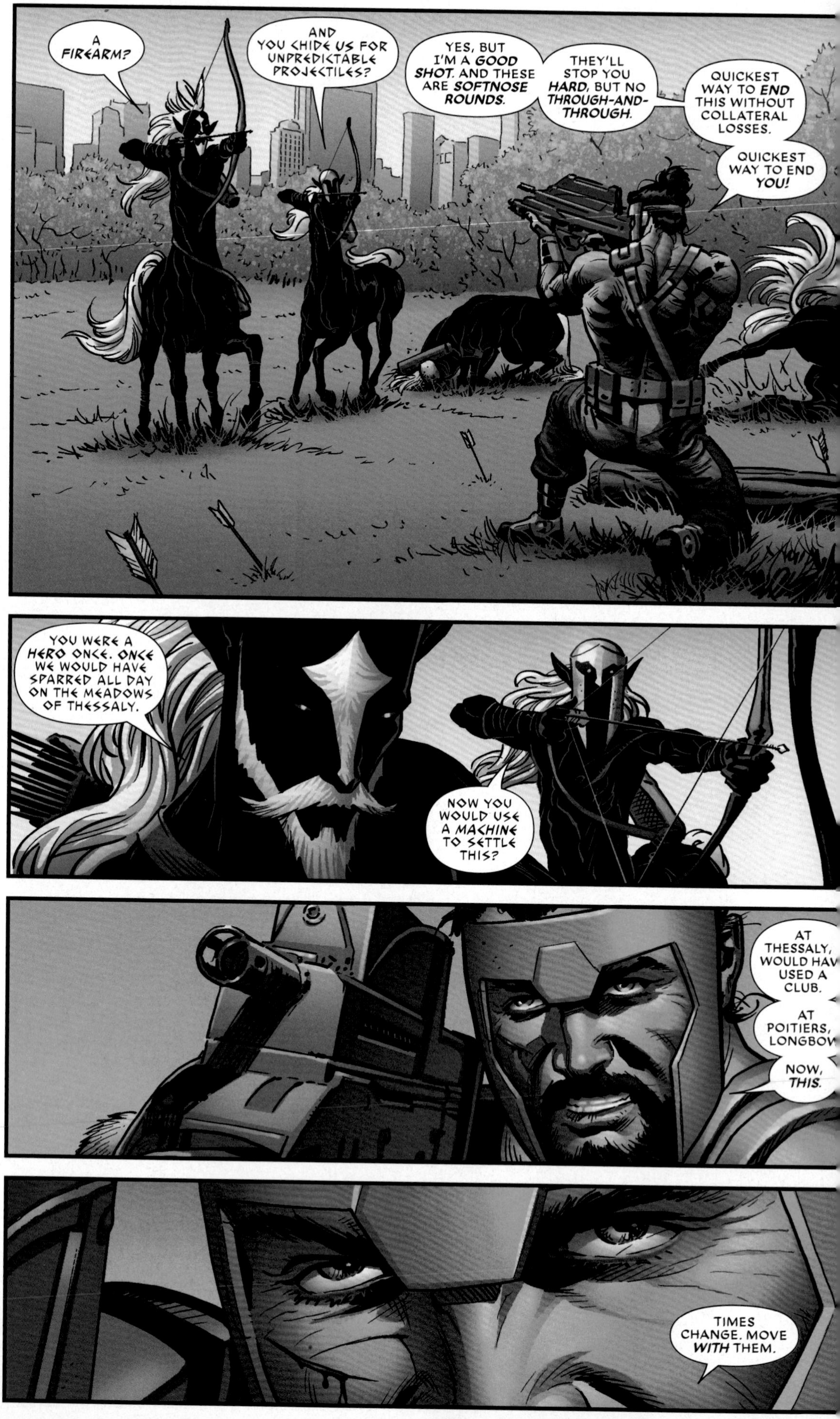
A FIREARM?
AND YOU CHIDE US FOR UNPREDICTABLE PROJECTILES?
YES, BUT I'M A GOOD SHOT. AND THESE ARE SOFTNOSE ROUNDS.
THEY'LL STOP YOU HARD, BUT NO THROUGH-AND-THROUGH.
QUICKEST WAY TO END THIS WITHOUT COLLATERAL LOSSES.
QUICKEST WAY TO END YOU!
YOU WERE A HERO ONCE. ONCE WE WOULD HAVE SPARRED ALL DAY ON THE MEADOWS OF THESSALY.
NOW YOU WOULD USE A MACHINE TO SETTLE THIS?
AT THESSALY, WOULD HAV USED A CLUB.
AT POITIERS, LONGBOV
NOW, THIS.
TIMES CHANGE. MOVE WITH THEM.

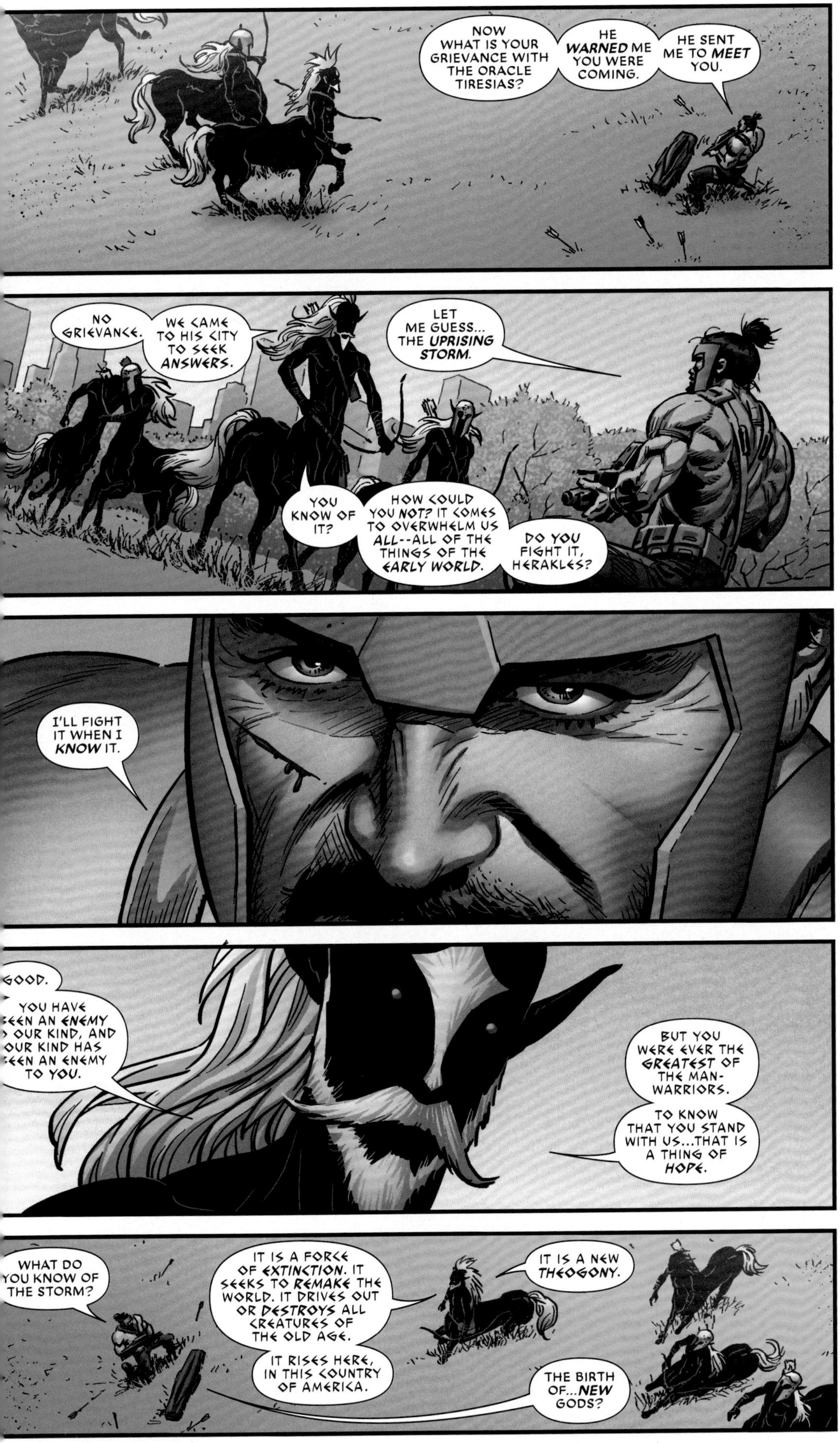
NOW WHAT IS YOUR GRIEVANCE WITH THE ORACLE TIRESIAS?
HE WARNED ME YOU WERE COMING.
HE SENT ME TO MEET YOU.
NO GRIEVANCE.
WE CAME TO HIS CITY TO SEEK ANSWERS.
LET ME GUESS... THE UPRISING STORM.
YOU KNOW OF IT?
HOW COULD YOU NOT? IT COMES TO OVERWHELM US ALL--ALL OF THE THINGS OF THE EARLY WORLD.
DO YOU FIGHT IT, HERAKLES?
I'LL FIGHT IT WHEN I KNOW IT.
GOOD.
YOU HAVE EEN AN ENEMY O OUR KIND, AND OUR KIND HAS EEN AN ENEMY TO YOU.
BUT YOU WERE EVER THE GREATEST OF THE MAN-WARRIORS.
TO KNOW THAT YOU STAND WITH US...THAT IS A THING OF HOPE.
WHAT DO YOU KNOW OF THE STORM?
IT IS A FORCE OF EXTINCTION. IT SEEKS TO REMAKE THE WORLD. IT DRIVES OUT OR DESTROYS ALL CREATURES OF THE OLD AGE.
IT RISES HERE, IN THIS COUNTRY OF AMERICA.
IT IS A NEW THEOGONY.
THE BIRTH OF...NEW GODS?

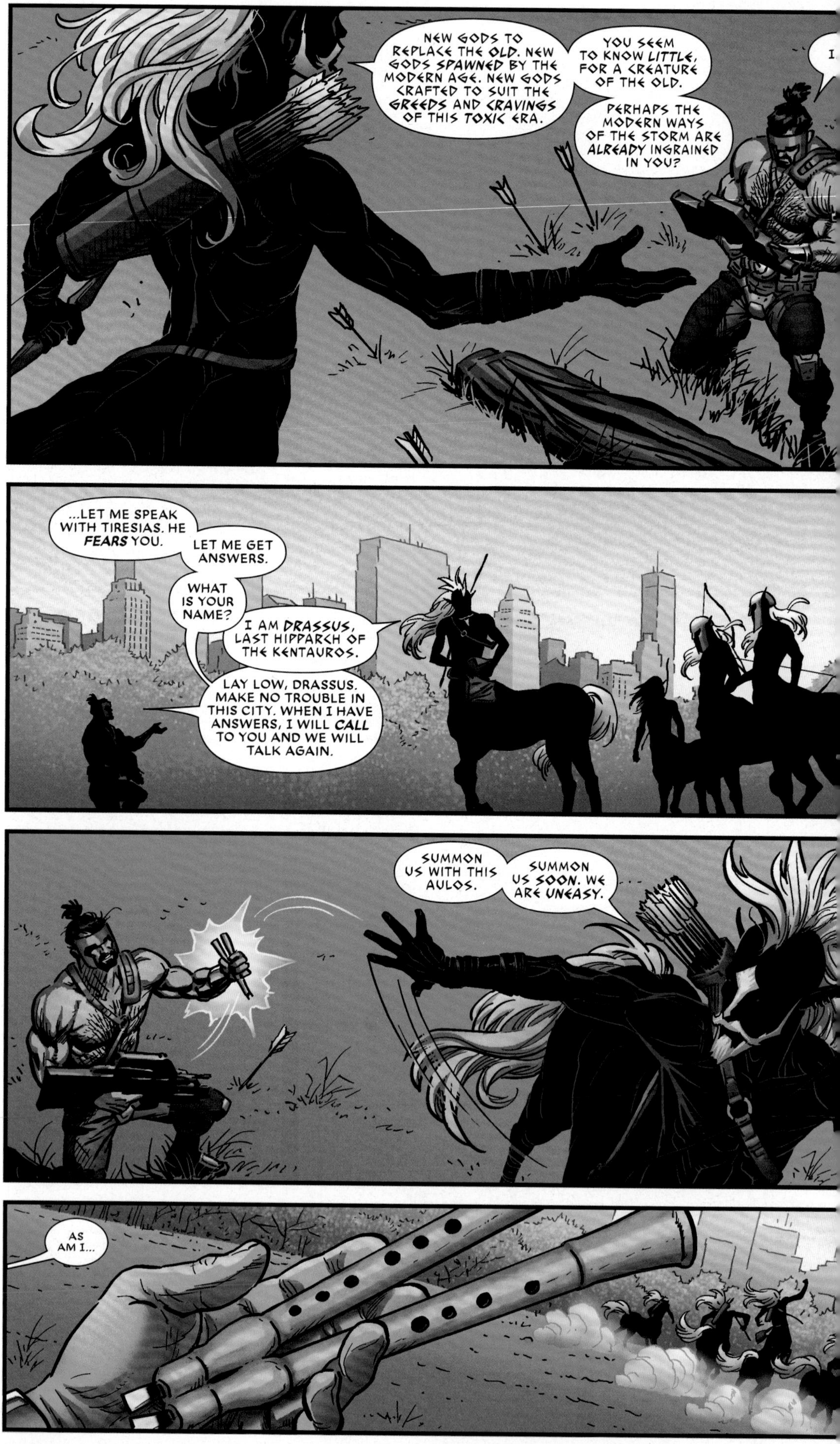
NEW GODS TO REPLACE THE OLD. NEW GODS SPAWNED BY THE MODERN AGE. NEW GODS CRAFTED TO SUIT THE GREEDS AND CRAVINGS OF THIS TOXIC ERA.
YOU SEEM TO KNOW LITTLE, FOR A CREATURE OF THE OLD.
PERHAPS THE MODERN WAYS OF THE STORM ARE ALREADY INGRAINED IN YOU?
I...
...LET ME SPEAK WITH TIRESIAS. HE FEARS YOU.
LET ME GET ANSWERS.
WHAT IS YOUR NAME?
I AM DRASSUS, LAST HIPPARCH OF THE KENTAUROS.
LAY LOW, DRASSUS. MAKE NO TROUBLE IN THIS CITY. WHEN I HAVE ANSWERS, I WILL CALL TO YOU AND WE WILL TALK AGAIN.
SUMMON US WITH THIS AULOS.
SUMMON US SOON. WE ARE UNEASY.
AS AM I...

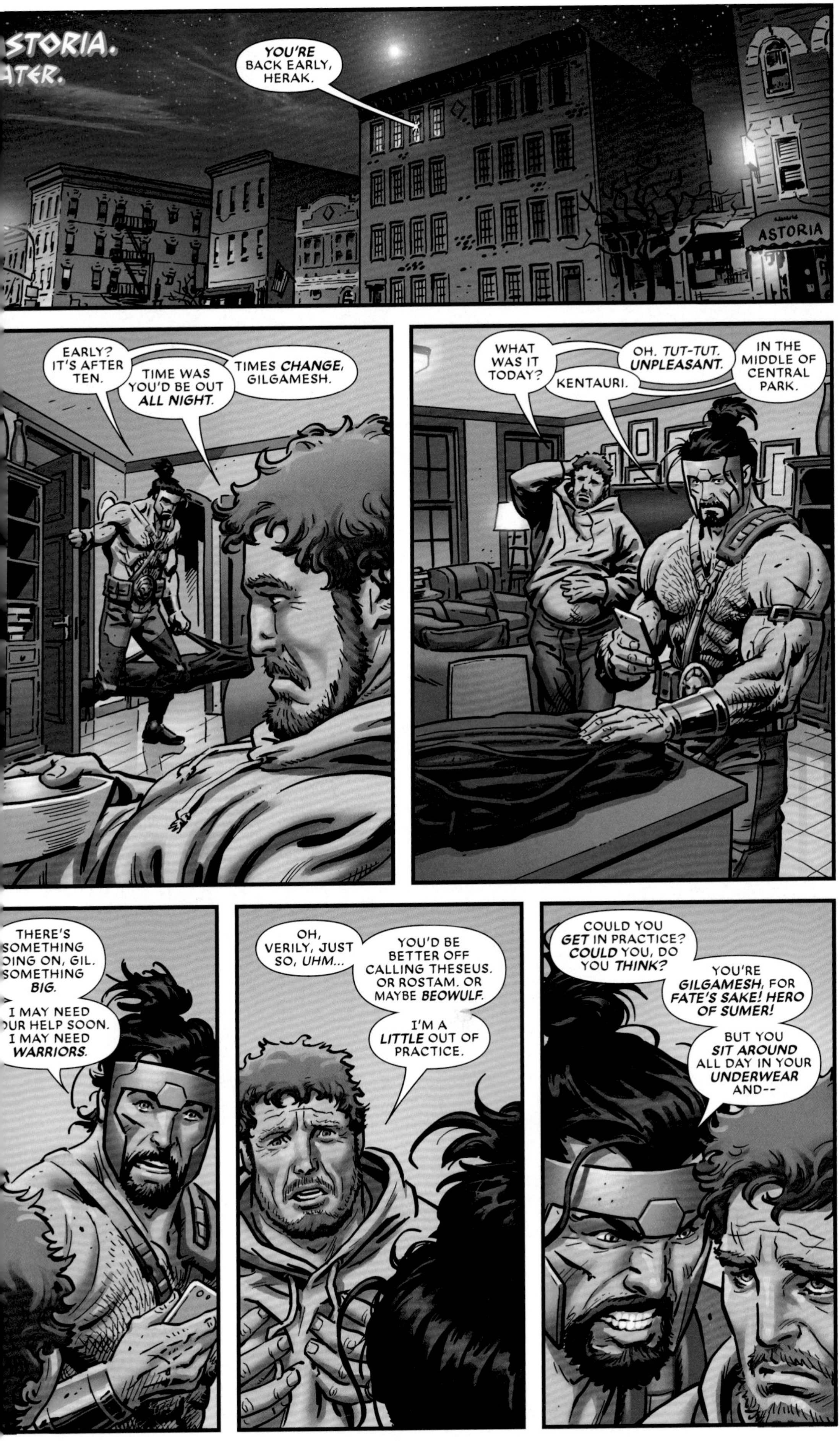
STORIA.
ATER.
YOU'RE BACK EARLY, HERAK.
ASTORIA
EARLY? IT'S AFTER TEN.
TIME WAS YOU'D BE OUT ALL NIGHT.
TIMES CHANGE, GILGAMESH.
WHAT WAS IT TODAY?
KENTAURI.
OH. TUT-TUT. UNPLEASANT.
IN THE MIDDLE OF CENTRAL PARK.
THERE'S SOMETHING OING ON, GIL. SOMETHING BIG.
I MAY NEED UR HELP SOON. I MAY NEED WARRIORS.
OH, VERILY, JUST SO, UHM...
YOU'D BE BETTER OFF CALLING THESEUS. OR ROSTAM. OR MAYBE BEOWULF.
I'M A LITTLE OUT OF PRACTICE.
COULD YOU GET IN PRACTICE? COULD YOU, DO YOU THINK?
YOU'RE GILGAMESH, FOR FATE'S SAKE! HERO OF SUMER!
BUT YOU SIT AROUND ALL DAY IN YOUR UNDERWEAR AND--

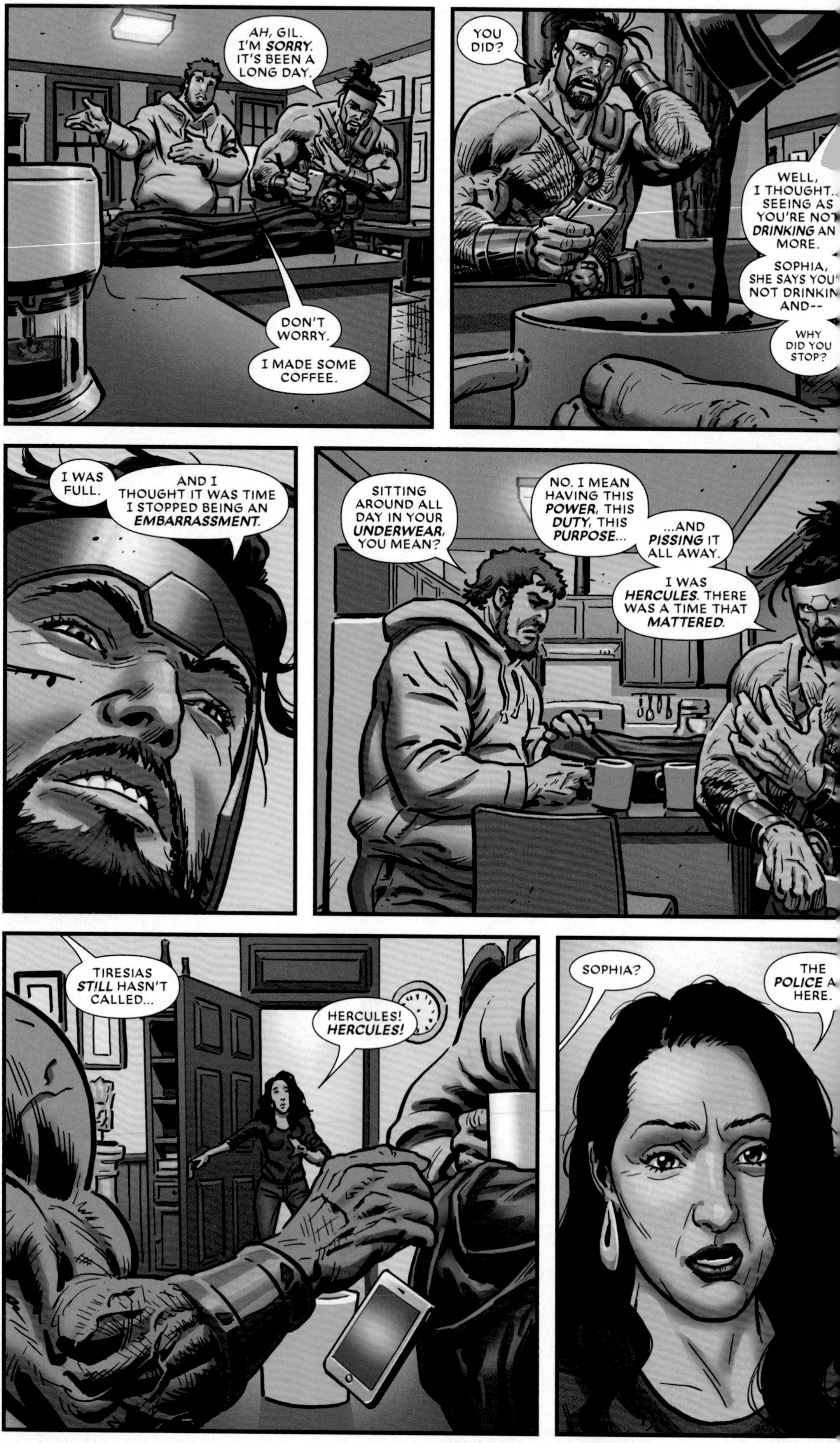
AH, GIL. I'M SORRY. IT'S BEEN A LONG DAY.
DON'T WORRY.
I MADE SOME COFFEE.
YOU DID?
WELL, I THOUGHT.. SEEING AS YOU'RE NOT DRINKING AN MORE.
SOPHIA, SHE SAYS YOU NOT DRINKIN AND--
WHY DID YOU STOP?
I WAS FULL.
AND I THOUGHT IT WAS TIME I STOPPED BEING AN EMBARRASSMENT.
SITTING AROUND ALL DAY IN YOUR UNDERWEAR, YOU MEAN?
NO. I MEAN HAVING THIS POWER, THIS DUTY, THIS PURPOSE...
...AND PISSING IT ALL AWAY.
I WAS HERCULES. THERE WAS A TIME THAT MATTERED.
TIRESIAS STILL HASN'T CALLED...
HERCULES! HERCULES!
SOPHIA?
THE POLICE A HERE.

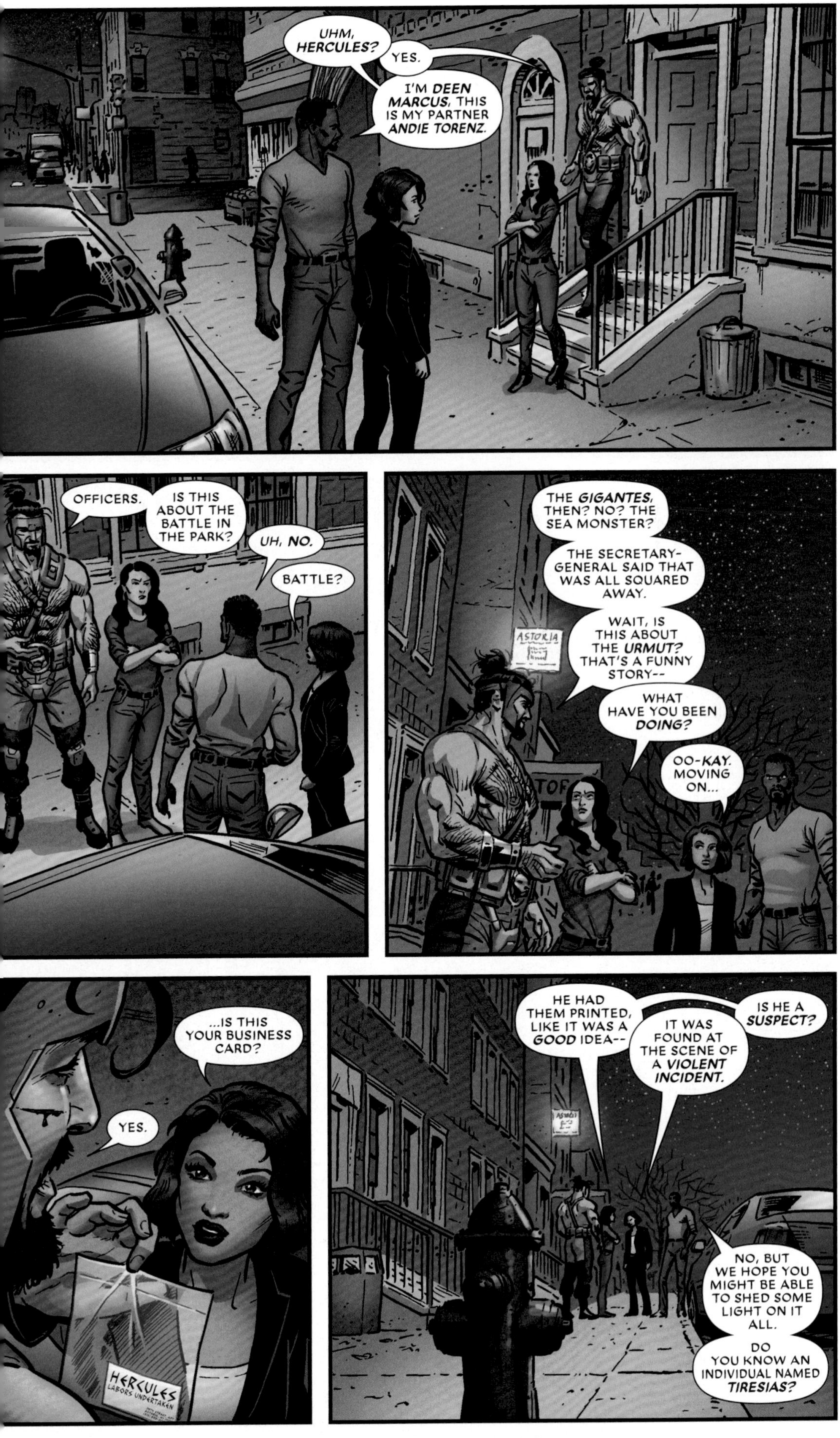
UHM, HERCULES?
YES.
I'M DEEN MARCUS, THIS IS MY PARTNER ANDIE TORENZ.
OFFICERS.
IS THIS ABOUT THE BATTLE IN THE PARK?
UH, NO.
BATTLE?
THE GIGANTES, THEN? NO? THE SEA MONSTER?
THE SECRETARY-GENERAL SAID THAT WAS ALL SQUARED AWAY.
WAIT, IS THIS ABOUT THE URMUT? THAT'S A FUNNY STORY--
WHAT HAVE YOU BEEN DOING?
OO-KAY. MOVING ON...
ASTORIA
...IS THIS YOUR BUSINESS CARD?
YES.
HERCULES
LABORS UNDERTAKEN
HE HAD THEM PRINTED, LIKE IT WAS A GOOD IDEA--
IT WAS FOUND AT THE SCENE OF A VIOLENT INCIDENT.
IS HE A SUSPECT?
NO, BUT WE HOPE YOU MIGHT BE ABLE TO SHED SOME LIGHT ON IT ALL.
DO YOU KNOW AN INDIVIDUAL NAMED TIRESIAS?

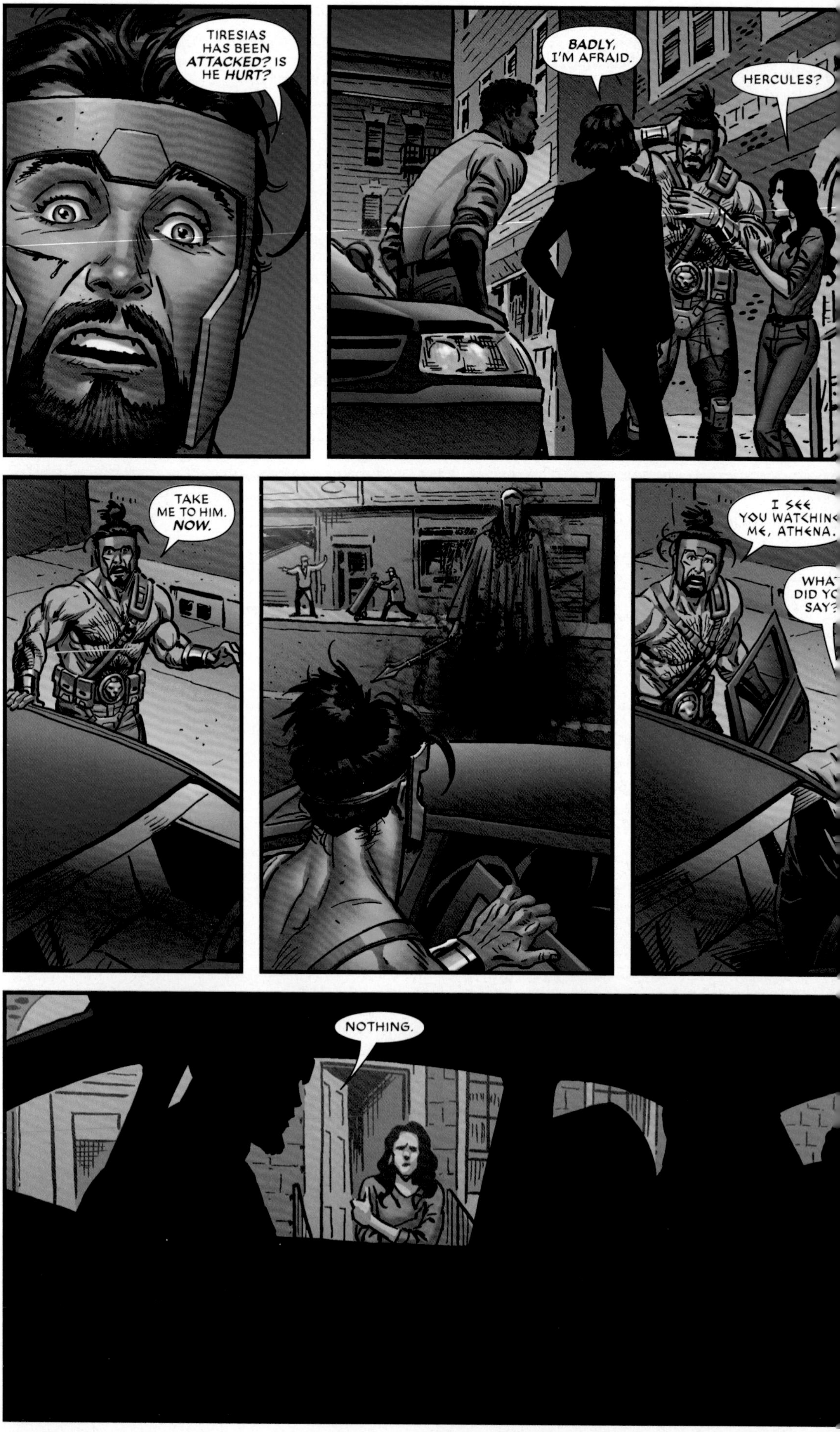
TIRESIAS HAS BEEN ATTACKED? IS HE HURT?
BADLY, I'M AFRAID.
HERCULES?
TAKE ME TO HIM. NOW.
I SEE YOU WATCHIN
ME, ATHENA.
WHA
DID YO
SAY?
NOTHING.

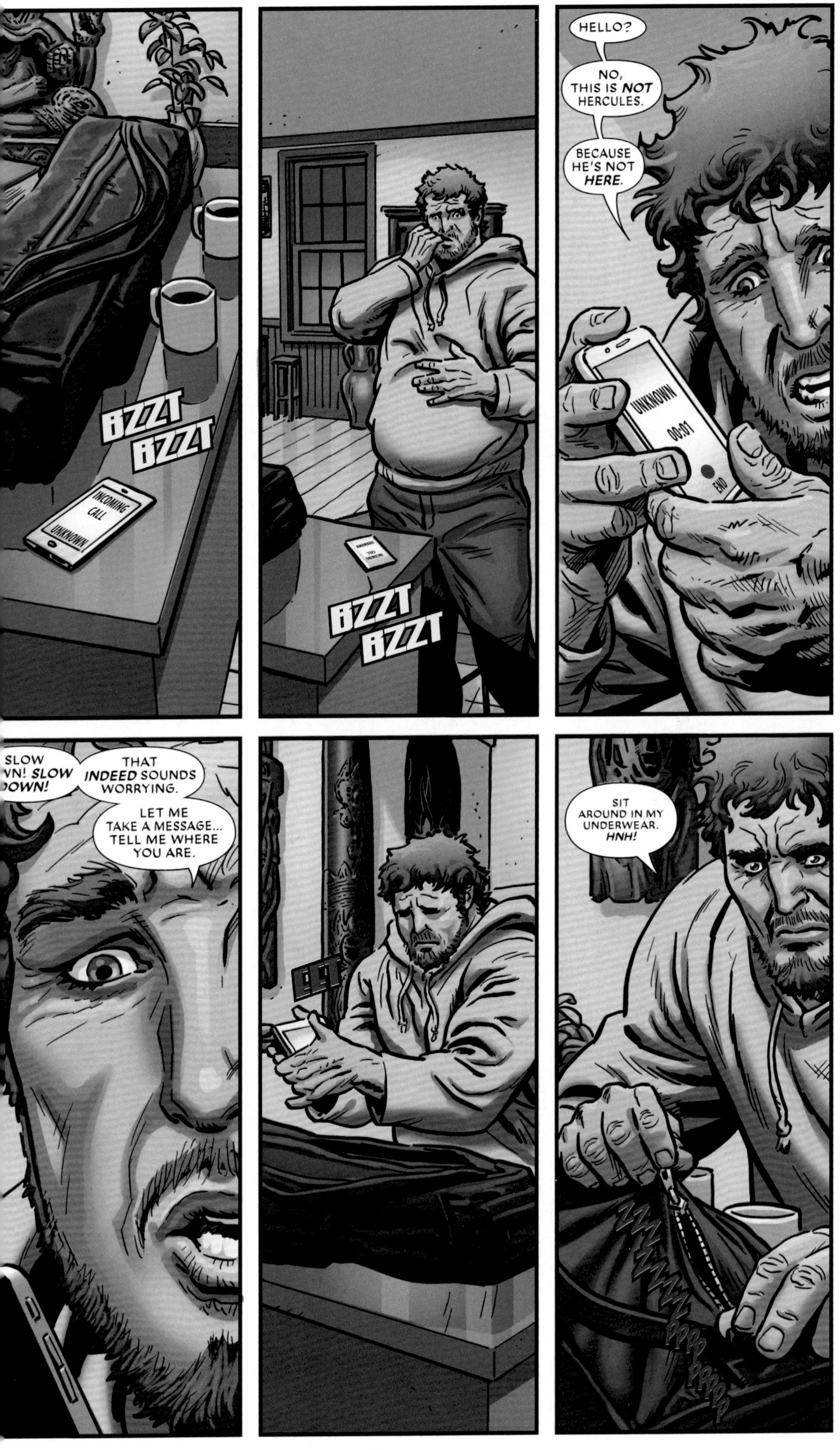
BZZT BZZT
INCOMING CALL
UNKNOWN
BZZT BZZT
HELLO?
NO, THIS IS *NOT* HERCULES.
BECAUSE HE'S NOT *HERE*.
UNKNOWN
00:01
END
SLOW
WN! *SLOW*
DOWN!
THAT *INDEED* SOUNDS WORRYING.
LET ME TAKE A MESSAGE... TELL ME WHERE YOU ARE.
SIT AROUND IN MY UNDERWEAR. *HNH!*

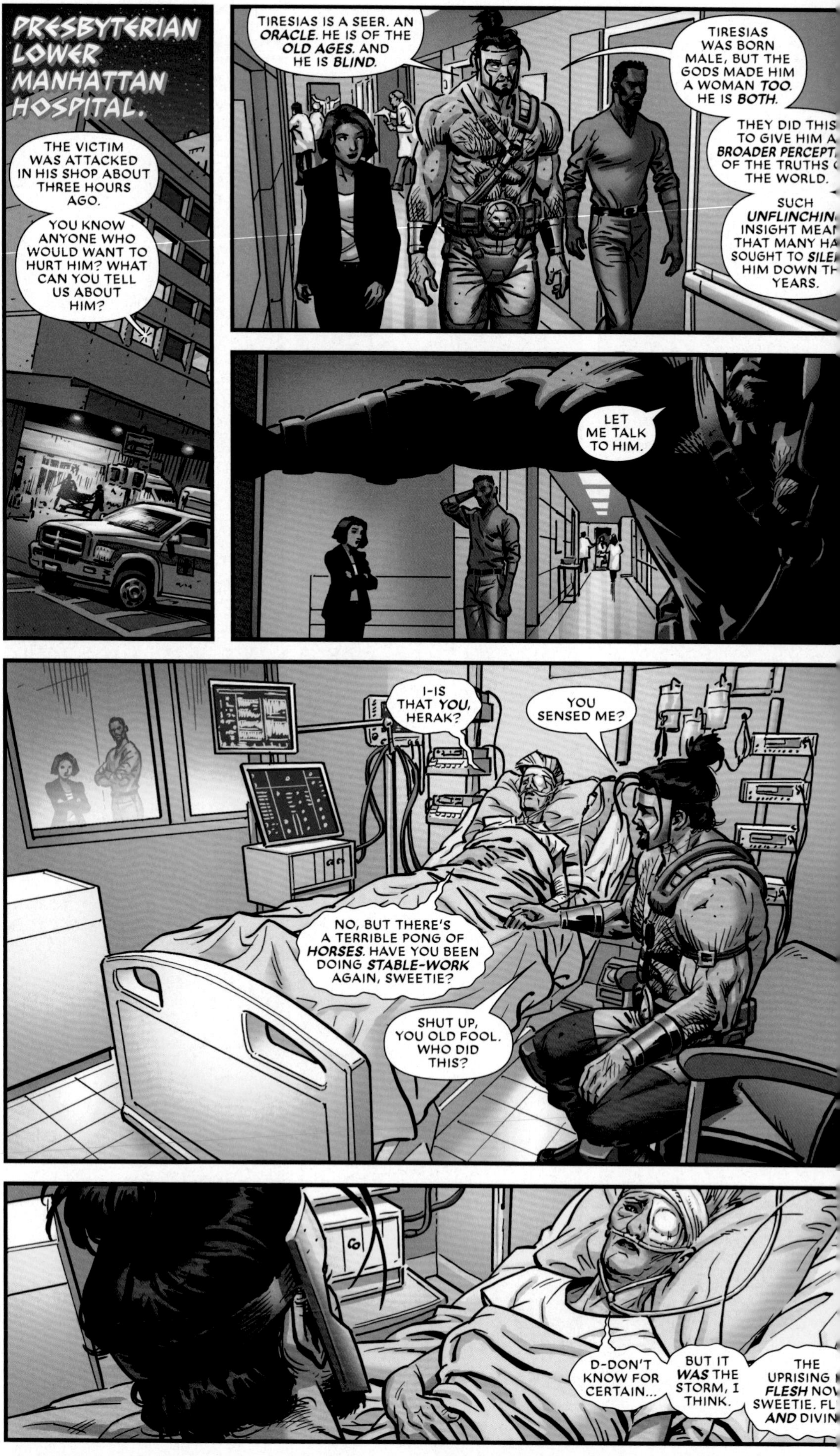
PRESBYTERIAN LOWER MANHATTAN HOSPITAL.
THE VICTIM WAS ATTACKED IN HIS SHOP ABOUT THREE HOURS AGO.
YOU KNOW ANYONE WHO WOULD WANT TO HURT HIM? WHAT CAN YOU TELL US ABOUT HIM?
TIRESIAS IS A SEER. AN ORACLE. HE IS OF THE OLD AGES. AND HE IS BLIND.
TIRESIAS WAS BORN MALE, BUT THE GODS MADE HIM A WOMAN TOO. HE IS BOTH.
THEY DID THIS TO GIVE HIM A BROADER PERCEPT OF THE TRUTHS THE WORLD.
SUCH UNFLINCHIN INSIGHT MEA THAT MANY HA SOUGHT TO SILE HIM DOWN TH YEARS.
LET ME TALK TO HIM.
I-IS THAT YOU, HERAK?
YOU SENSED ME?
NO, BUT THERE'S A TERRIBLE PONG OF HORSES. HAVE YOU BEEN DOING STABLE-WORK AGAIN, SWEETIE?
SHUT UP, YOU OLD FOOL. WHO DID THIS?
D-DON'T KNOW FOR CERTAIN...
BUT IT WAS THE STORM, I THINK.
THE UPRISING FLESH NOV SWEETIE. FL AND DIVIN

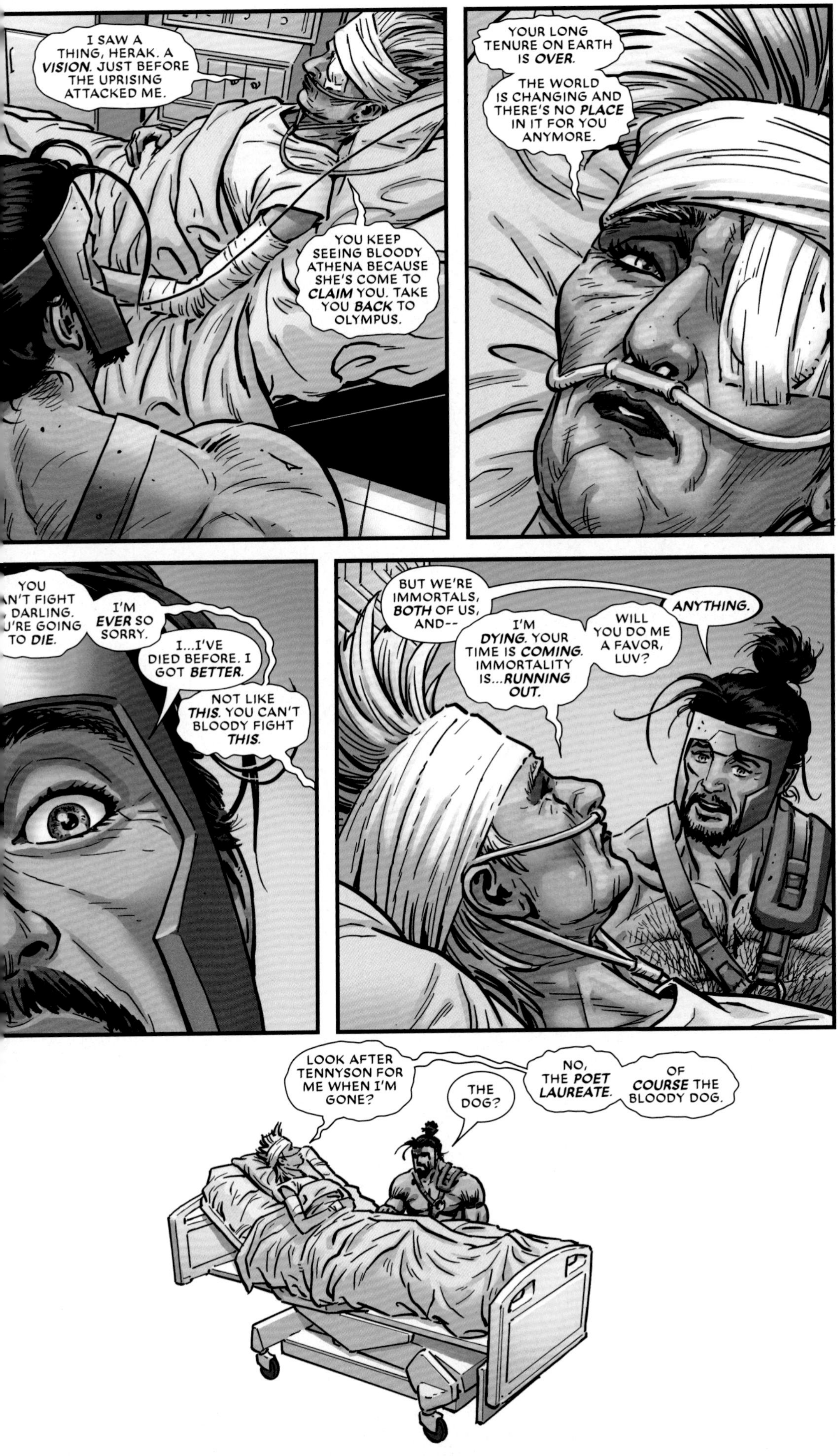
I SAW A THING, HERAK. A VISION. JUST BEFORE THE UPRISING ATTACKED ME.
YOU KEEP SEEING BLOODY ATHENA BECAUSE SHE'S COME TO CLAIM YOU. TAKE YOU BACK TO OLYMPUS.
YOUR LONG TENURE ON EARTH IS OVER.
THE WORLD IS CHANGING AND THERE'S NO PLACE IN IT FOR YOU ANYMORE.
YOU CAN'T FIGHT IT, DARLING. YOU'RE GOING TO DIE.
I'M EVER SO SORRY.
I...I'VE DIED BEFORE. I GOT BETTER.
NOT LIKE THIS. YOU CAN'T BLOODY FIGHT THIS.
BUT WE'RE IMMORTALS, BOTH OF US, AND--
I'M DYING. YOUR TIME IS COMING. IMMORTALITY IS...RUNNING OUT.
WILL YOU DO ME A FAVOR, LUV?
ANYTHING.
LOOK AFTER TENNYSON FOR ME WHEN I'M GONE?
THE DOG?
NO, THE POET LAUREATE.
OF COURSE THE BLOODY DOG.

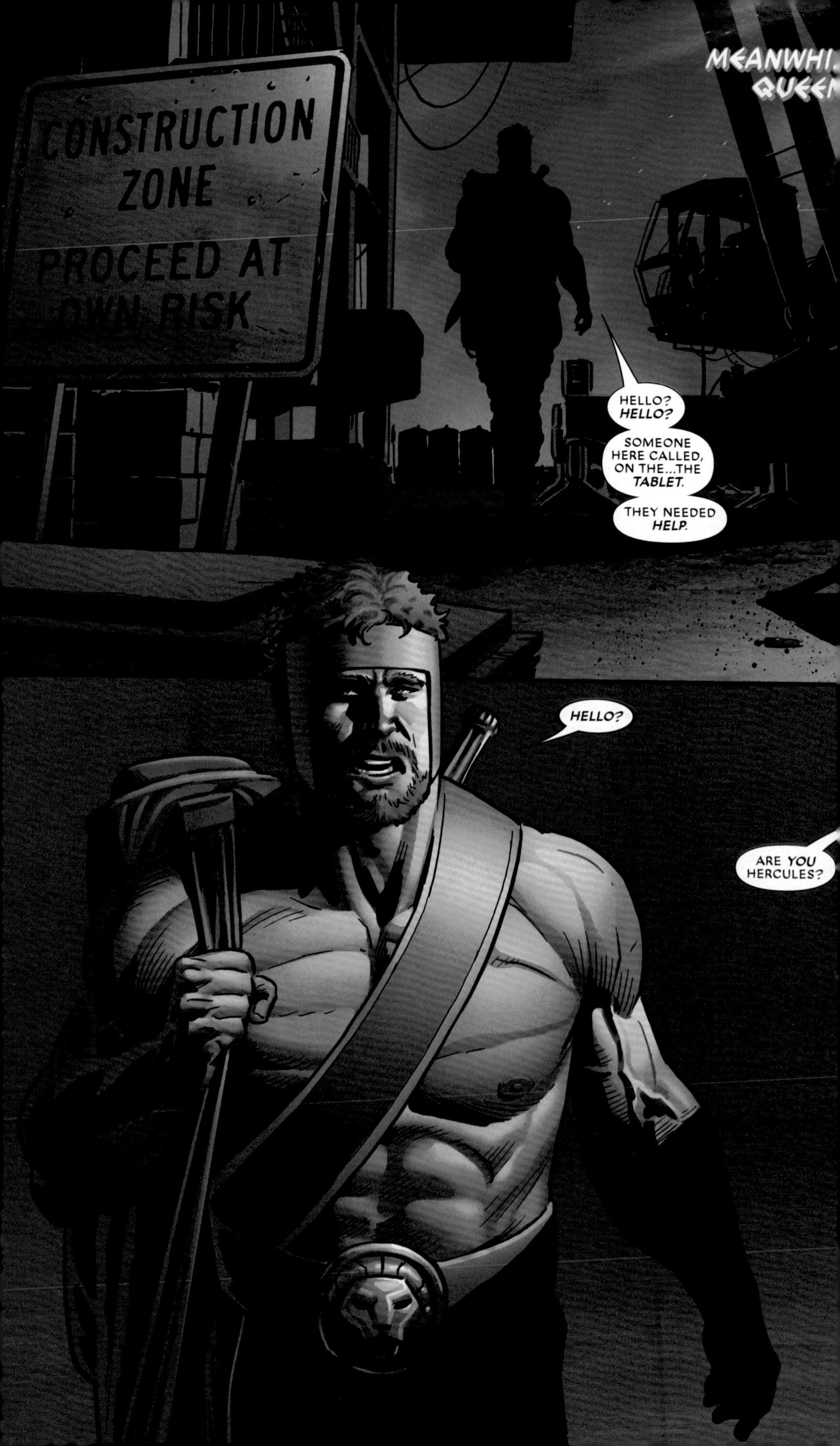

MEANWHI
QUEE
CONSTRUCTION
ZONE
PROCEED AT
OWN RISK
HELLO? *HELLO?*
SOMEONE HERE CALLED, ON THE...THE *TABLET*.
THEY NEEDED *HELP*.
HELLO?
ARE *YOU* HERCULES?

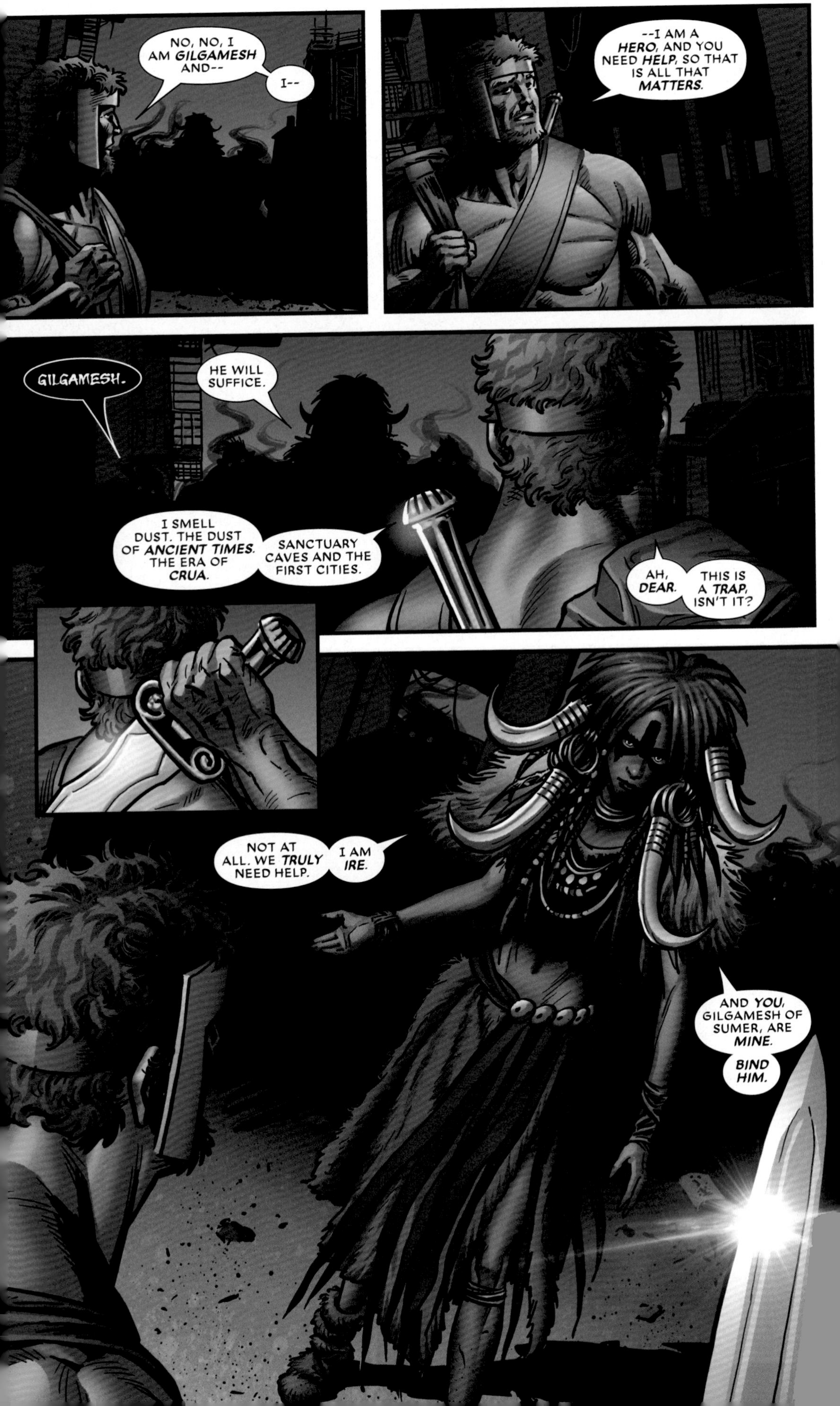
NO, NO, I AM GILGAMESH AND--
I--
--I AM A HERO, AND YOU NEED HELP, SO THAT IS ALL THAT MATTERS.
GILGAMESH.
HE WILL SUFFICE.
I SMELL DUST. THE DUST OF ANCIENT TIMES. THE ERA OF CRUA.
SANCTUARY CAVES AND THE FIRST CITIES.
AH, DEAR.
THIS IS A TRAP, ISN'T IT?
NOT AT ALL. WE TRULY NEED HELP.
I AM IRE.
AND YOU, GILGAMESH OF SUMER, ARE MINE.
BIND HIM.

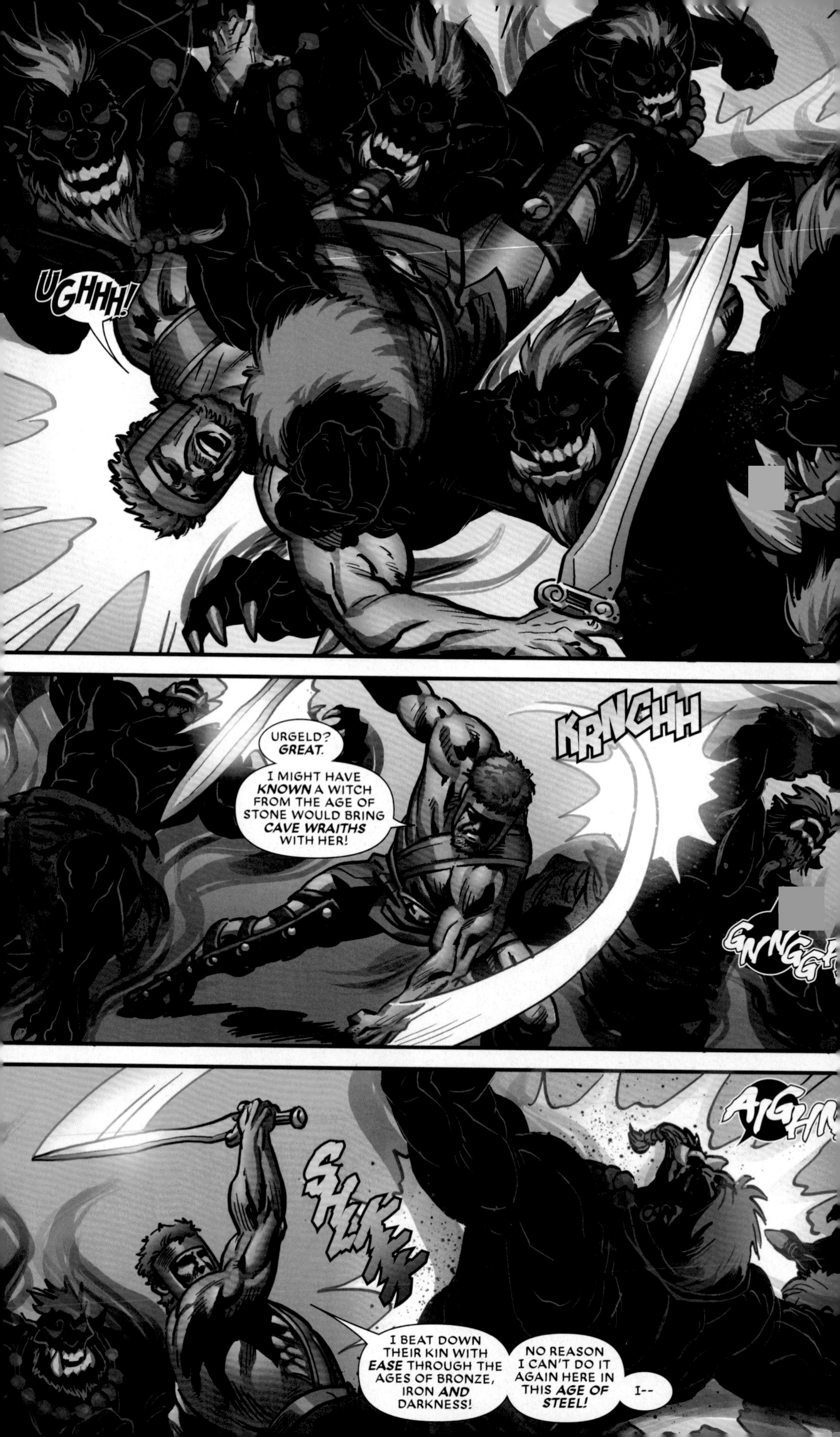
UGHHH!
URGELD? *GREAT.*
I MIGHT HAVE *KNOWN* A WITCH FROM THE AGE OF STONE WOULD BRING *CAVE WRAITHS* WITH HER!
KRNCHH
SHLUNK
I BEAT DOWN THEIR KIN WITH *EASE* THROUGH THE AGES OF BRONZE, IRON *AND* DARKNESS!
NO REASON I CAN'T DO IT AGAIN HERE IN THIS *AGE OF STEEL!*
I--

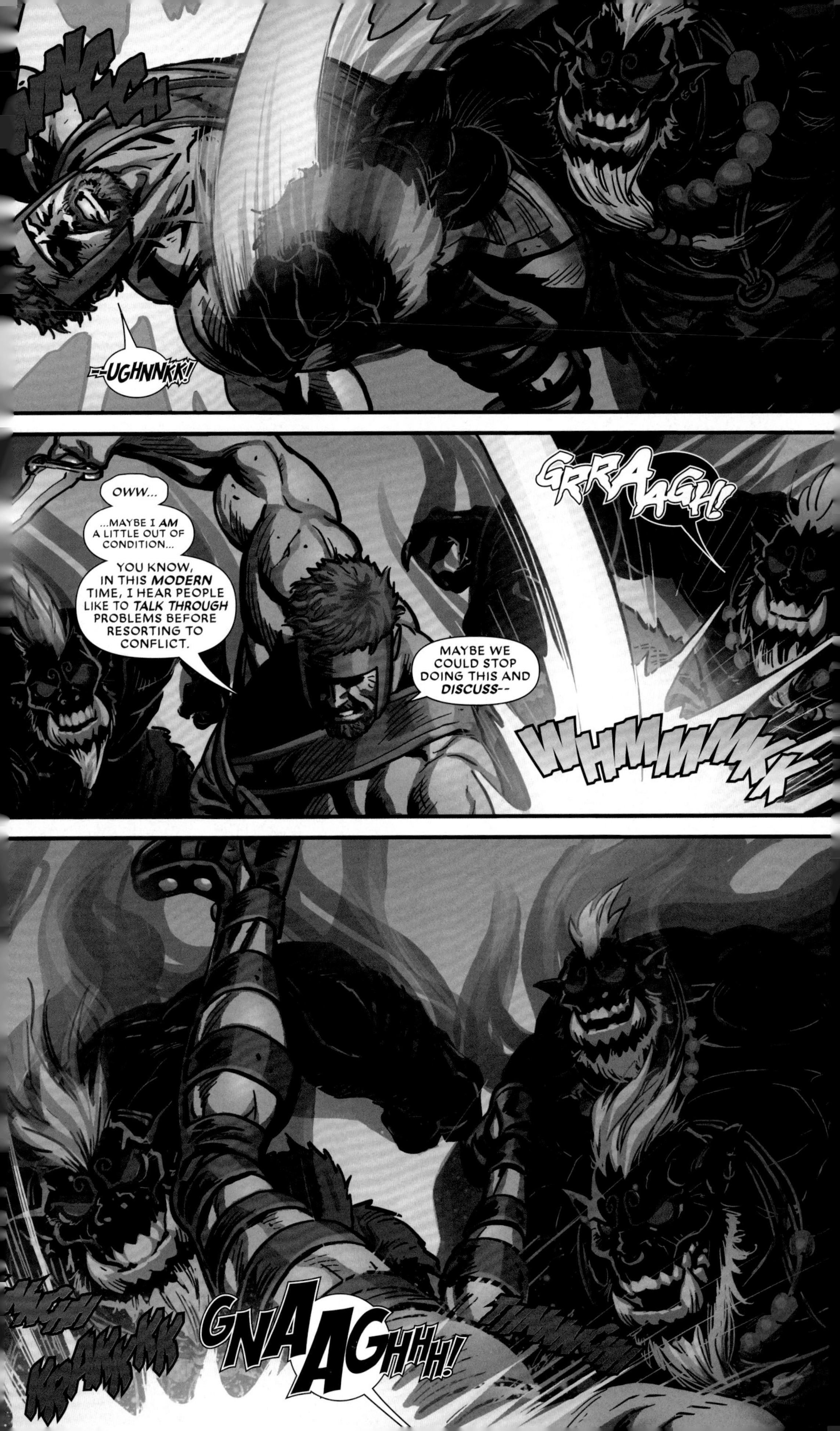
--UGHNNKK!
GRRAAGH!
OWW...
...MAYBE I *AM* A LITTLE OUT OF CONDITION...
YOU KNOW, IN THIS *MODERN* TIME, I HEAR PEOPLE LIKE TO *TALK THROUGH* PROBLEMS BEFORE RESORTING TO CONFLICT.
MAYBE WE COULD STOP DOING THIS AND *DISCUSS*--
WHMMMMKK
GNAAAGHHH!

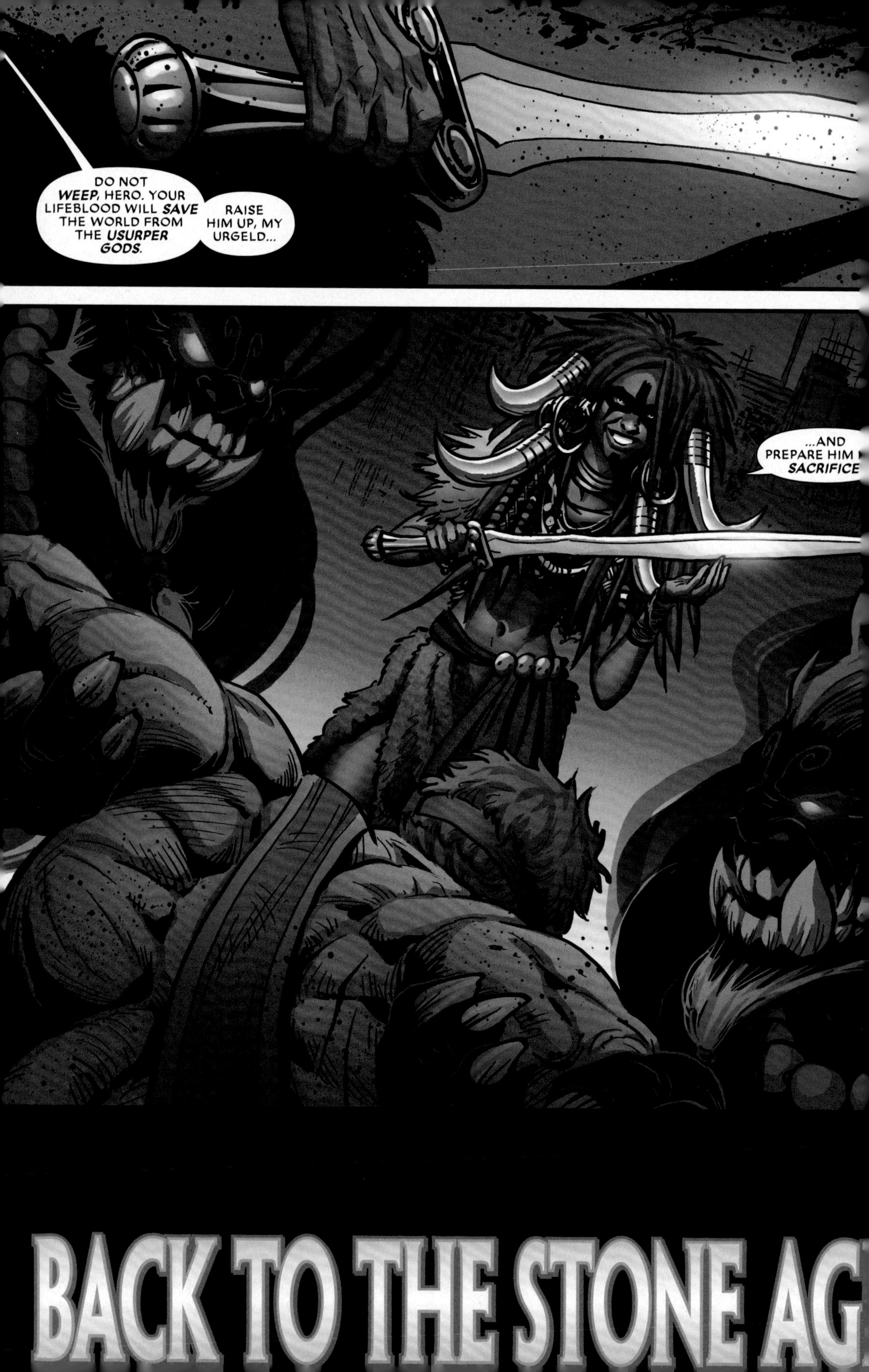
DO NOT WEEP, HERO. YOUR LIFEBLOOD WILL SAVE THE WORLD FROM THE USURPER GODS.
RAISE HIM UP, MY URGELD...
...AND PREPARE HIM SACRIFICE
BACK TO THE STONE AG

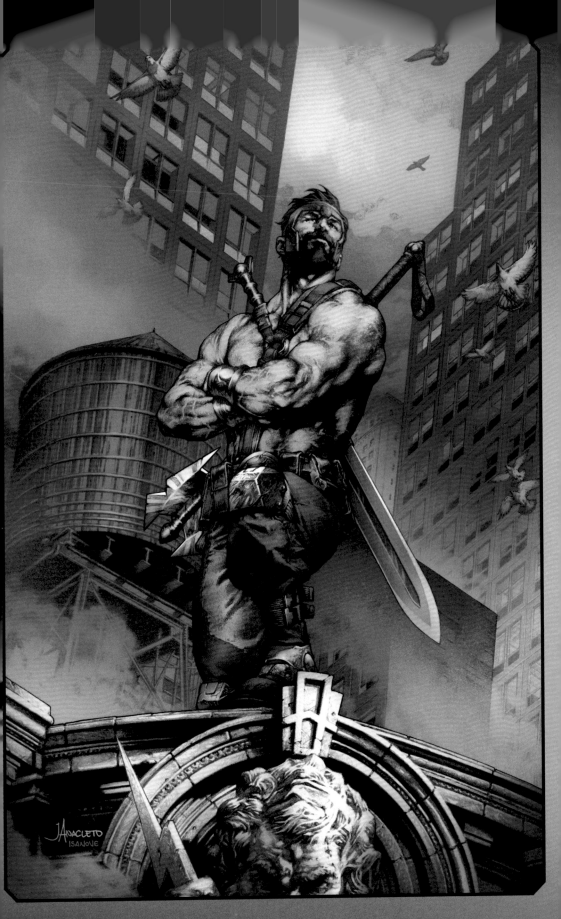

No. 1 VARIANT BY JAY ANACLETO & RICHARD ISANOVE

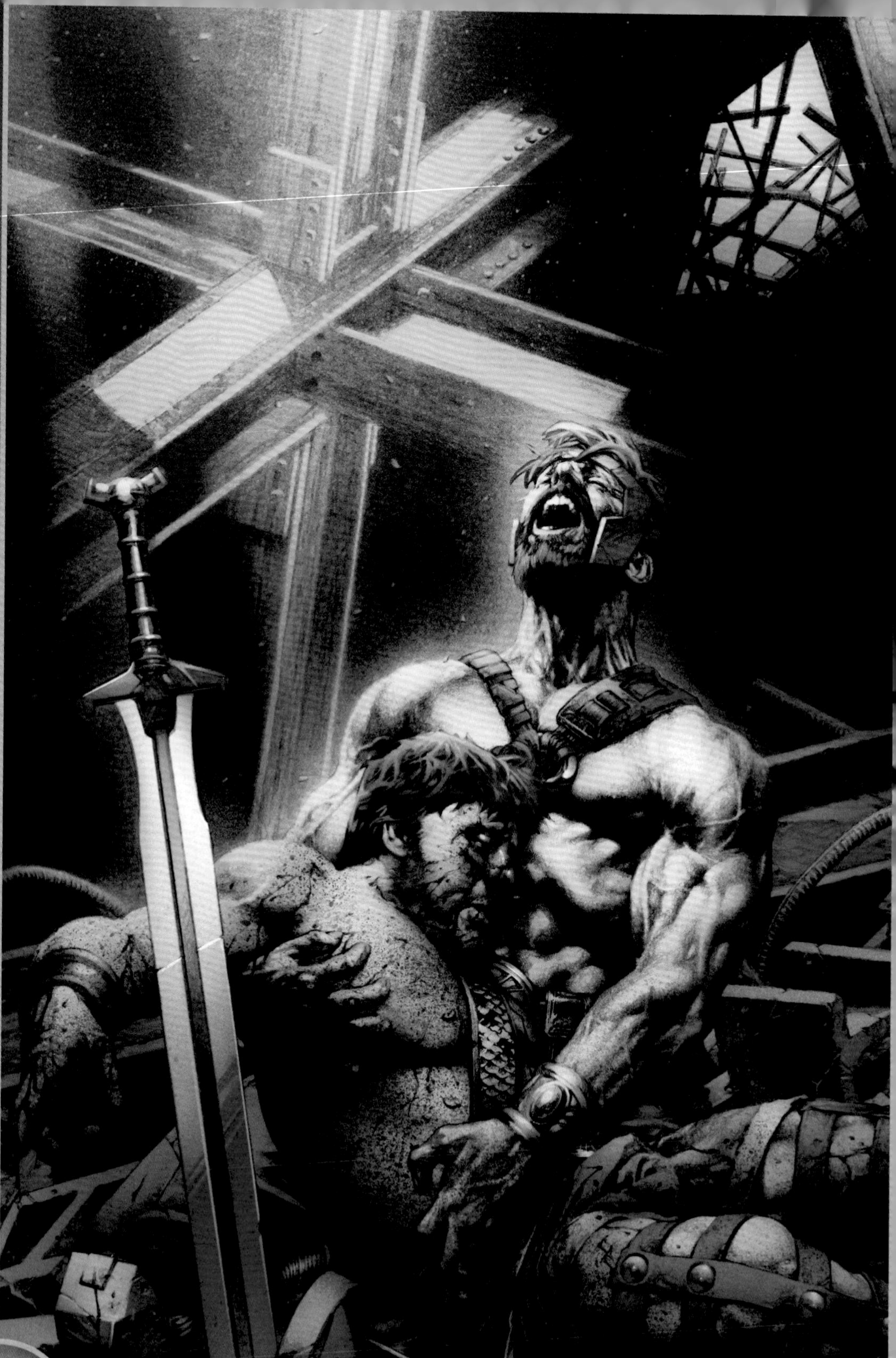

4 LET THERE BE BLOOD

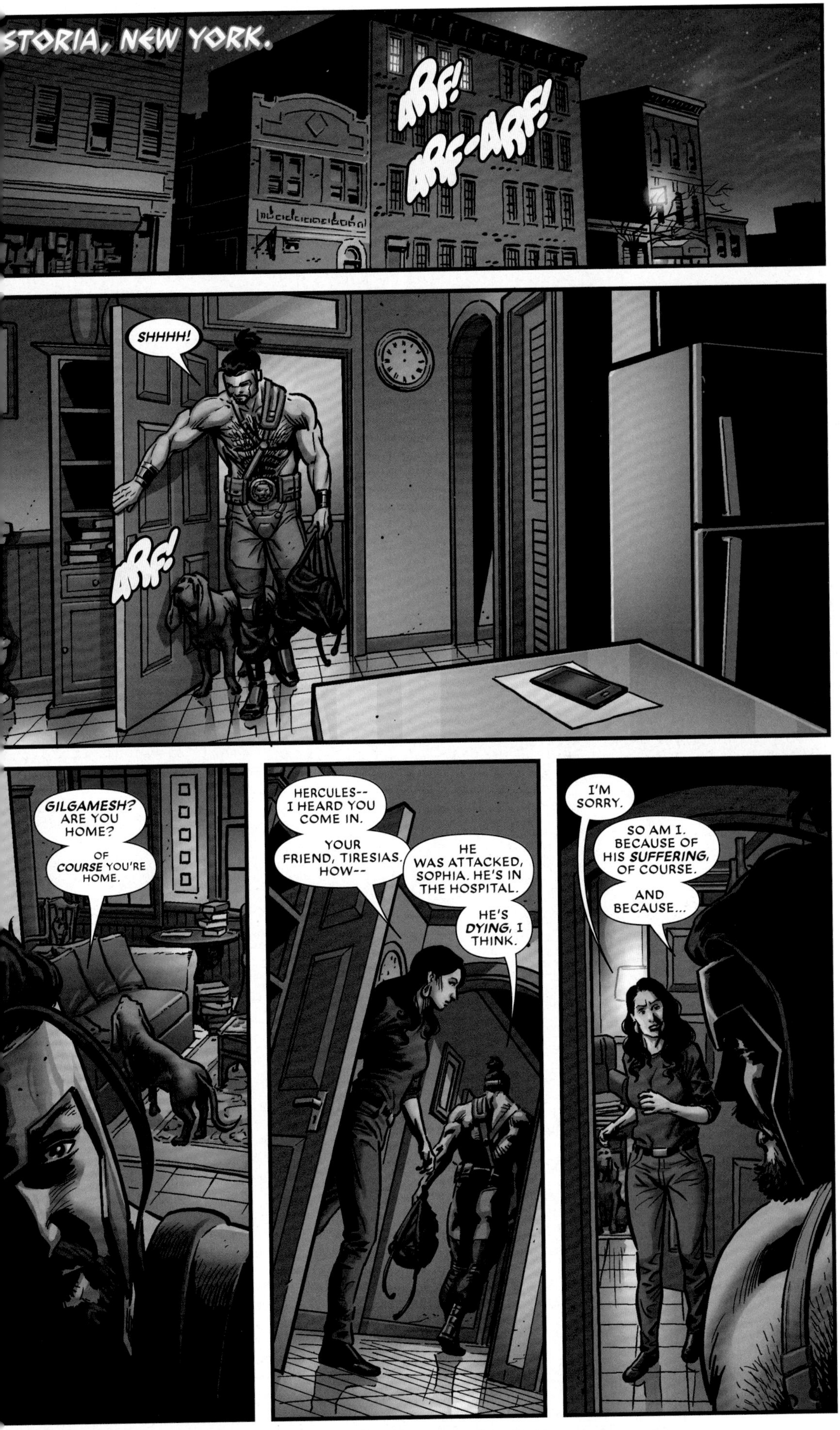
STORIA, NEW YORK.
ARF! ARF-ARF!
SHHHH!
ARF!
GILGAMESH? ARE YOU HOME?
OF COURSE YOU'RE HOME.
HERCULES-- I HEARD YOU COME IN.
YOUR FRIEND, TIRESIAS. HOW--
HE WAS ATTACKED, SOPHIA. HE'S IN THE HOSPITAL.
HE'S DYING, I THINK.
I'M SORRY.
SO AM I. BECAUSE OF HIS SUFFERING, OF COURSE.
AND BECAUSE...

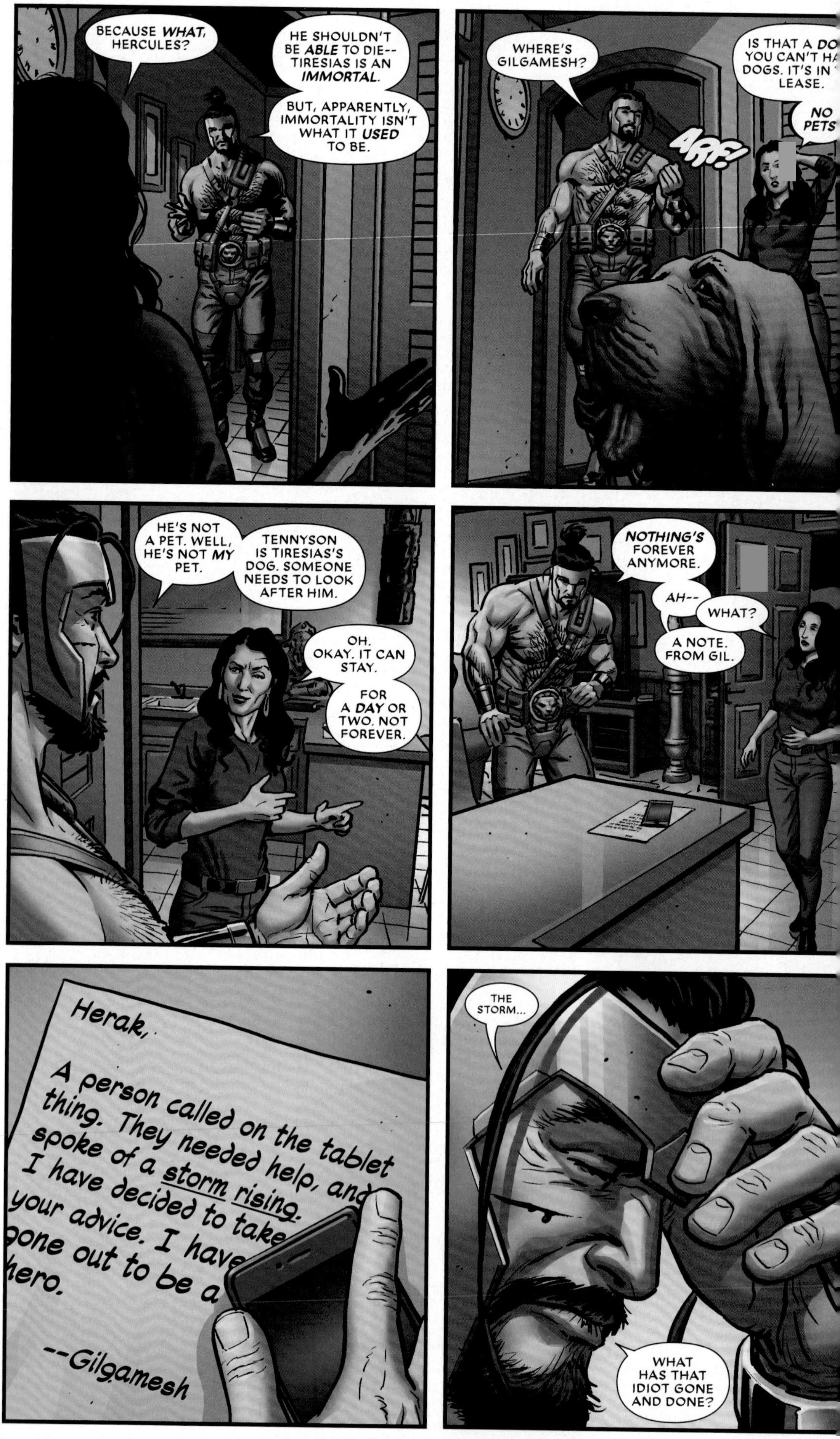

BECAUSE WHAT, HERCULES?
HE SHOULDN'T BE ABLE TO DIE-- TIRESIAS IS AN IMMORTAL.
BUT, APPARENTLY, IMMORTALITY ISN'T WHAT IT USED TO BE.
WHERE'S GILGAMESH?
IS THAT A DO YOU CAN'T HA DOGS. IT'S IN LEASE.
NO PETS
ARF!
HE'S NOT A PET. WELL, HE'S NOT MY PET.
TENNYSON IS TIRESIAS'S DOG. SOMEONE NEEDS TO LOOK AFTER HIM.
OH. OKAY. IT CAN STAY.
FOR A DAY OR TWO. NOT FOREVER.
NOTHING'S FOREVER ANYMORE.
AH--
WHAT?
A NOTE. FROM GIL.
Herak,
A person called on the tablet thing. They needed help, and spoke of a storm rising. I have decided to take your advice. I have gone out to be a hero.
--Gilgamesh
THE STORM...
WHAT HAS THAT IDIOT GONE AND DONE?

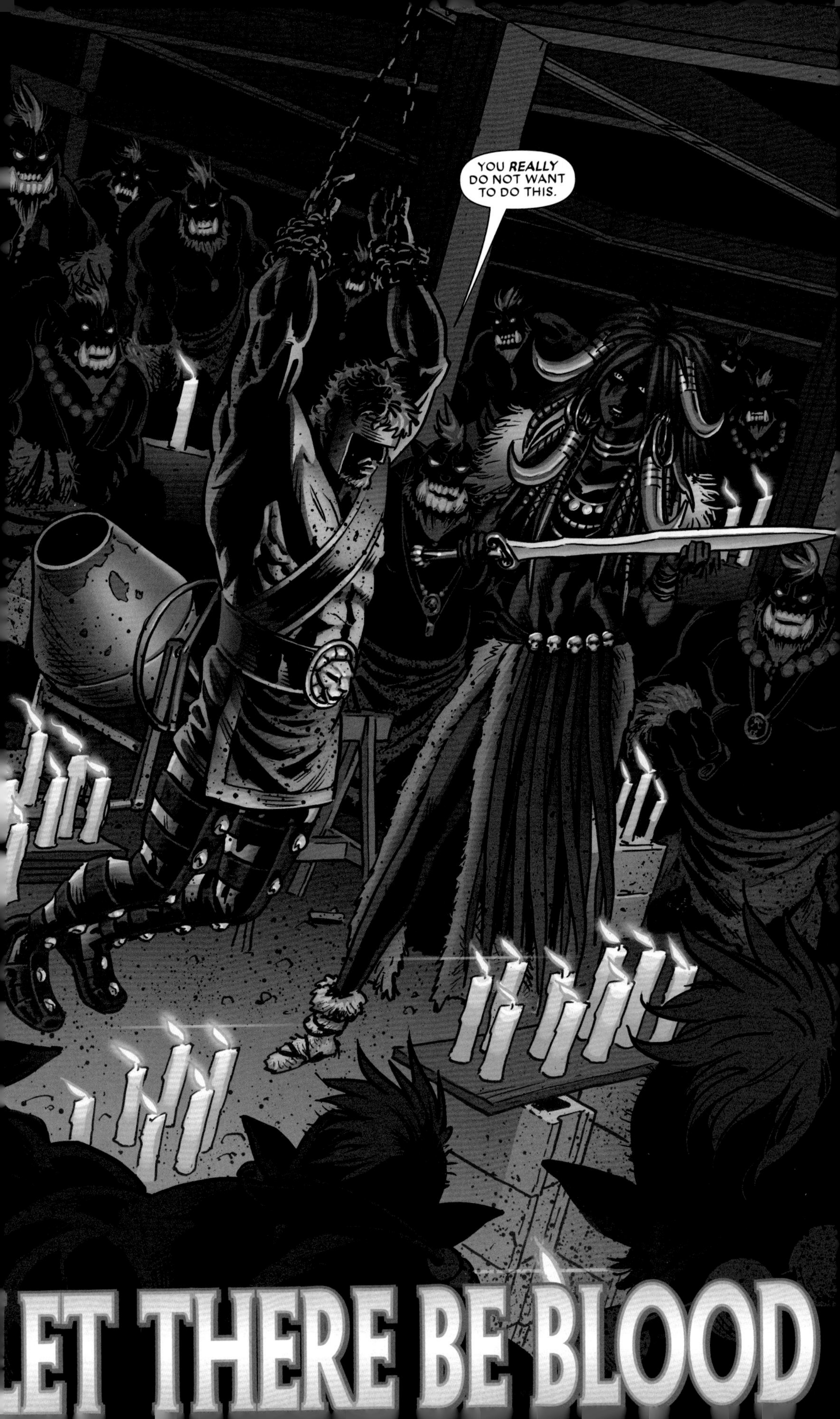
YOU REALLY DO NOT WANT TO DO THIS.
LET THERE BE BLOOD

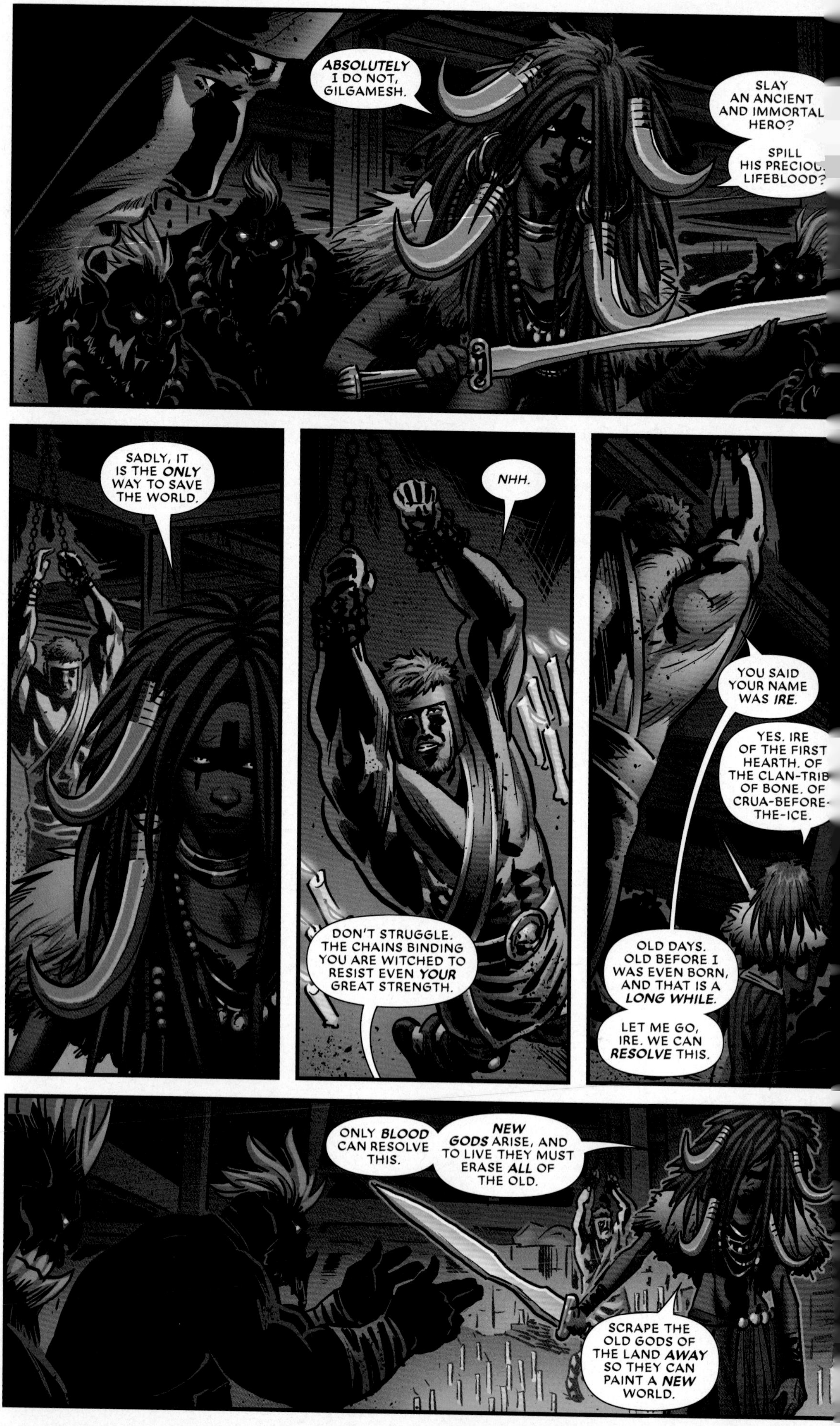
ABSOLUTELY I DO NOT, GILGAMESH.
SLAY AN ANCIENT AND IMMORTAL HERO?
SPILL HIS PRECIOU LIFEBLOOD?
SADLY, IT IS THE ONLY WAY TO SAVE THE WORLD.
NHH.
DON'T STRUGGLE. THE CHAINS BINDING YOU ARE WITCHED TO RESIST EVEN YOUR GREAT STRENGTH.
YOU SAID YOUR NAME WAS IRE.
YES. IRE OF THE FIRST HEARTH. OF THE CLAN-TRIB OF BONE. OF CRUA-BEFORE-THE-ICE.
OLD DAYS. OLD BEFORE I WAS EVEN BORN, AND THAT IS A LONG WHILE.
LET ME GO, IRE. WE CAN RESOLVE THIS.
ONLY BLOOD CAN RESOLVE THIS.
NEW GODS ARISE, AND TO LIVE THEY MUST ERASE ALL OF THE OLD.
SCRAPE THE OLD GODS OF THE LAND AWAY SO THEY CAN PAINT A NEW WORLD.

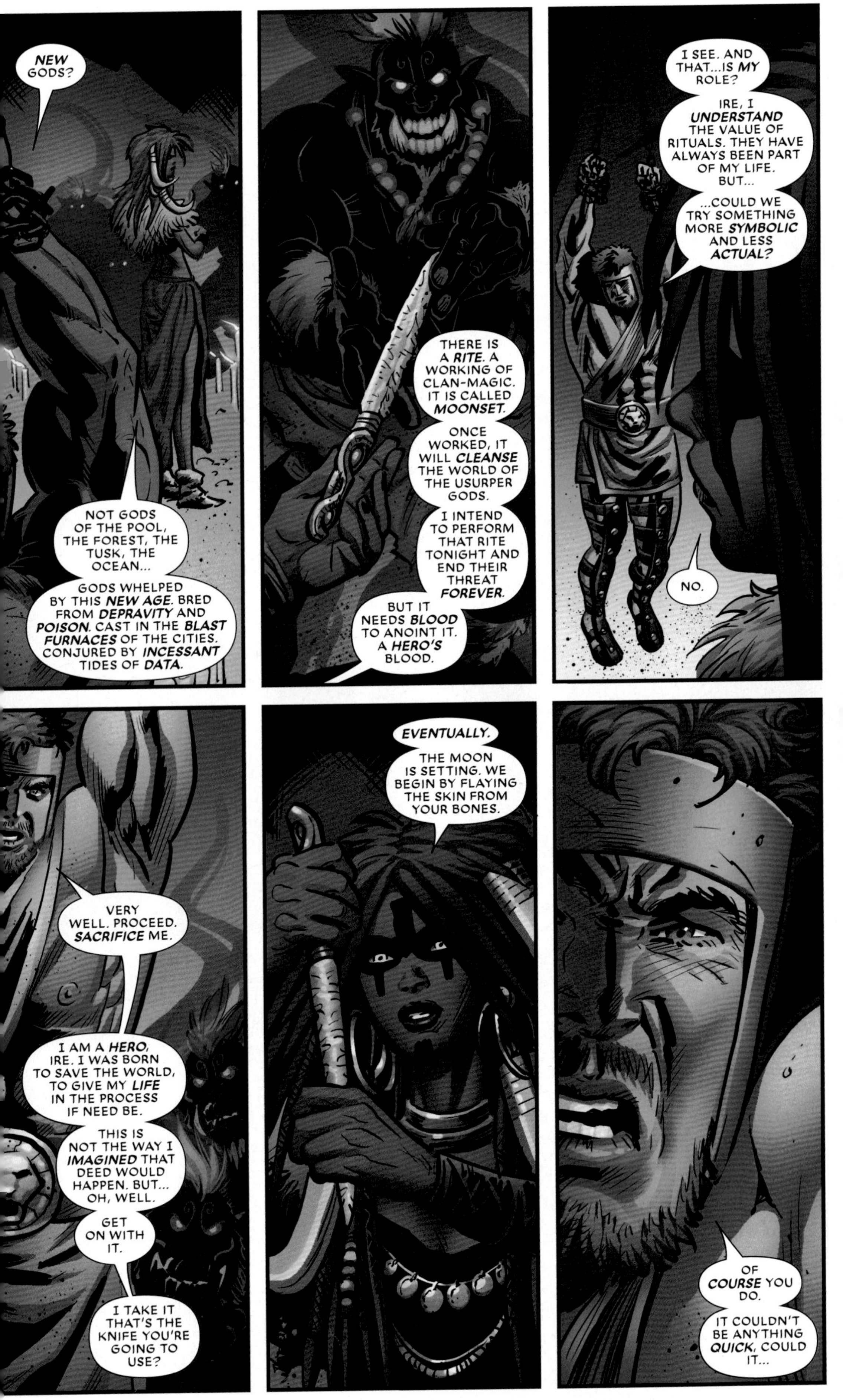
NEW GODS?
NOT GODS OF THE POOL, THE FOREST, THE TUSK, THE OCEAN...
GODS WHELPED BY THIS NEW AGE. BRED FROM DEPRAVITY AND POISON. CAST IN THE BLAST FURNACES OF THE CITIES. CONJURED BY INCESSANT TIDES OF DATA.
THERE IS A RITE. A WORKING OF CLAN-MAGIC. IT IS CALLED MOONSET.
ONCE WORKED, IT WILL CLEANSE THE WORLD OF THE USURPER GODS.
I INTEND TO PERFORM THAT RITE TONIGHT AND END THEIR THREAT FOREVER.
BUT IT NEEDS BLOOD TO ANOINT IT. A HERO'S BLOOD.
I SEE. AND THAT...IS MY ROLE?
IRE, I UNDERSTAND THE VALUE OF RITUALS. THEY HAVE ALWAYS BEEN PART OF MY LIFE. BUT...
...COULD WE TRY SOMETHING MORE SYMBOLIC AND LESS ACTUAL?
NO.
VERY WELL. PROCEED. SACRIFICE ME.
I AM A HERO, IRE. I WAS BORN TO SAVE THE WORLD, TO GIVE MY LIFE IN THE PROCESS IF NEED BE.
THIS IS NOT THE WAY I IMAGINED THAT DEED WOULD HAPPEN. BUT... OH, WELL.
GET ON WITH IT.
I TAKE IT THAT'S THE KNIFE YOU'RE GOING TO USE?
EVENTUALLY.
THE MOON IS SETTING. WE BEGIN BY FLAYING THE SKIN FROM YOUR BONES.
OF COURSE YOU DO.
IT COULDN'T BE ANYTHING QUICK, COULD IT...

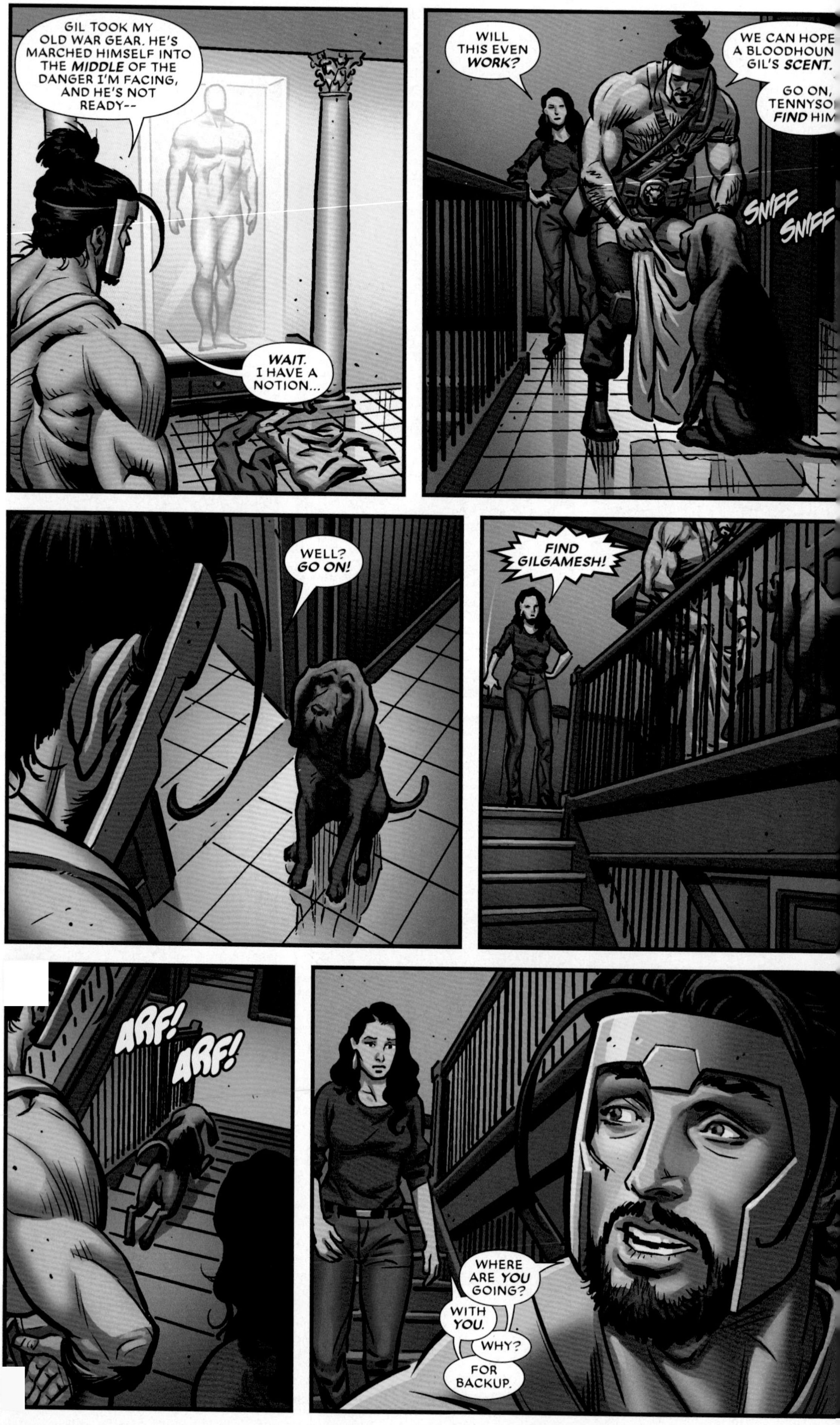

GIL TOOK MY OLD WAR GEAR. HE'S MARCHED HIMSELF INTO THE *MIDDLE* OF THE DANGER I'M FACING, AND HE'S NOT READY--
WAIT. I HAVE A NOTION...
WILL THIS EVEN *WORK?*
WE CAN HOPE A BLOODHOUN GIL'S *SCENT.*
GO ON, TENNYSO *FIND* HIM
SNIFF SNIFF
WELL? *GO ON!*
FIND GILGAMESH!
ARF! ARF!
WHERE ARE *YOU* GOING?
WITH *YOU.*
WHY?
FOR BACKUP.

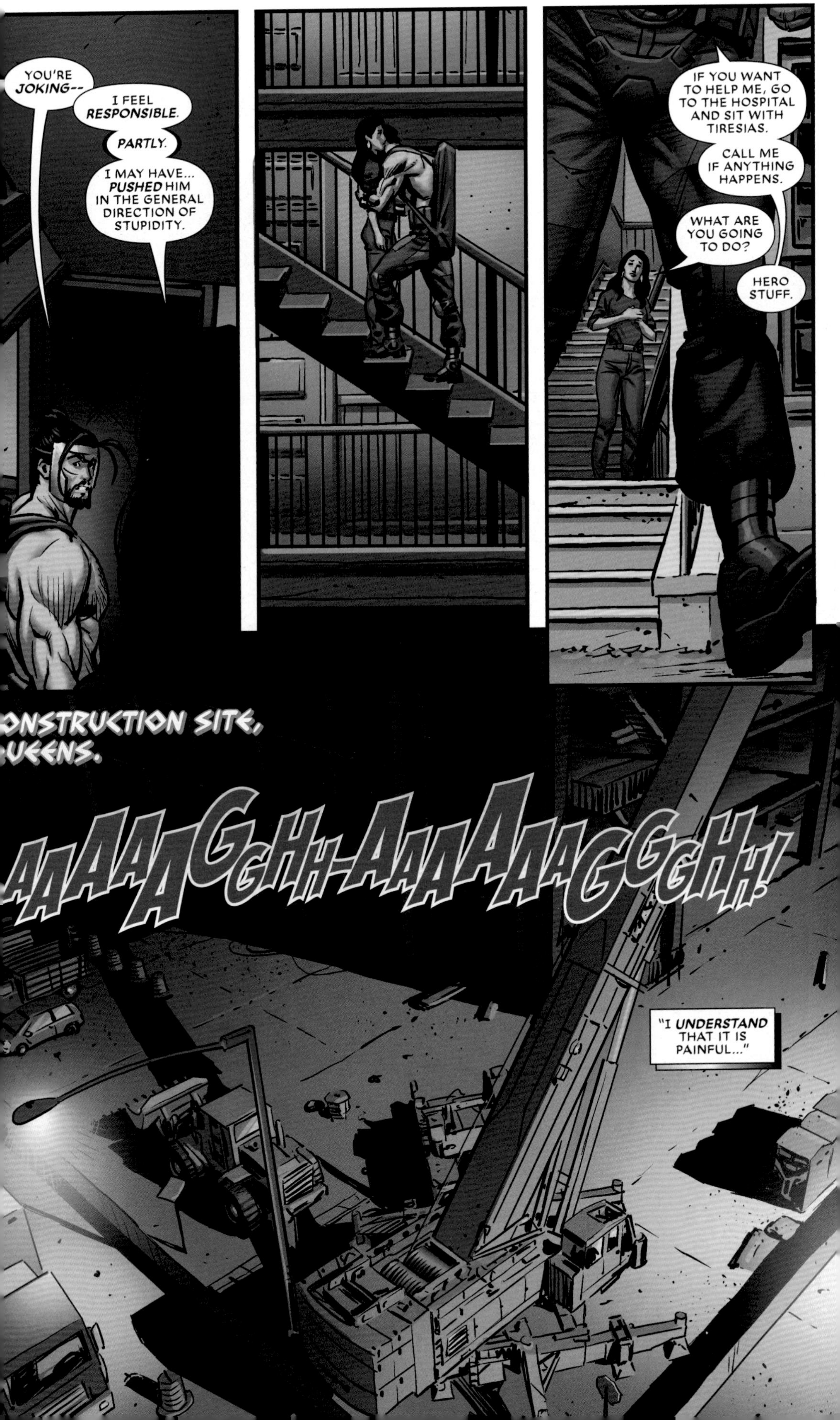

YOU'RE JOKING--
I FEEL RESPONSIBLE.
PARTLY.
I MAY HAVE... PUSHED HIM IN THE GENERAL DIRECTION OF STUPIDITY.
IF YOU WANT TO HELP ME, GO TO THE HOSPITAL AND SIT WITH TIRESIAS.
CALL ME IF ANYTHING HAPPENS.
WHAT ARE YOU GOING TO DO?
HERO STUFF.
ONSTRUCTION SITE, UEENS.
AAAAAGGHH-AAAAAAAGGGHH!
"I UNDERSTAND THAT IT IS PAINFUL..."

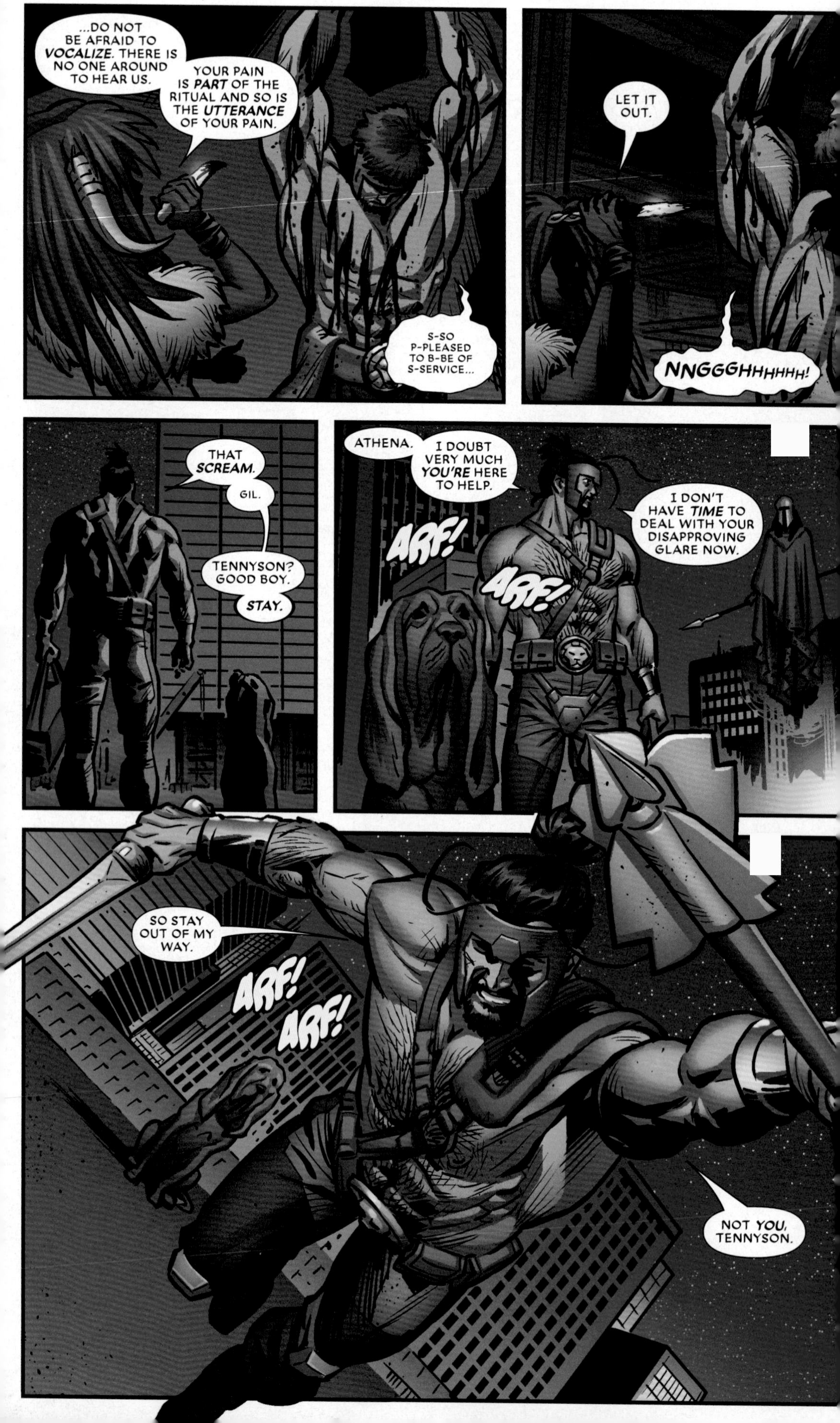

...DO NOT BE AFRAID TO *VOCALIZE.* THERE IS NO ONE AROUND TO HEAR US.
YOUR PAIN IS *PART* OF THE RITUAL AND SO IS THE *UTTERANCE* OF YOUR PAIN.
S-SO P-PLEASED TO B-BE OF S-SERVICE...
LET IT OUT.
NNGGGHHHHHH!
THAT *SCREAM.*
GIL.
TENNYSON? GOOD BOY.
STAY.
ATHENA.
I DOUBT VERY MUCH *YOU'RE* HERE TO HELP.
ARF!
ARF!
I DON'T HAVE *TIME* TO DEAL WITH YOUR DISAPPROVING GLARE NOW.
SO STAY OUT OF MY WAY.
ARF!
ARF!
NOT *YOU,* TENNYSON.

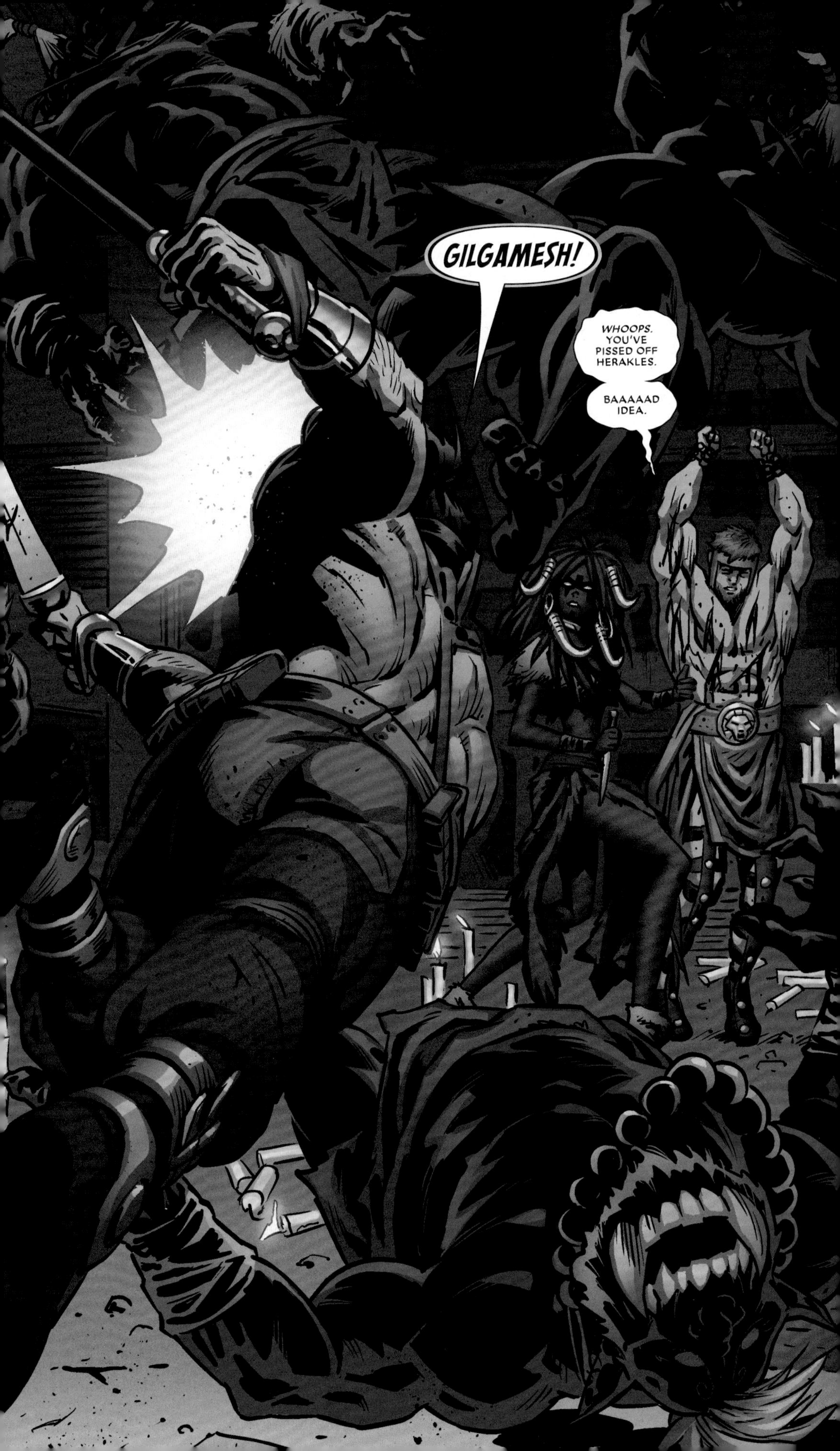
GILGAMESH!
WHOOPS. YOU'VE PISSED OFF HERAKLES.
BAAAAAD IDEA.

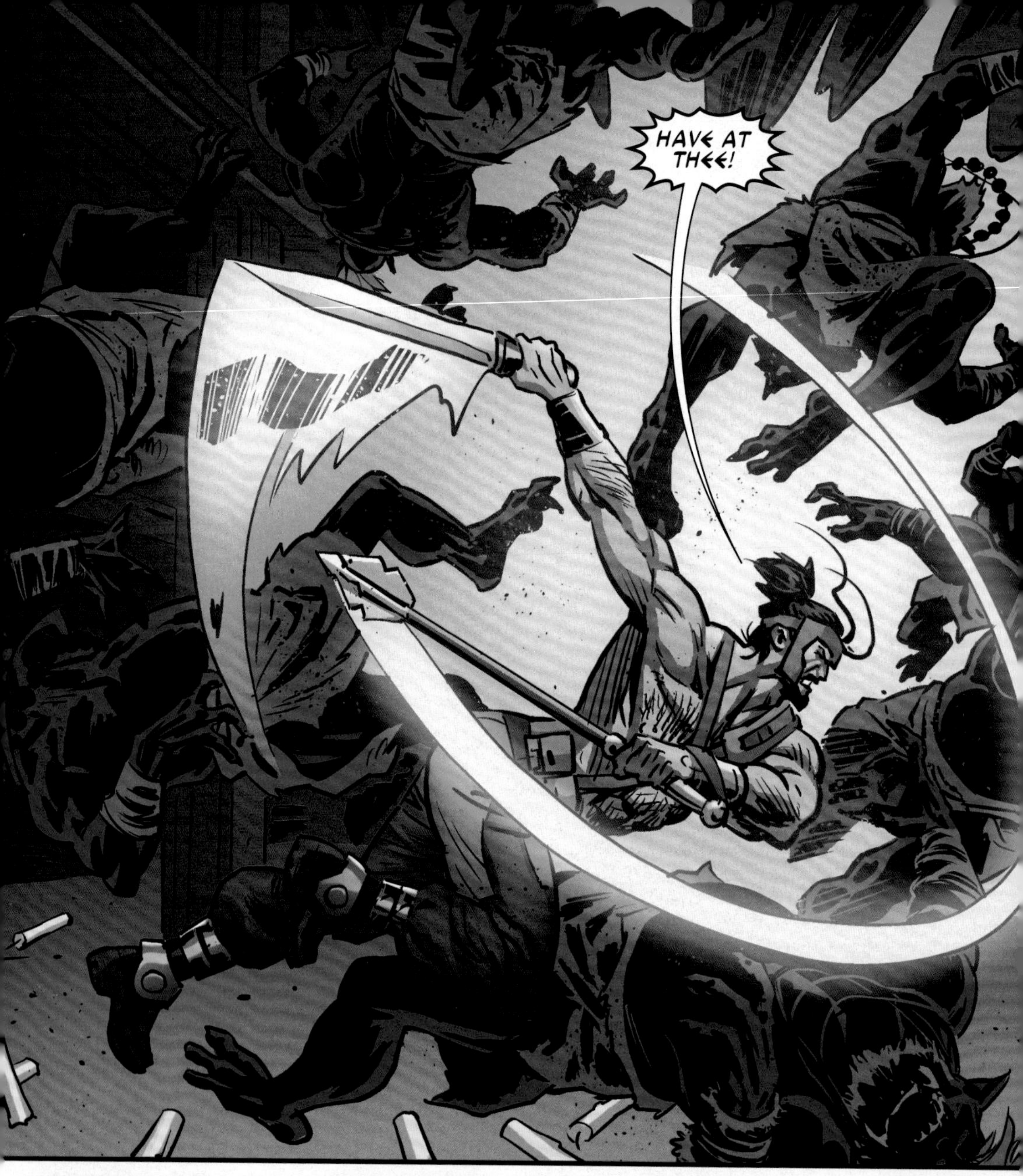
HAVE AT THEE!

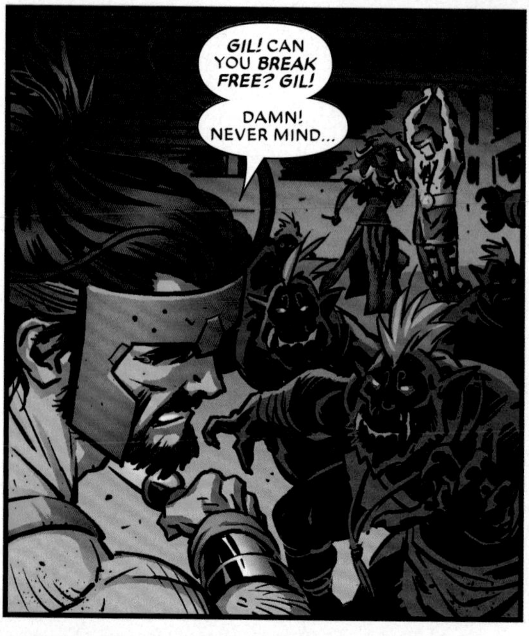
GIL! CAN YOU BREAK FREE? GIL!
DAMN! NEVER MIND...

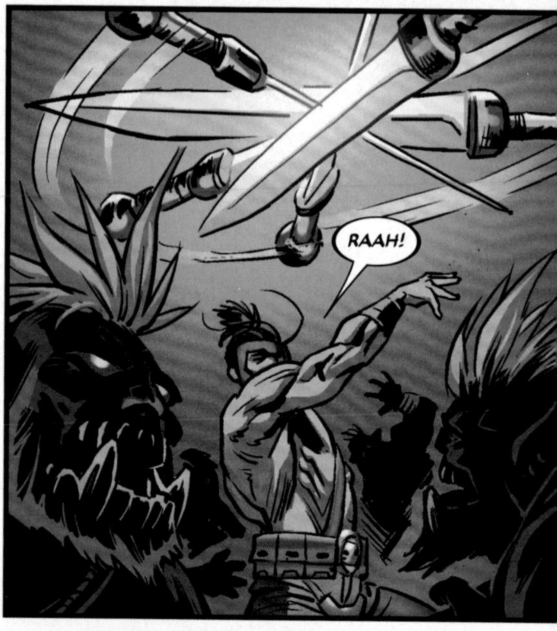
RAAH!

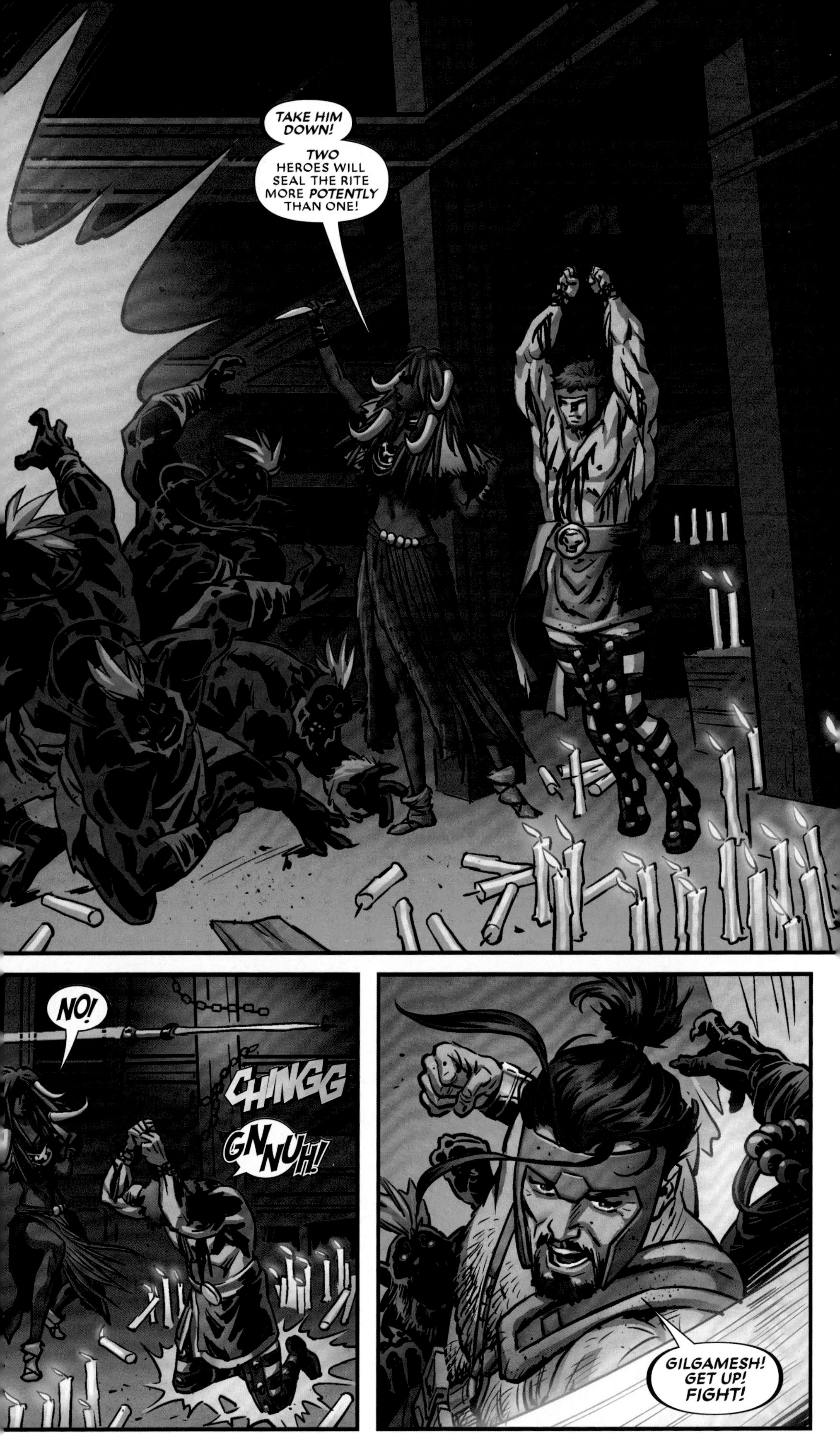
TAKE HIM DOWN!
TWO HEROES WILL SEAL THE RITE MORE POTENTLY THAN ONE!
NO!
CHINGG
GNNUH!
GILGAMESH! GET UP! FIGHT!

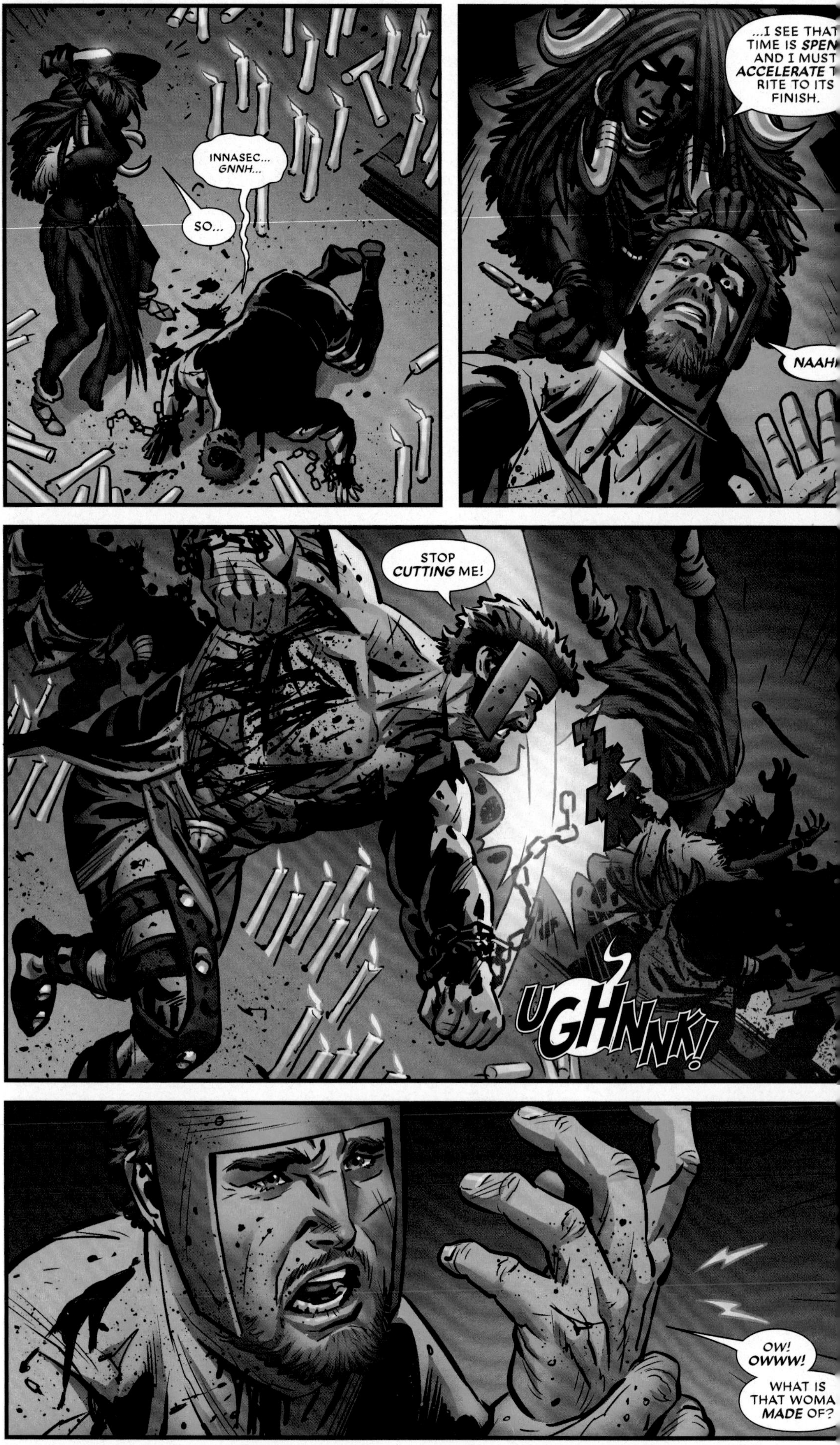
INNASEC... GNNH...
SO...
...I SEE THAT TIME IS SPEN AND I MUST ACCELERATE T RITE TO ITS FINISH.
NAAH
STOP CUTTING ME!
UGHNNK!
OW! OWWW!
WHAT IS THAT WOMA MADE OF?

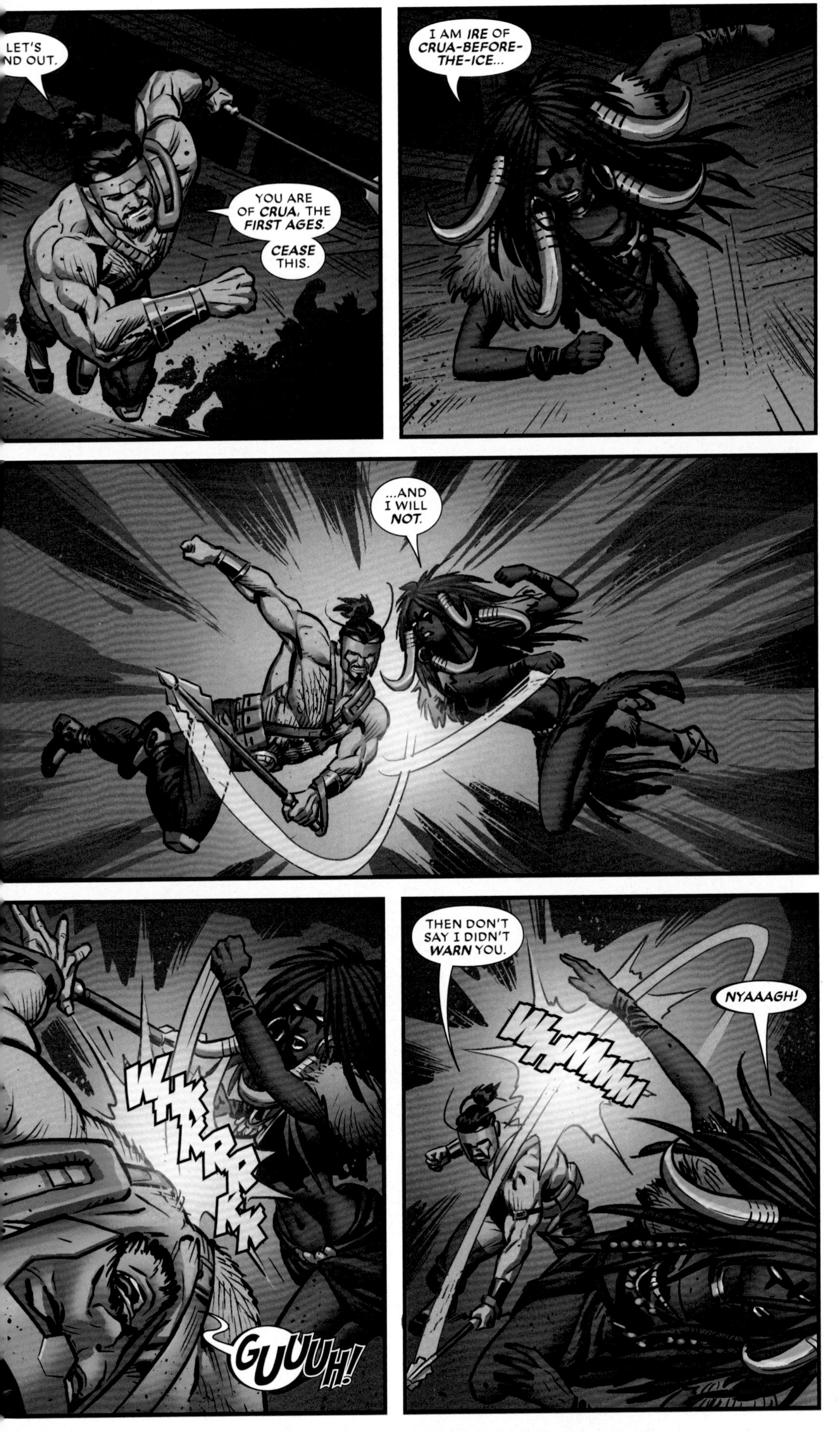
LET'S
ND OUT.
YOU ARE OF CRUA, THE FIRST AGES.
CEASE THIS.
I AM IRE OF CRUA-BEFORE-THE-ICE...
...AND I WILL NOT.
WHRRRKK
GUUUH!
THEN DON'T SAY I DIDN'T WARN YOU.
NYAAAGH!

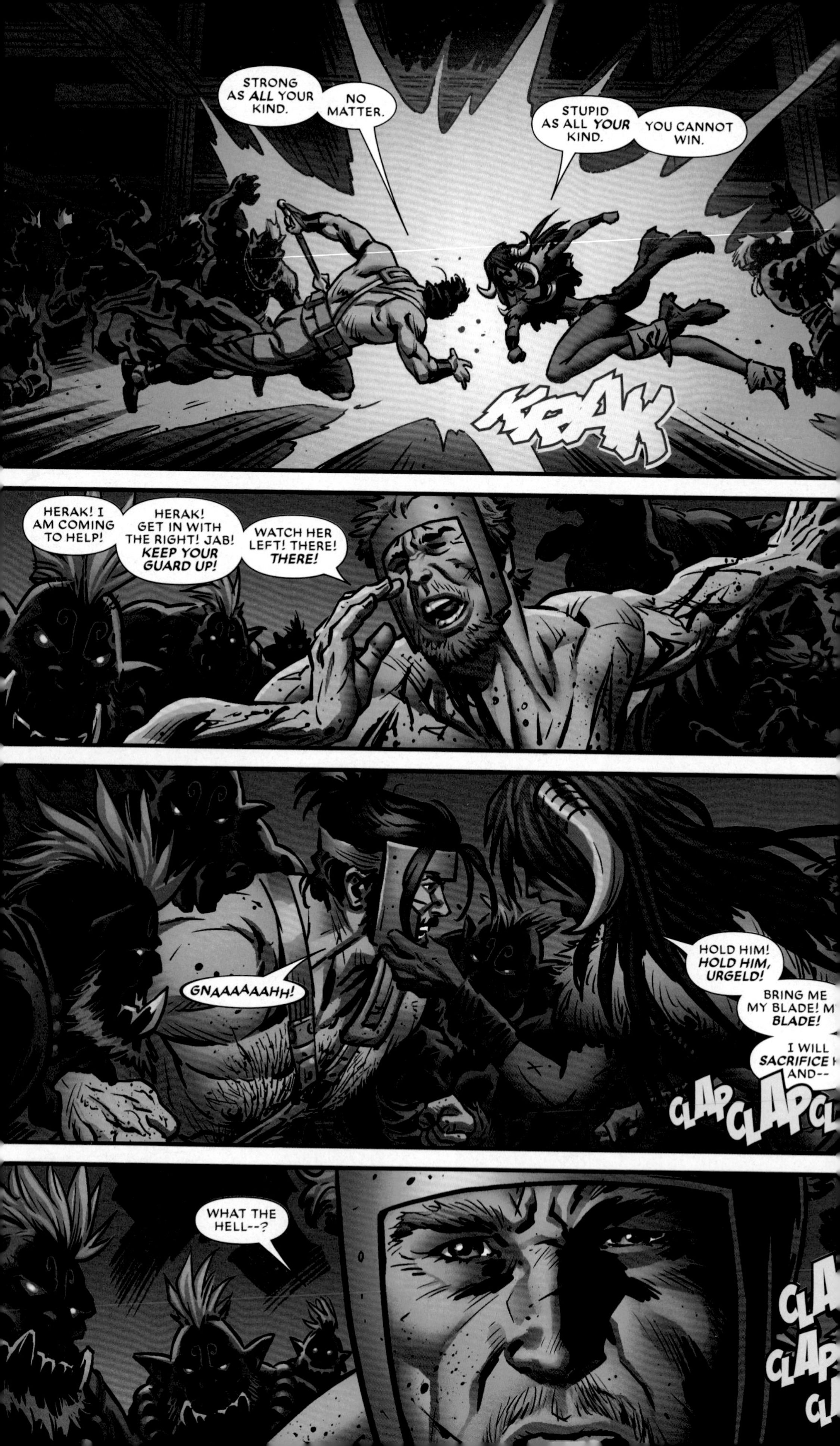
STRONG AS ALL YOUR KIND.
NO MATTER.
STUPID AS ALL YOUR KIND.
YOU CANNOT WIN.
KRAAK
HERAK! I AM COMING TO HELP!
HERAK! GET IN WITH THE RIGHT! JAB! KEEP YOUR GUARD UP!
WATCH HER LEFT! THERE! THERE!
GNAAAAAAHH!
HOLD HIM! HOLD HIM, URGELD!
BRING ME MY BLADE! M BLADE!
I WILL SACRIFICE AND--
CLAP CLAP
WHAT THE HELL--?

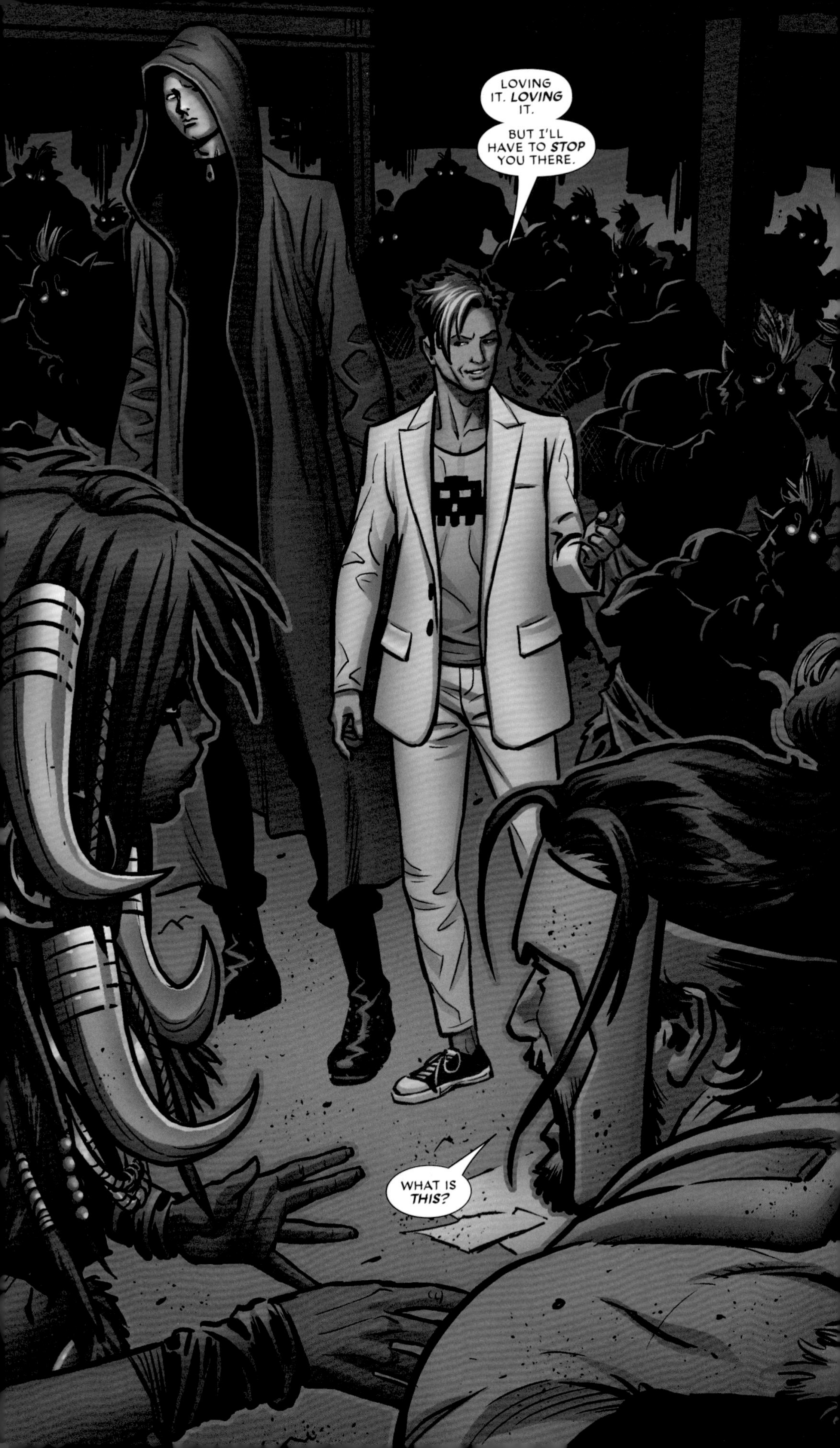
LOVING IT. *LOVING* IT.
BUT I'LL HAVE TO *STOP* YOU THERE.
WHAT IS *THIS?*

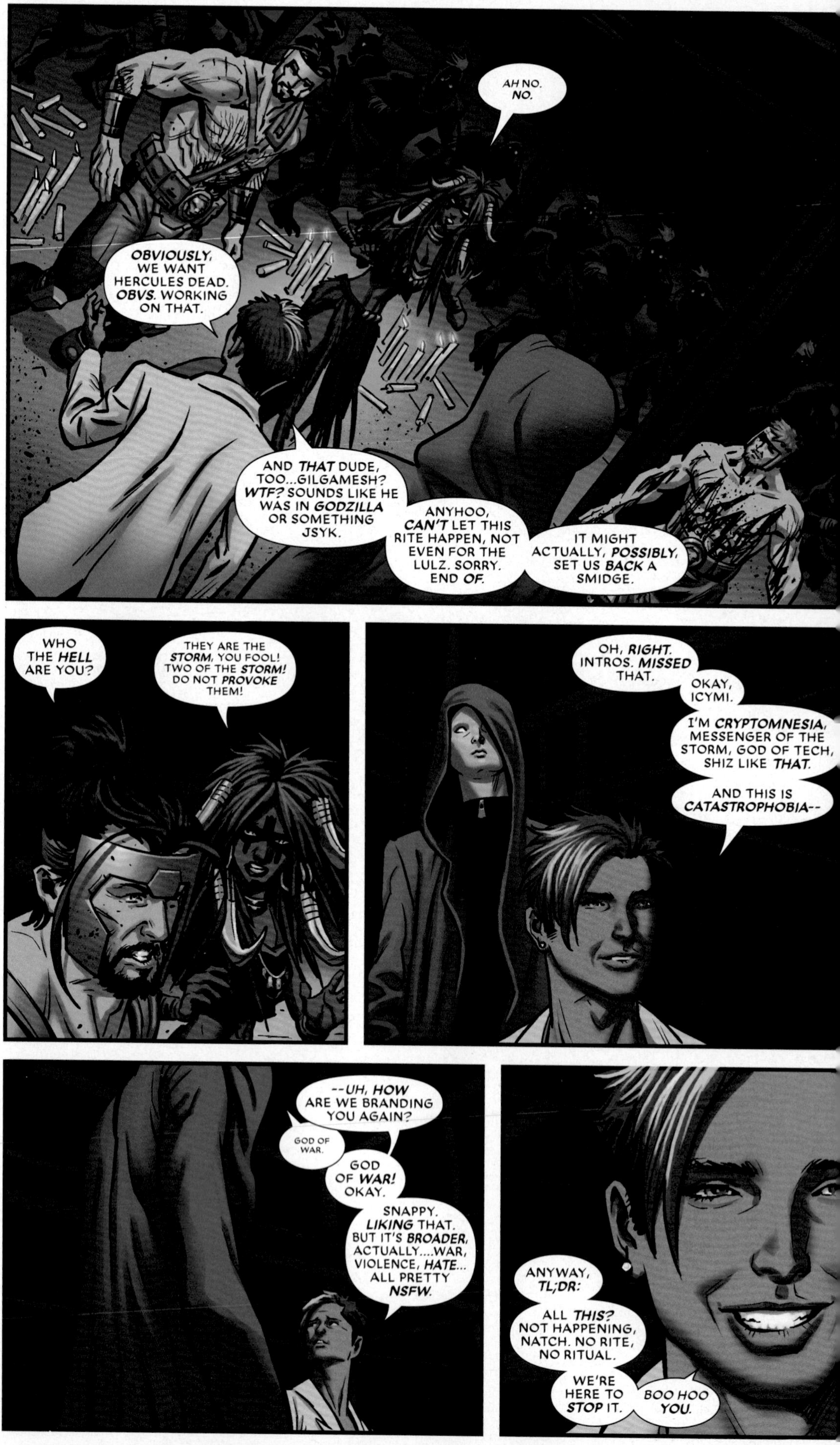

AH NO. NO.
OBVIOUSLY, WE WANT HERCULES DEAD. OBVS. WORKING ON THAT.
AND THAT DUDE, TOO...GILGAMESH? WTF? SOUNDS LIKE HE WAS IN GODZILLA OR SOMETHING JSYK.
ANYHOO, CAN'T LET THIS RITE HAPPEN, NOT EVEN FOR THE LULZ. SORRY. END OF.
IT MIGHT ACTUALLY, POSSIBLY, SET US BACK A SMIDGE.
WHO THE HELL ARE YOU?
THEY ARE THE STORM, YOU FOOL! TWO OF THE STORM! DO NOT PROVOKE THEM!
OH, RIGHT. INTROS. MISSED THAT.
OKAY, ICYMI.
I'M CRYPTOMNESIA, MESSENGER OF THE STORM, GOD OF TECH, SHIZ LIKE THAT.
AND THIS IS CATASTROPHOBIA--
--UH, HOW ARE WE BRANDING YOU AGAIN?
GOD OF WAR.
GOD OF WAR! OKAY.
SNAPPY. LIKING THAT. BUT IT'S BROADER, ACTUALLY....WAR, VIOLENCE, HATE... ALL PRETTY NSFW.
ANYWAY, TL;DR:
ALL THIS? NOT HAPPENING, NATCH. NO RITE, NO RITUAL.
WE'RE HERE TO STOP IT.
BOO HOO YOU.

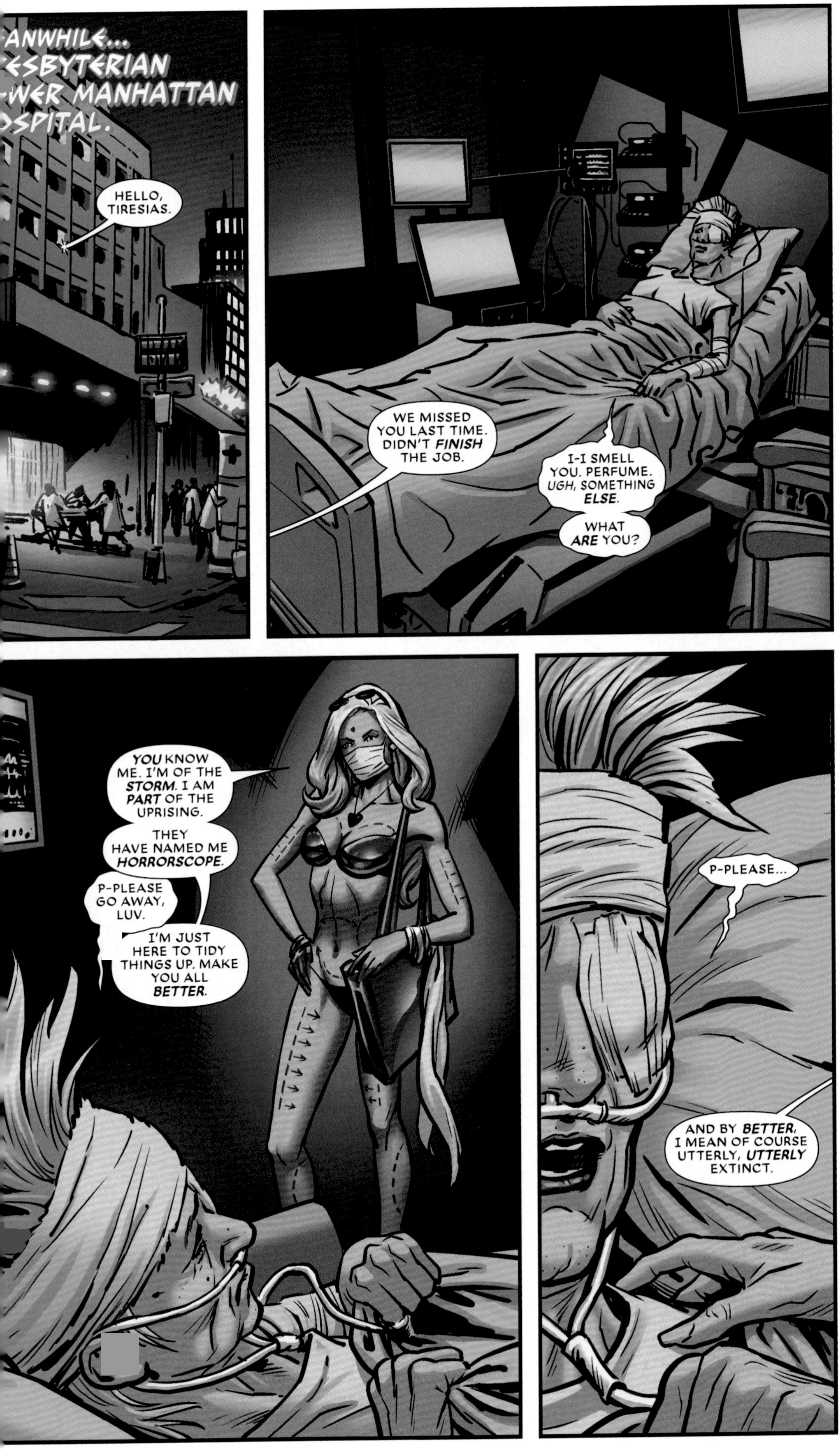
ANWHILE...
ESBYTERIAN
WER MANHATTAN
SPITAL.
HELLO, TIRESIAS.
WE MISSED YOU LAST TIME. DIDN'T *FINISH* THE JOB.
I-I SMELL YOU. PERFUME. *UGH*, SOMETHING *ELSE*.
WHAT *ARE* YOU?
YOU KNOW ME. I'M OF THE *STORM*. I AM *PART* OF THE UPRISING.
THEY HAVE NAMED ME *HORRORSCOPE*.
P-PLEASE GO AWAY, LUV.
I'M JUST HERE TO TIDY THINGS UP. MAKE YOU ALL *BETTER*.
P-PLEASE...
AND BY *BETTER*, I MEAN OF COURSE UTTERLY, *UTTERLY* EXTINCT.

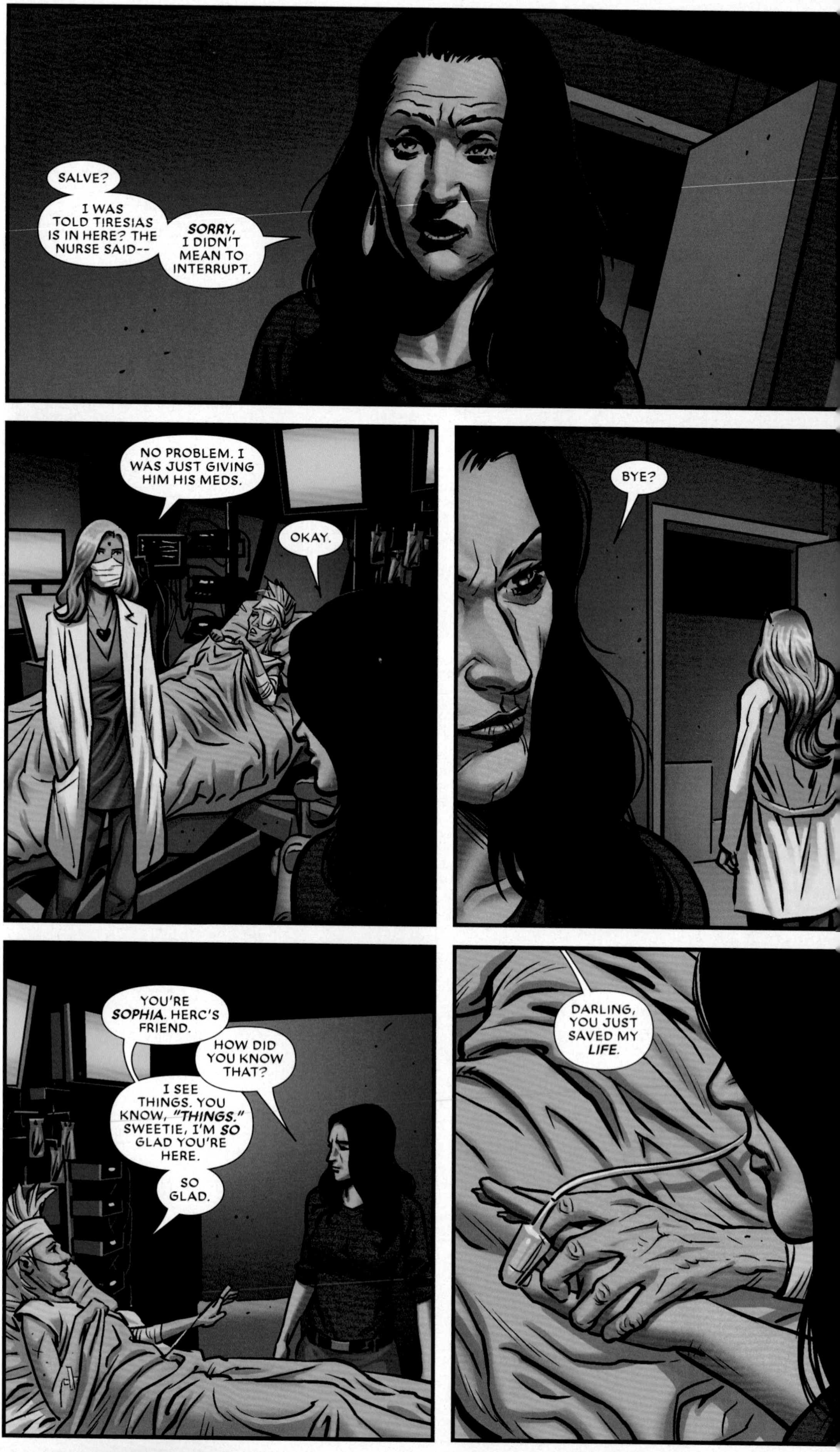
SALVE?
I WAS TOLD TIRESIAS IS IN HERE? THE NURSE SAID--
SORRY, I DIDN'T MEAN TO INTERRUPT.
NO PROBLEM. I WAS JUST GIVING HIM HIS MEDS.
OKAY.
BYE?
YOU'RE SOPHIA. HERC'S FRIEND.
HOW DID YOU KNOW THAT?
I SEE THINGS. YOU KNOW, "THINGS." SWEETIE, I'M SO GLAD YOU'RE HERE.
SO GLAD.
DARLING, YOU JUST SAVED MY LIFE.

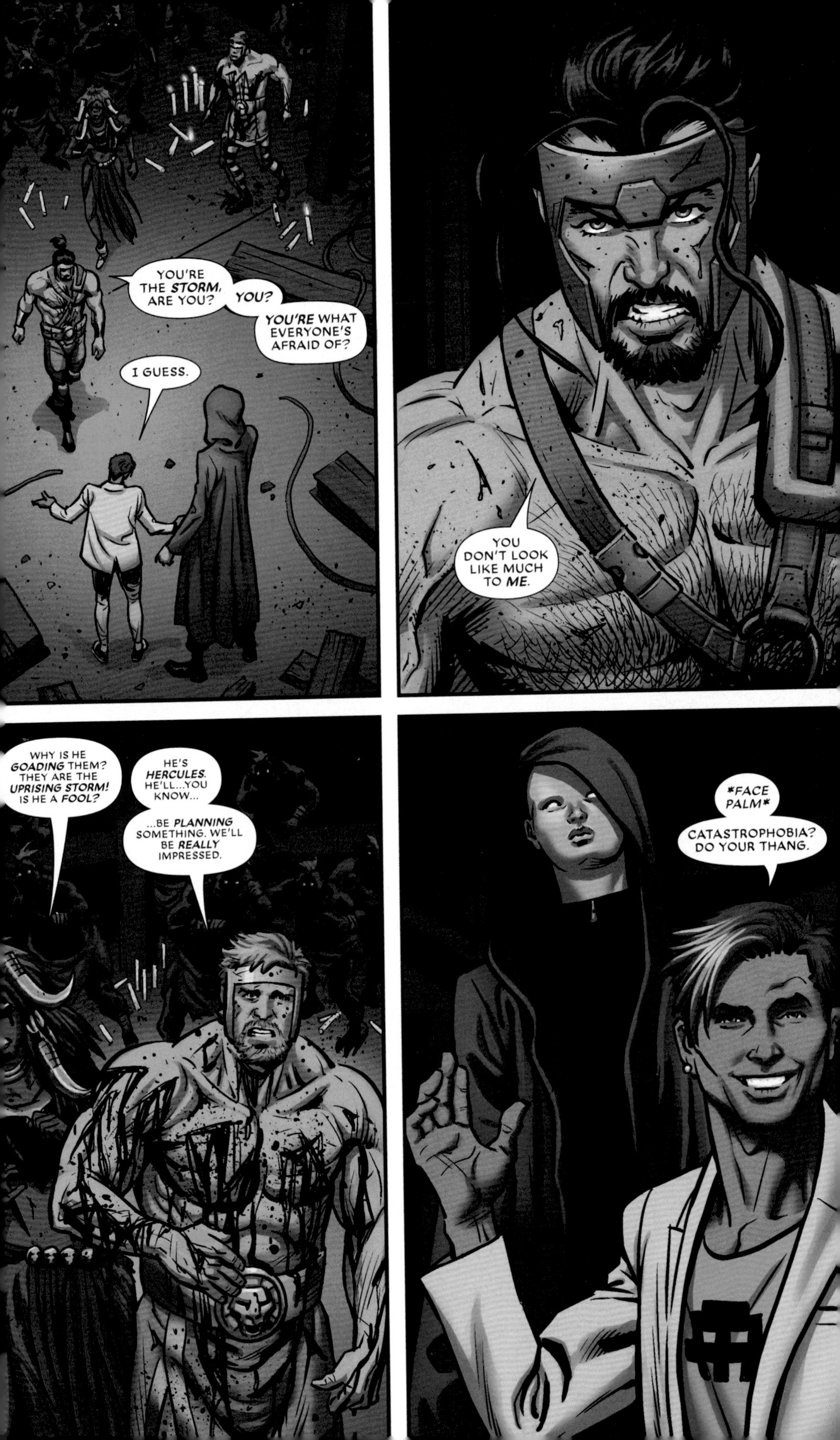
YOU'RE THE STORM, ARE YOU?
YOU?
YOU'RE WHAT EVERYONE'S AFRAID OF?
I GUESS.
YOU DON'T LOOK LIKE MUCH TO ME.
WHY IS HE GOADING THEM? THEY ARE THE UPRISING STORM! IS HE A FOOL?
HE'S HERCULES. HE'LL...YOU KNOW...
...BE PLANNING SOMETHING. WE'LL BE REALLY IMPRESSED.
FACE PALM
CATASTROPHOBIA? DO YOUR THANG.

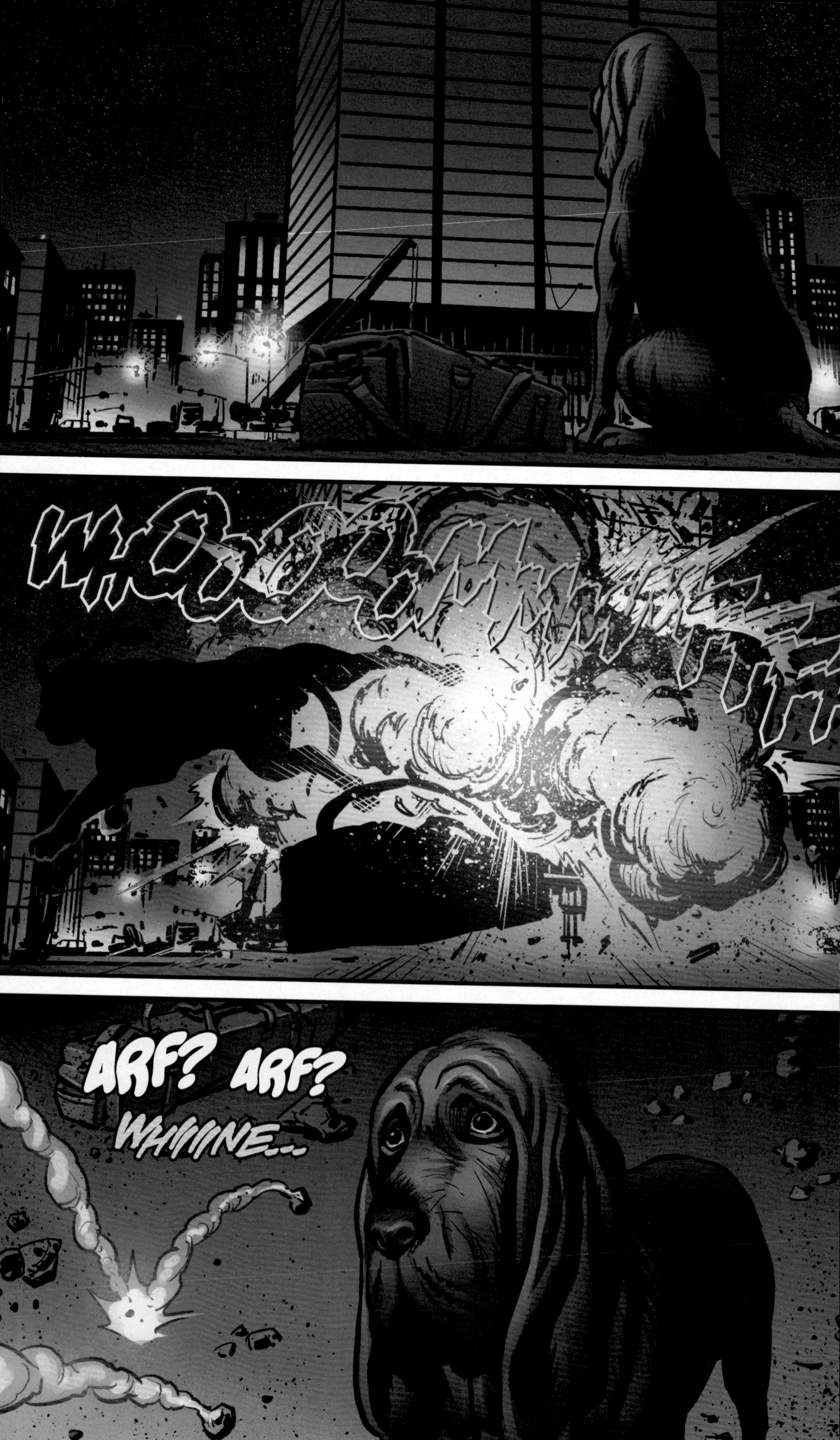
WHOOOOMMMFFF
ARF? ARF?
WHIIIINE...

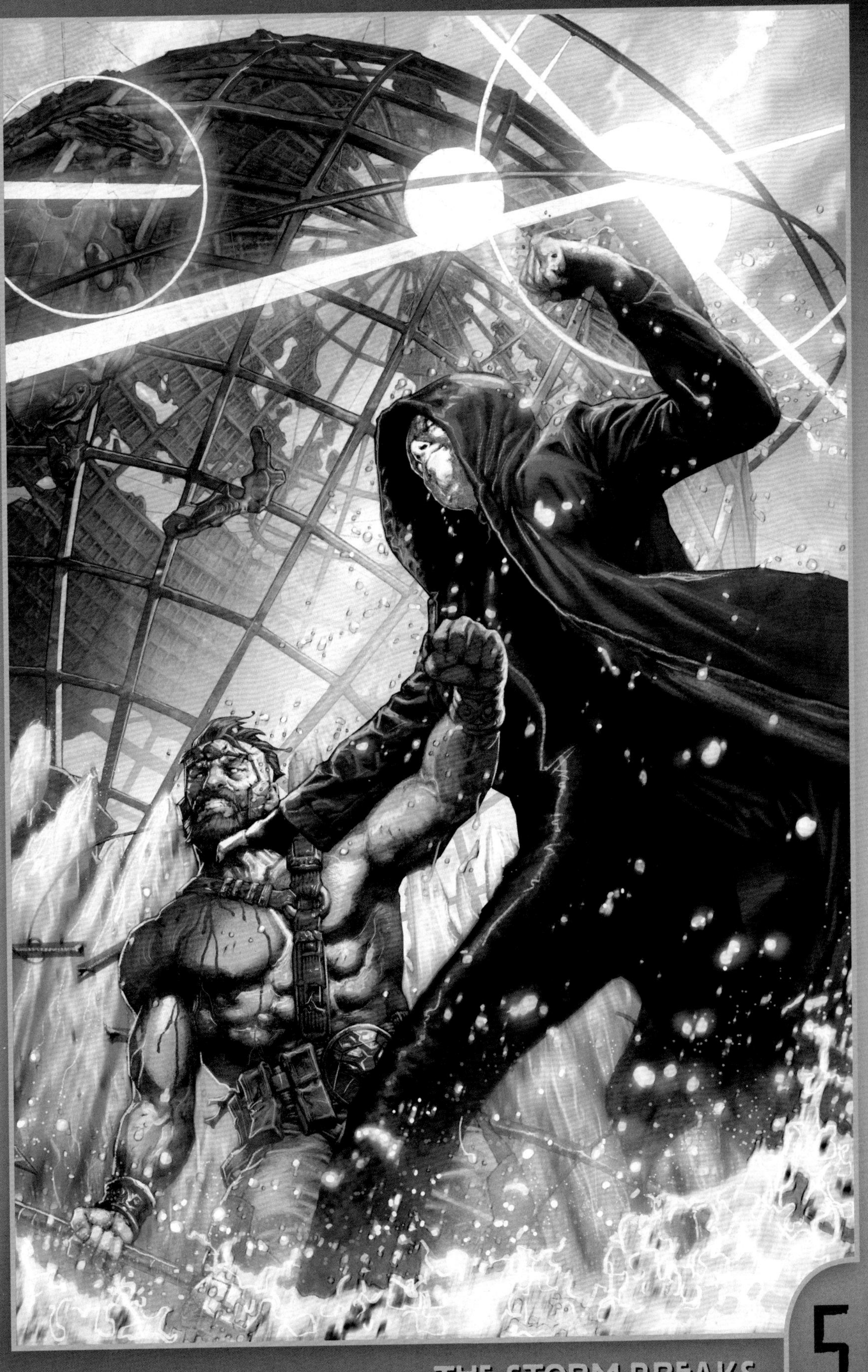

5

THE STORM BREAKS

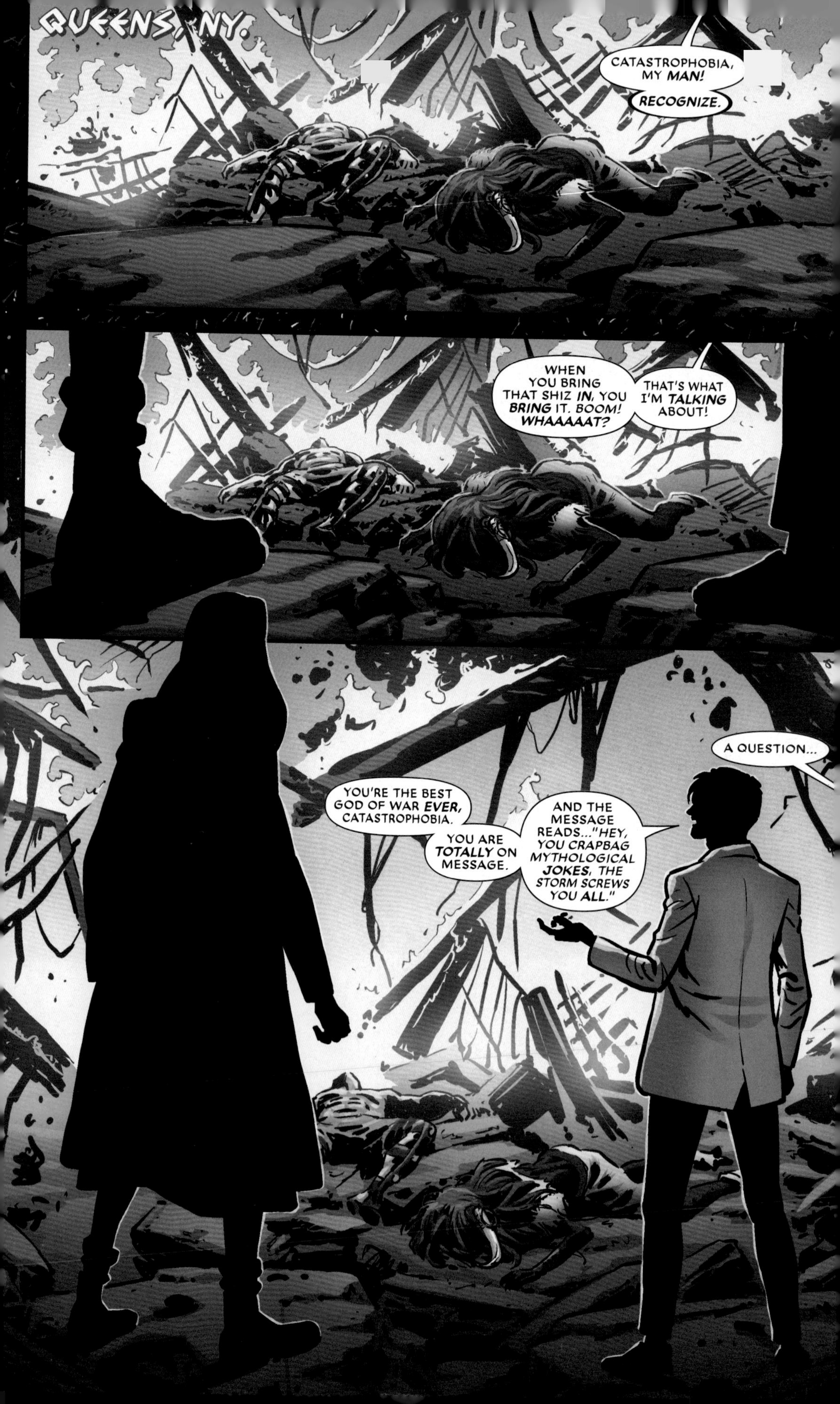
QUEENS, NY.
CATASTROPHOBIA, MY MAN!
RECOGNIZE.
WHEN YOU BRING THAT SHIZ IN, YOU BRING IT. BOOM! WHAAAAAT?
THAT'S WHAT I'M TALKING ABOUT!
YOU'RE THE BEST GOD OF WAR EVER, CATASTROPHOBIA.
YOU ARE TOTALLY ON MESSAGE.
AND THE MESSAGE READS..."HEY, YOU CRAPBAG MYTHOLOGICAL JOKES, THE STORM SCREWS YOU ALL."
A QUESTION...

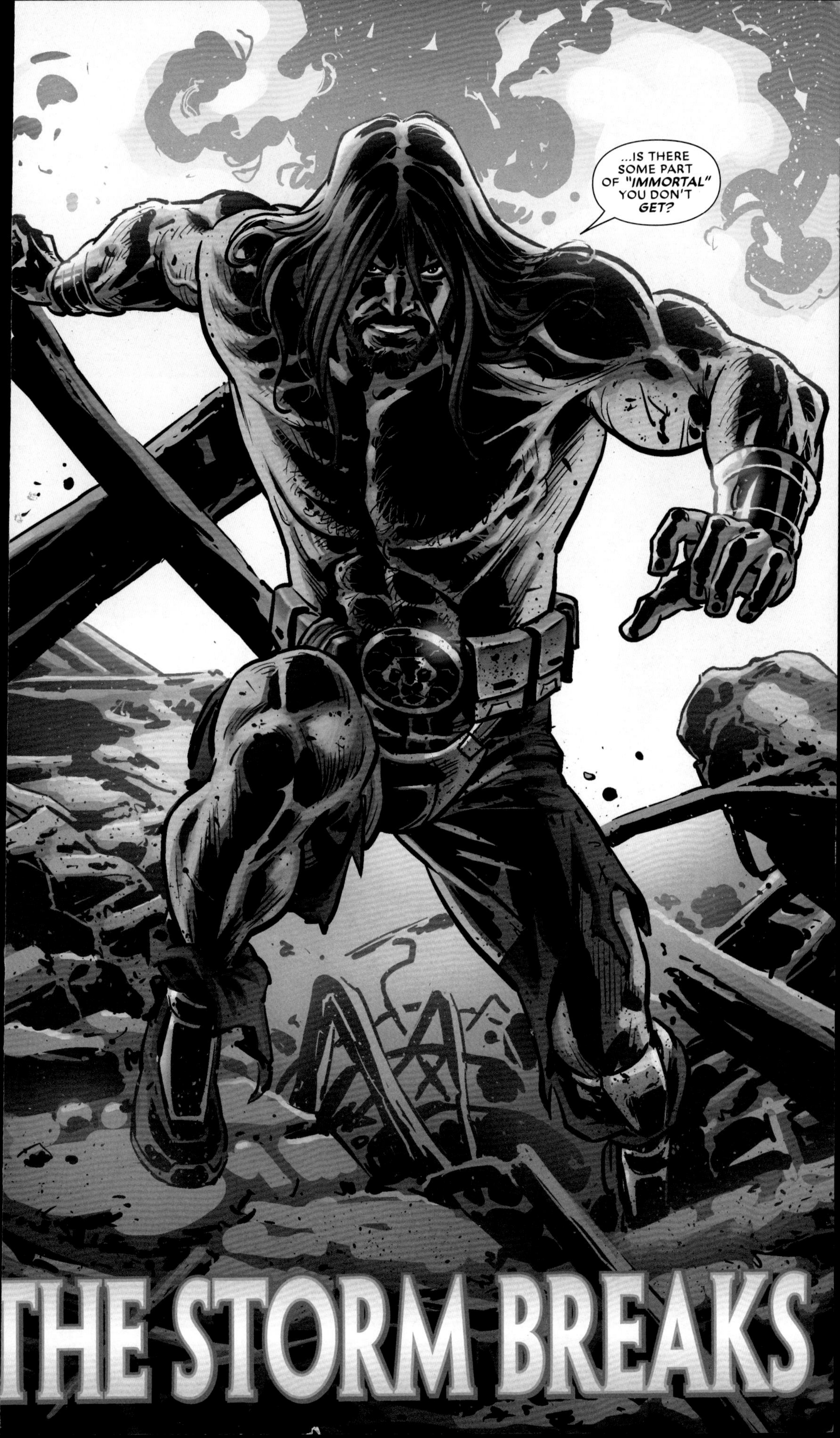
...IS THERE SOME PART OF "IMMORTAL" YOU DON'T GET?
THE STORM BREAKS

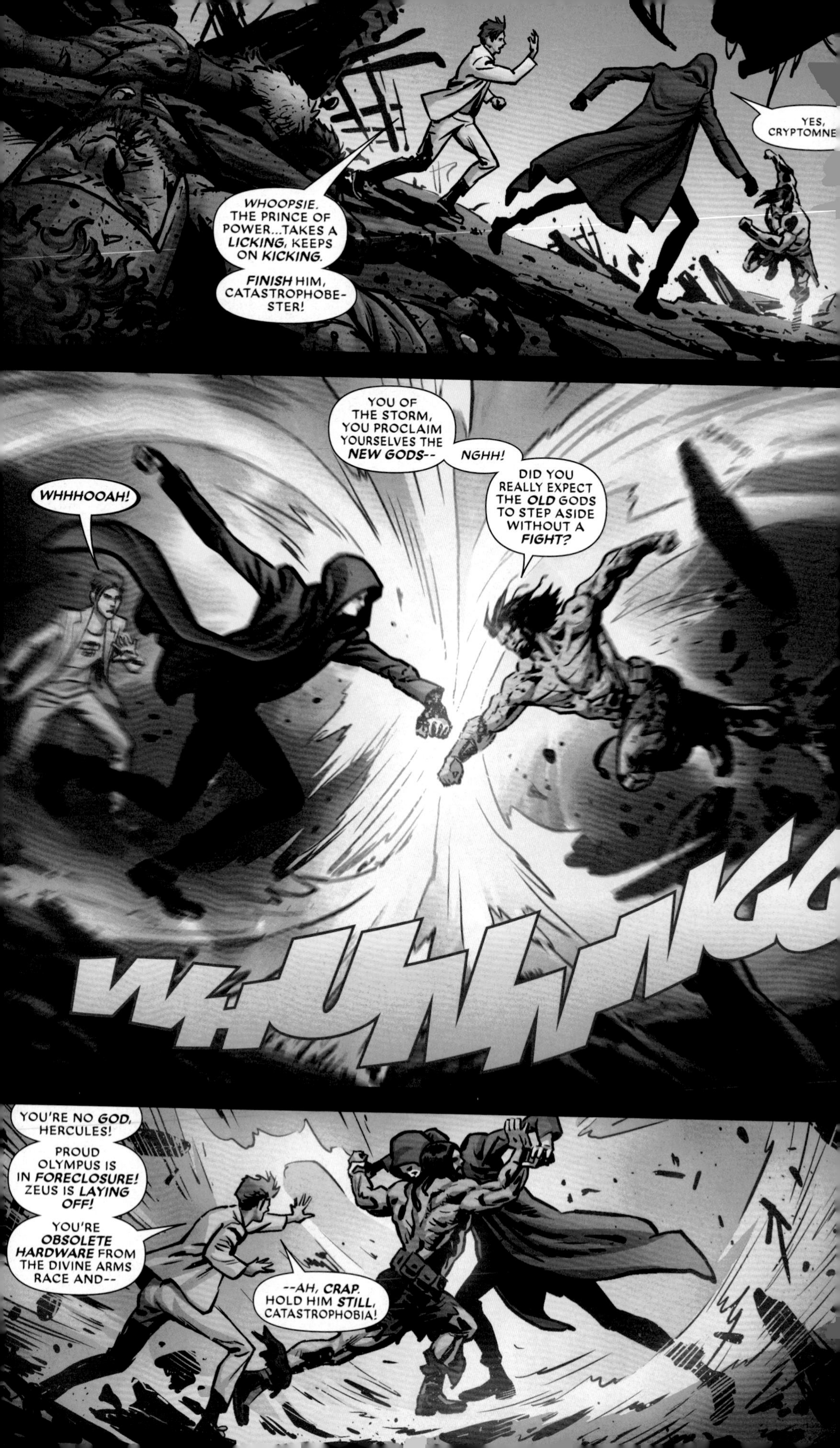
YES, CRYPTOMNE
WHOOPSIE. THE PRINCE OF POWER...TAKES A LICKING, KEEPS ON KICKING.
FINISH HIM, CATASTROPHOBE-STER!
YOU OF THE STORM, YOU PROCLAIM YOURSELVES THE NEW GODS--
NGHH!
DID YOU REALLY EXPECT THE OLD GODS TO STEP ASIDE WITHOUT A FIGHT?
WHHHOOAH!
WHUMMG
YOU'RE NO GOD, HERCULES!
PROUD OLYMPUS IS IN FORECLOSURE! ZEUS IS LAYING OFF!
YOU'RE OBSOLETE HARDWARE FROM THE DIVINE ARMS RACE AND--
--AH, CRAP. HOLD HIM STILL, CATASTROPHOBIA!

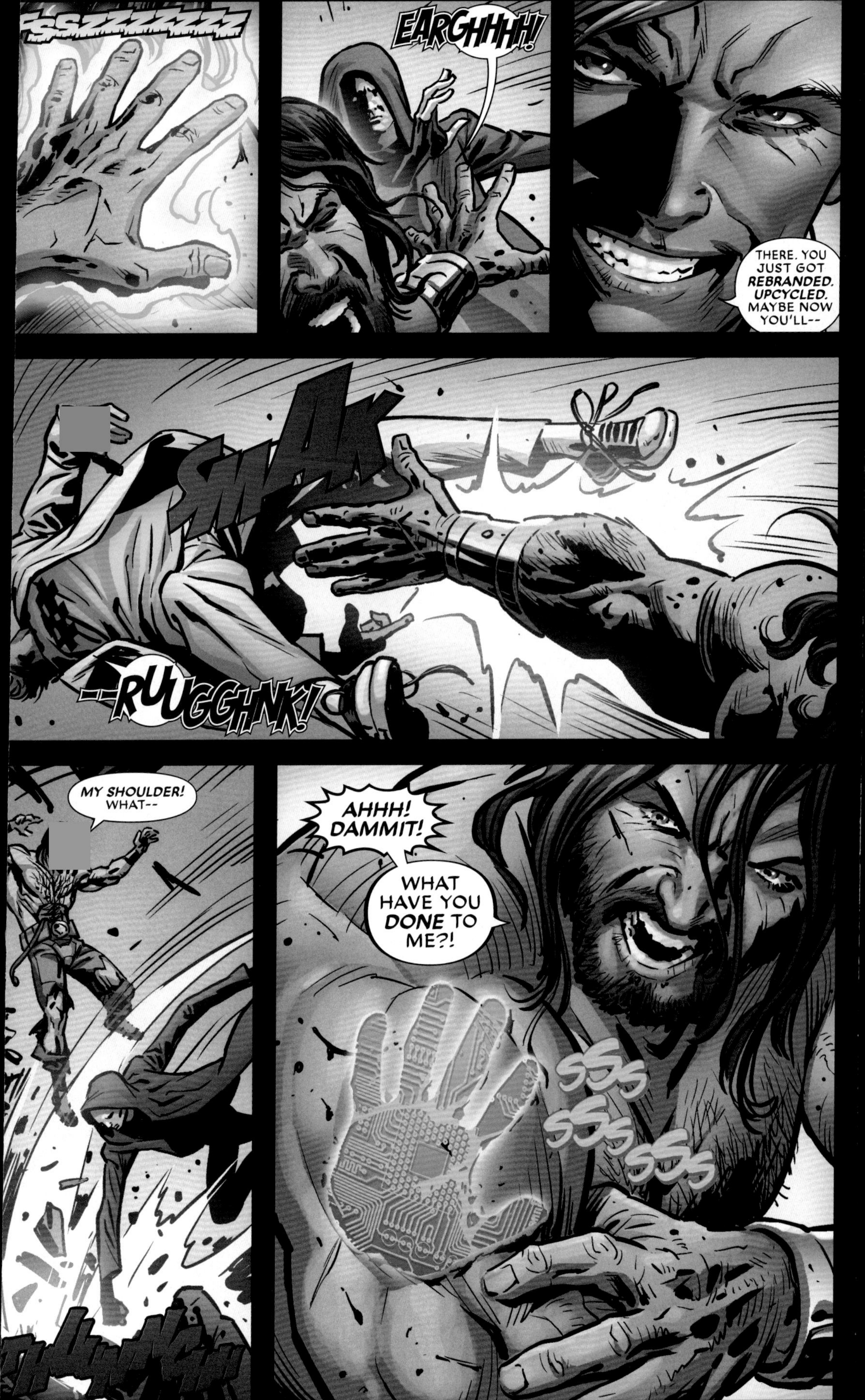
SSZZZZZZZZ
EARGHHHH!
THERE. YOU JUST GOT *REBRANDED. UPCYCLED.* MAYBE NOW YOU'LL--
--RUUGGHNK!
MY SHOULDER! WHAT--
AHHH! DAMMIT!
WHAT HAVE YOU *DONE* TO ME?!

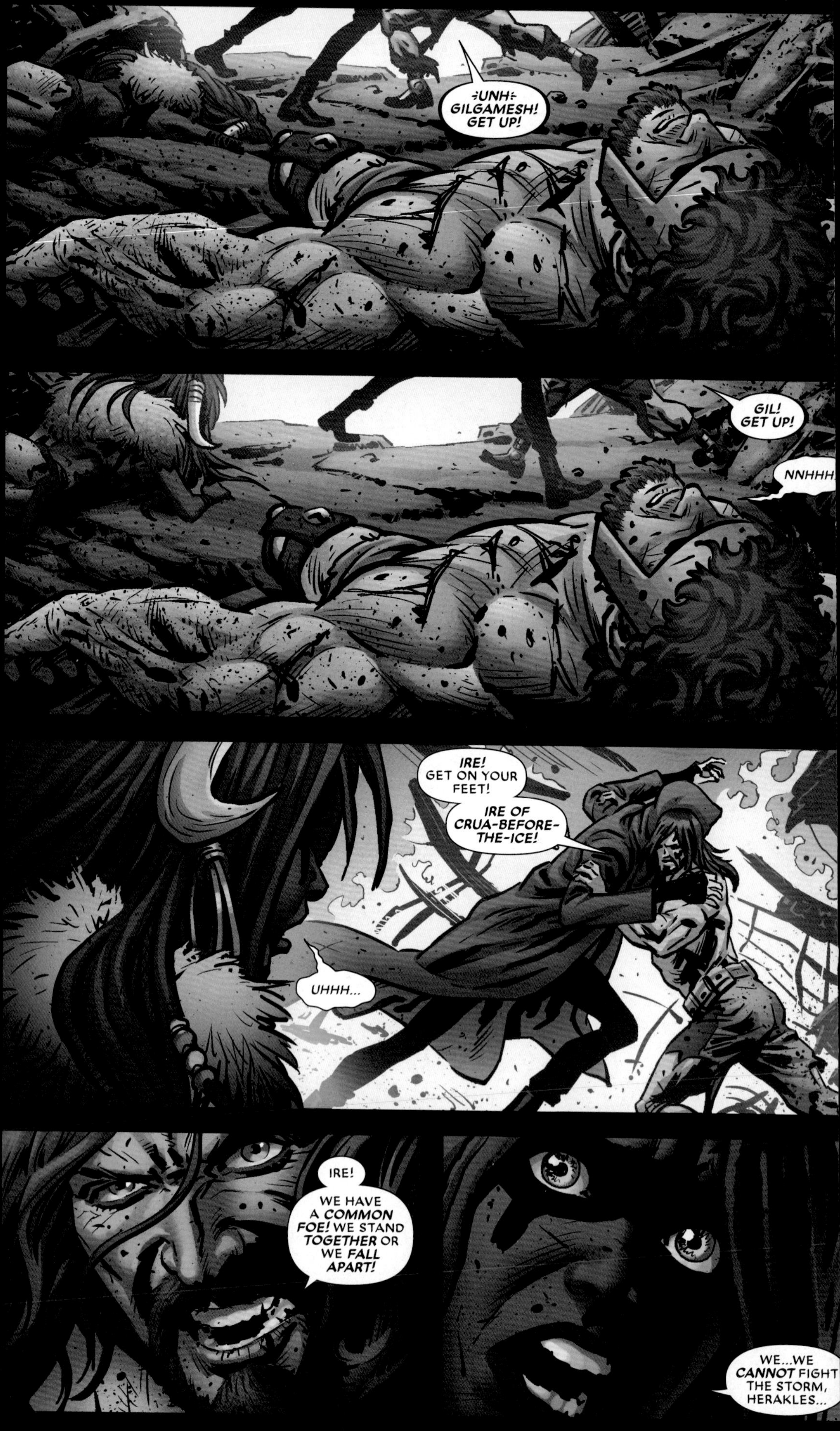

UNH
GILGAMESH! GET UP!
GIL! GET UP!
NNHHH
IRE! GET ON YOUR FEET!
IRE OF CRUA-BEFORE-THE-ICE!
UHHH...
IRE!
WE HAVE A COMMON FOE! WE STAND TOGETHER OR WE FALL APART!
WE...WE CANNOT FIGHT THE STORM, HERAKLES...

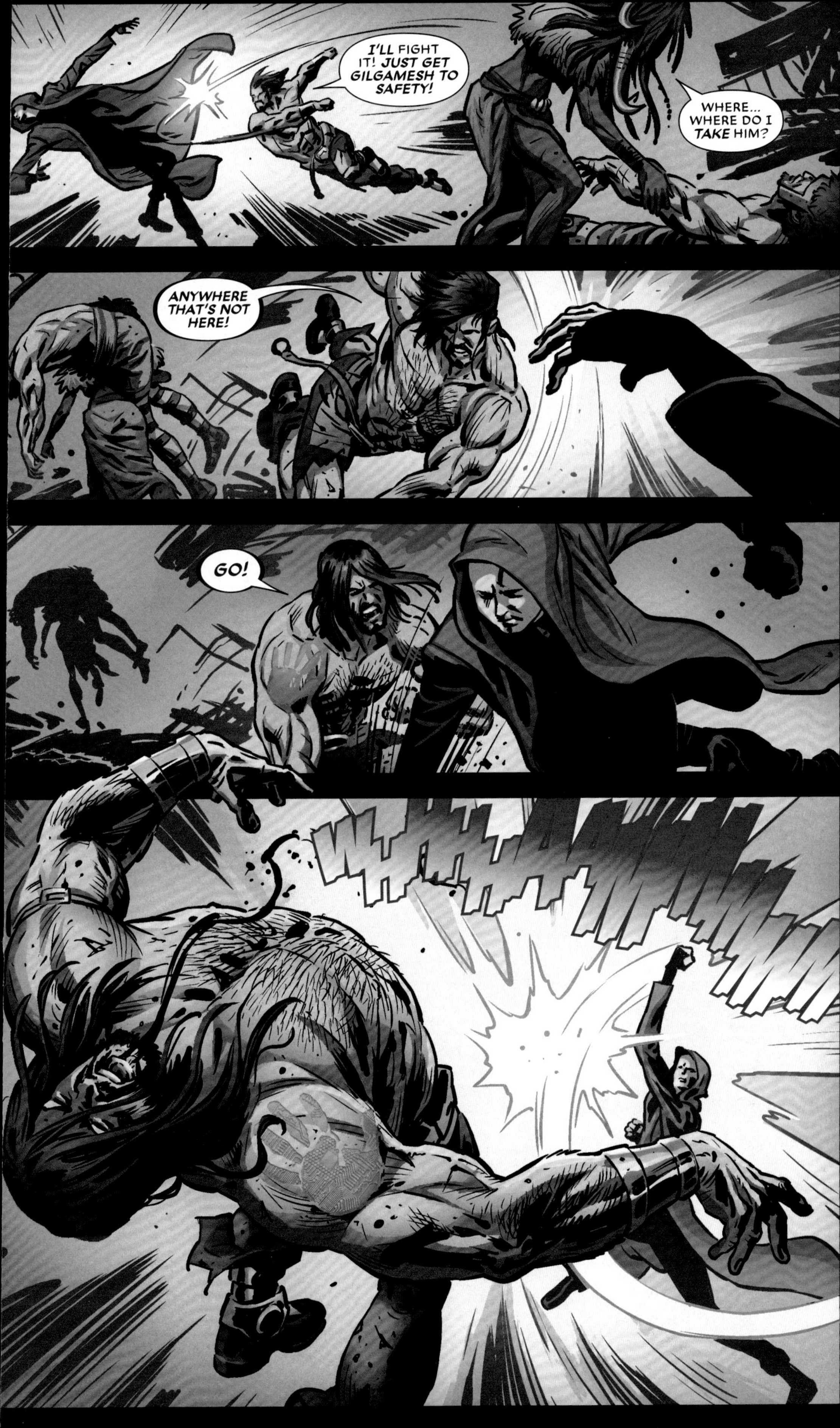
I'LL FIGHT IT! JUST GET GILGAMESH TO SAFETY!
WHERE... WHERE DO I TAKE HIM?
ANYWHERE THAT'S NOT HERE!
GO!
WHHHAAAM

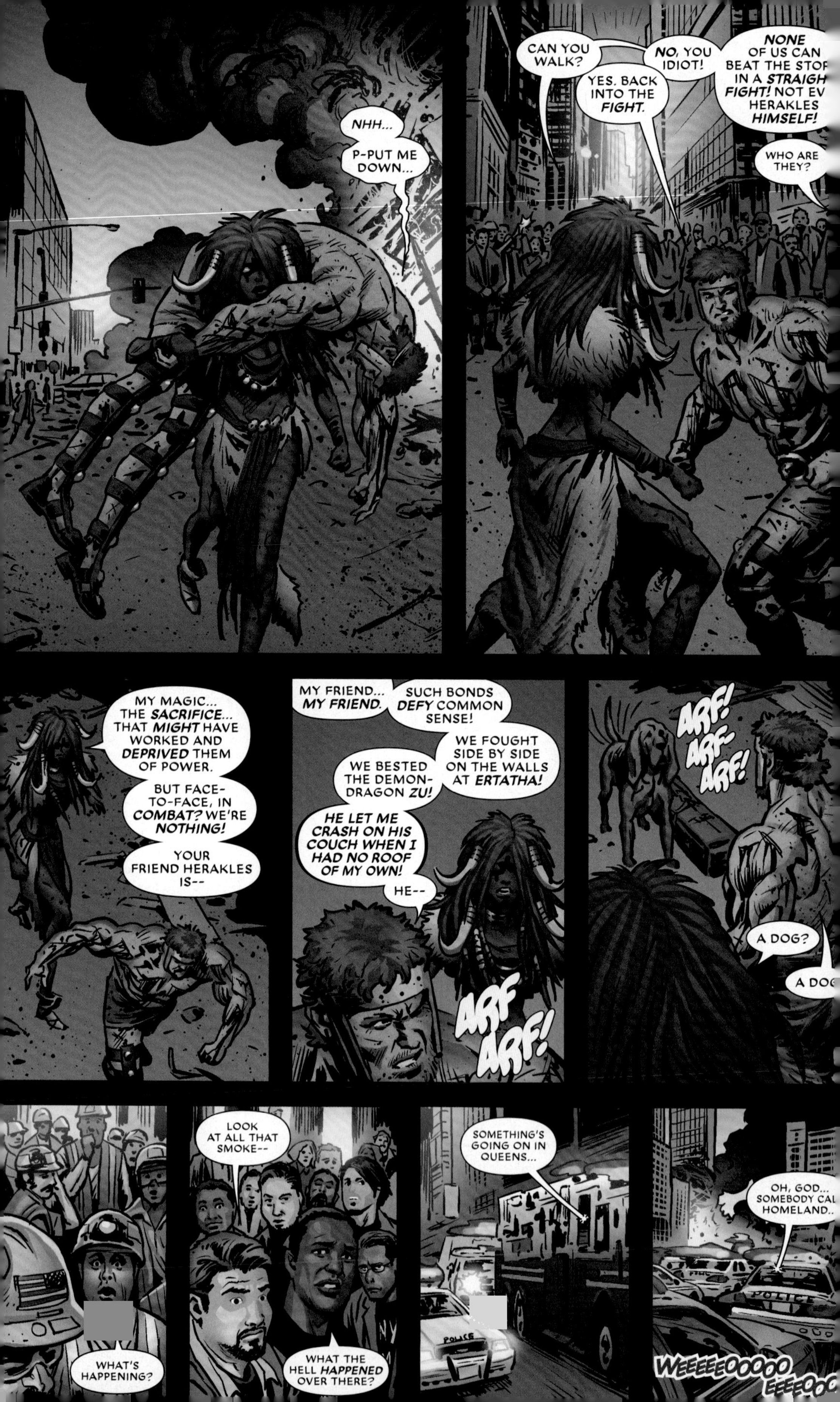
NHH...
P-PUT ME DOWN...
CAN YOU WALK?
YES. BACK INTO THE *FIGHT.*
NO, YOU IDIOT!
NONE OF US CAN BEAT THE STO IN A *STRAIGH FIGHT!* NOT EV HERAKLES *HIMSELF!*
WHO ARE THEY?
MY MAGIC... THE *SACRIFICE...* THAT *MIGHT* HAVE WORKED AND *DEPRIVED* THEM OF POWER.
BUT FACE-TO-FACE, IN *COMBAT?* WE'RE *NOTHING!*
YOUR FRIEND HERAKLES IS--
MY FRIEND... *MY FRIEND.*
SUCH BONDS *DEFY* COMMON SENSE!
WE FOUGHT SIDE BY SIDE ON THE WALLS AT *ERTATHA!*
WE BESTED THE DEMON-DRAGON *ZU!*
HE LET ME CRASH ON HIS COUCH WHEN I HAD NO ROOF OF MY OWN!
HE--
ARF ARF!
ARF! ARF-ARF!
A DOG?
A DO
WHAT'S HAPPENING?
LOOK AT ALL THAT SMOKE--
WHAT THE HELL *HAPPENED* OVER THERE?
SOMETHING'S GOING ON IN QUEENS...
OH, GOD... SOMEBODY CAL HOMELAND..
WEEEEEOOOOO EEEEOOO

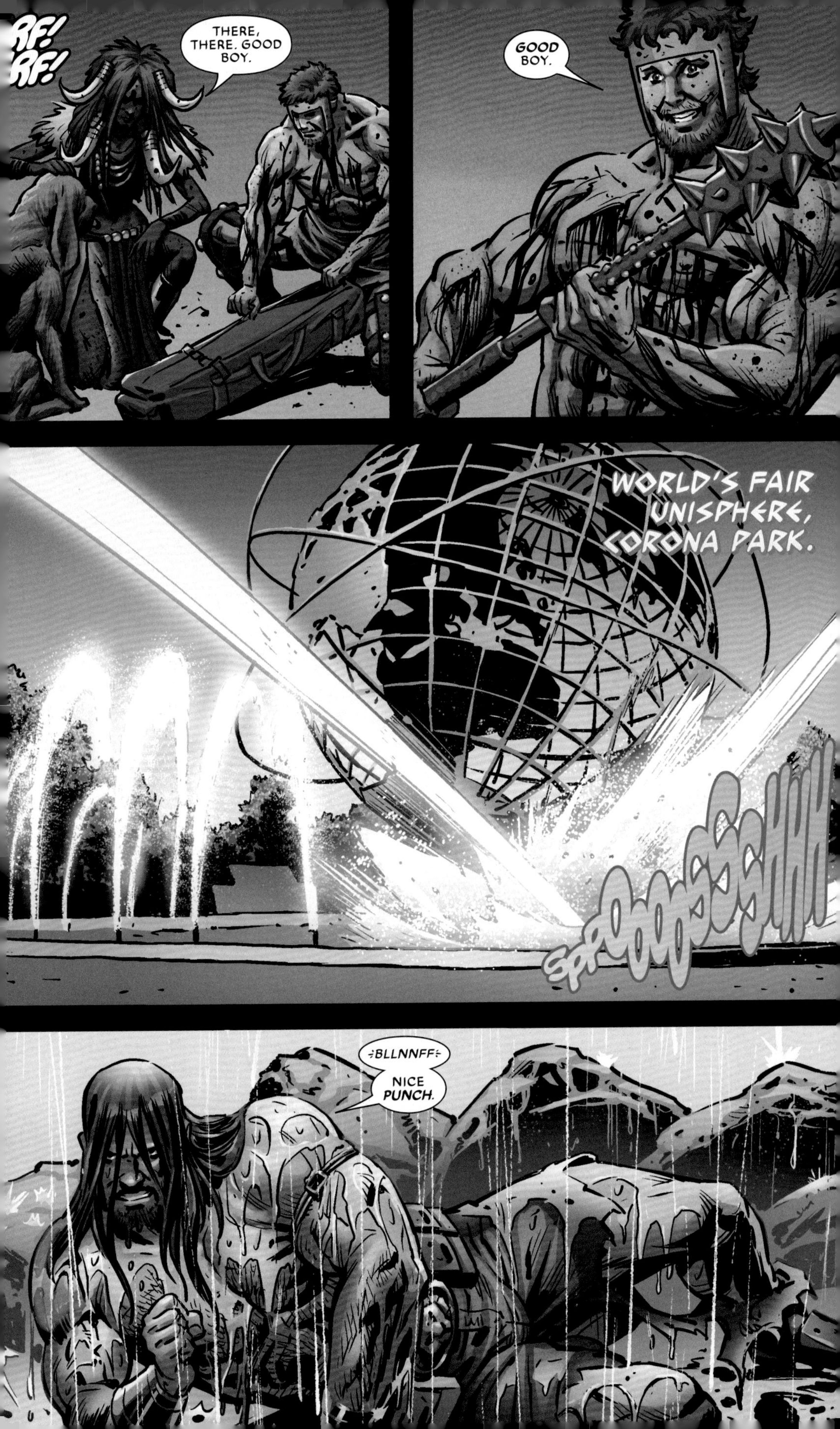
RF!
RF!
THERE, THERE. GOOD BOY.
GOOD BOY.
WORLD'S FAIR UNISPHERE, CORONA PARK.
SPLOOOOSSSHHH
BLLNNFF
NICE PUNCH.

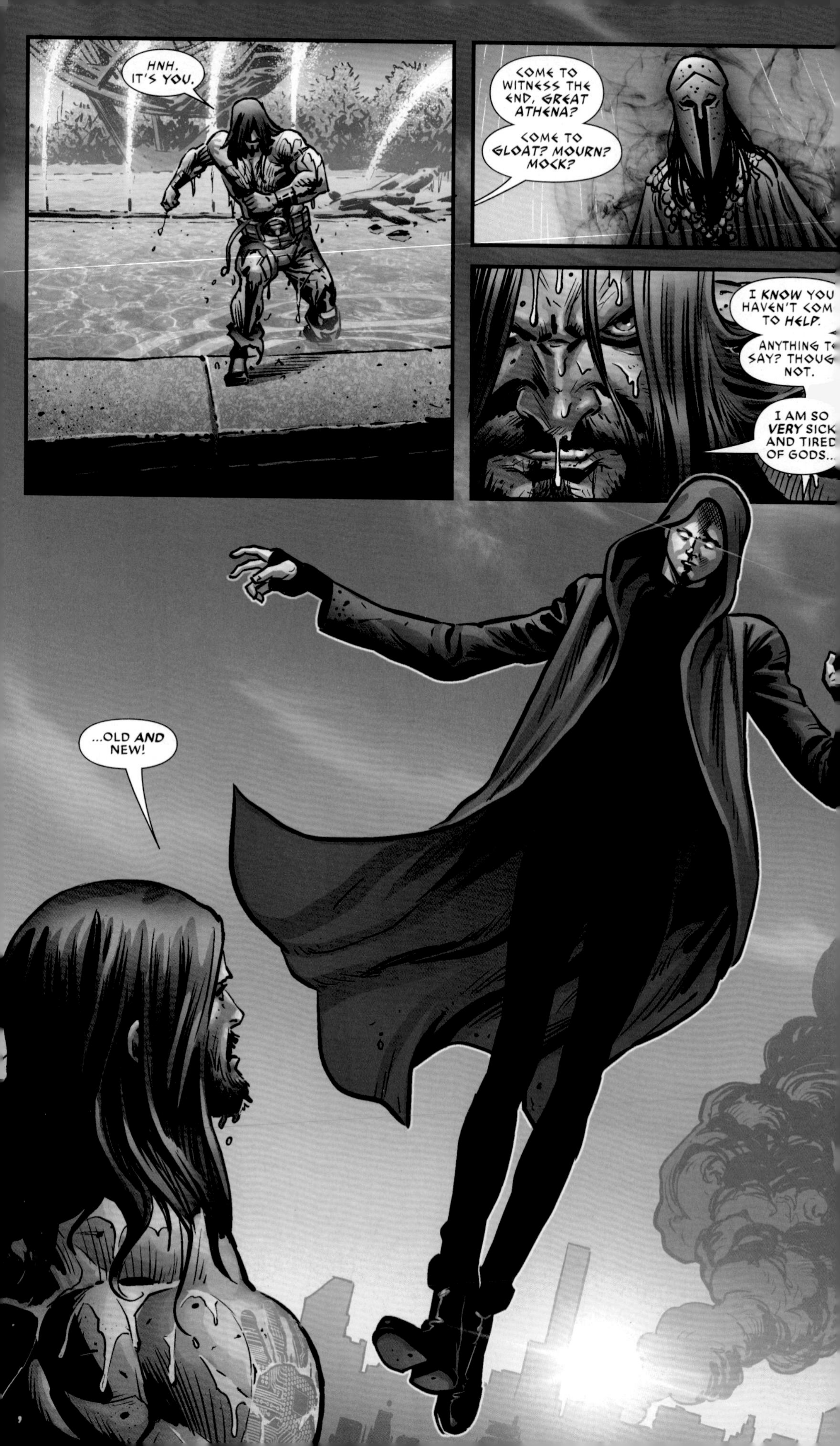
HNH. IT'S YOU.
COME TO WITNESS THE END, GREAT ATHENA?
COME TO GLOAT? MOURN? MOCK?
I KNOW YOU HAVEN'T COM TO HELP.
ANYTHING T SAY? THOUG NOT.
I AM SO VERY SICK AND TIRED OF GODS...
...OLD AND NEW!

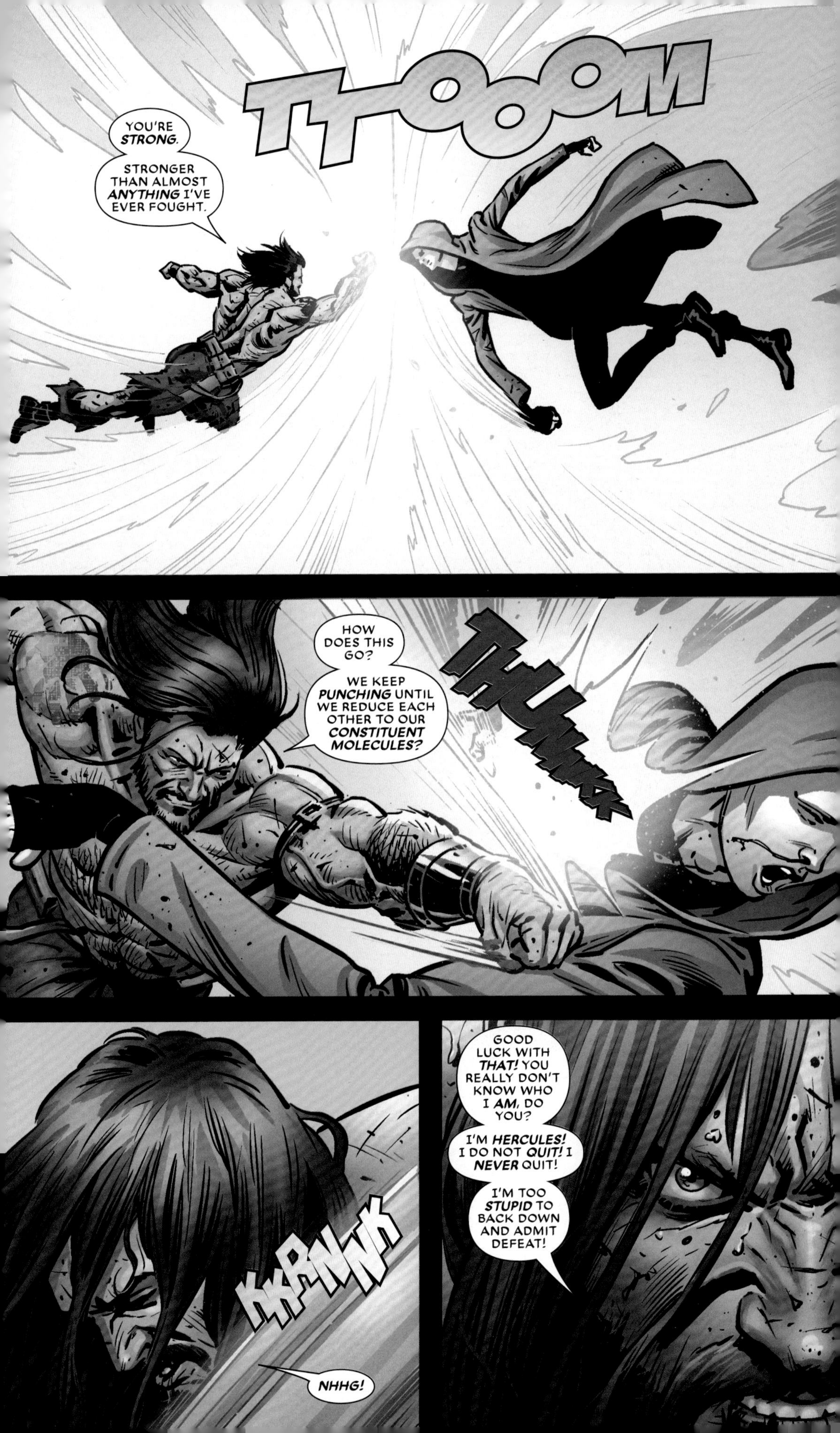

TTOOOM
YOU'RE STRONG.
STRONGER THAN ALMOST ANYTHING I'VE EVER FOUGHT.
HOW DOES THIS GO?
WE KEEP PUNCHING UNTIL WE REDUCE EACH OTHER TO OUR CONSTITUENT MOLECULES?
THUNKK
KKRNNK
NHHG!
GOOD LUCK WITH THAT! YOU REALLY DON'T KNOW WHO I AM, DO YOU?
I'M HERCULES! I DO NOT QUIT! I NEVER QUIT!
I'M TOO STUPID TO BACK DOWN AND ADMIT DEFEAT!

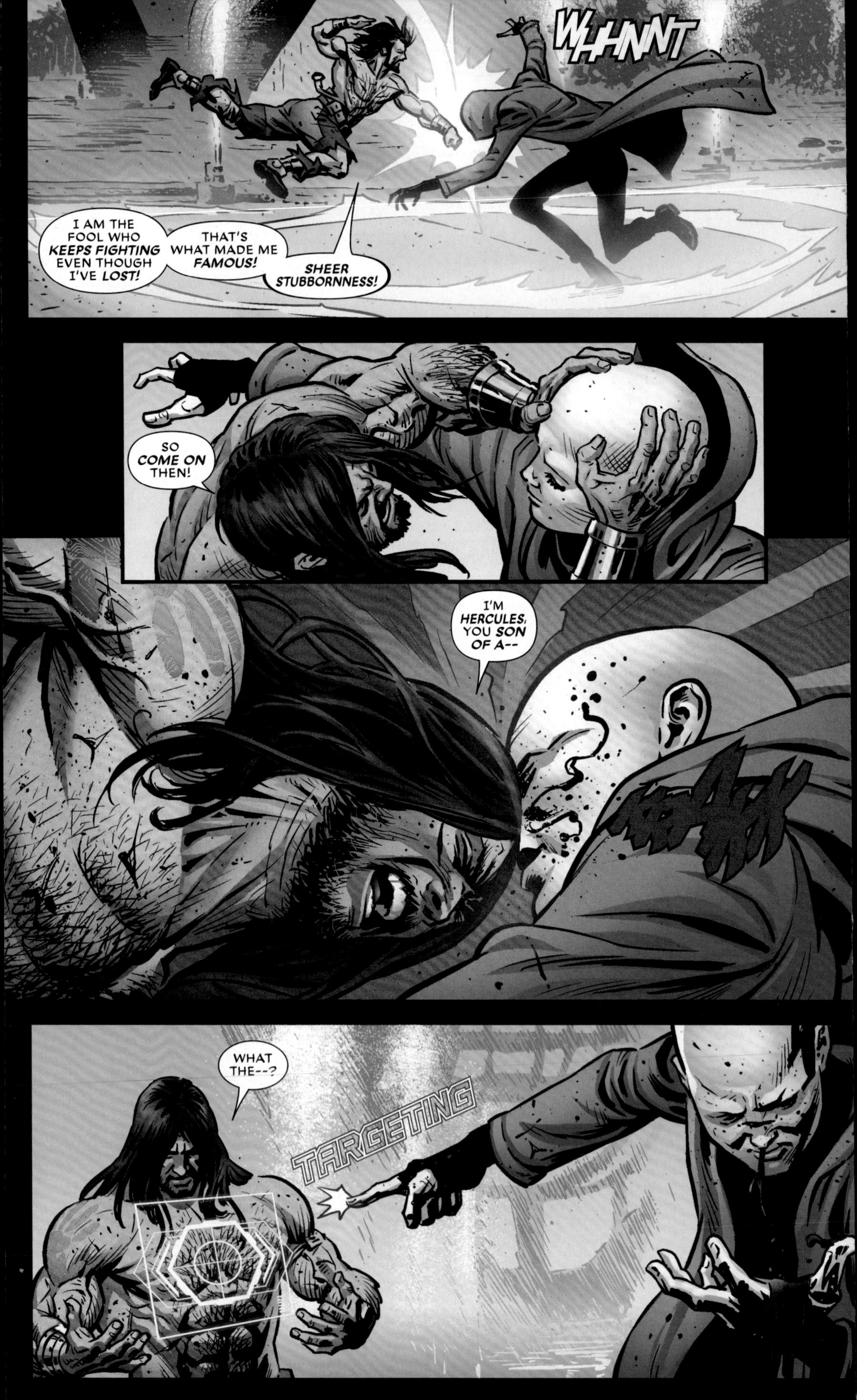
WHHNNT
I AM THE FOOL WHO KEEPS FIGHTING EVEN THOUGH I'VE LOST!
THAT'S WHAT MADE ME FAMOUS!
SHEER STUBBORNNESS!
SO COME ON THEN!
I'M HERCULES, YOU SON OF A--
WHAT THE--?
TARGETING

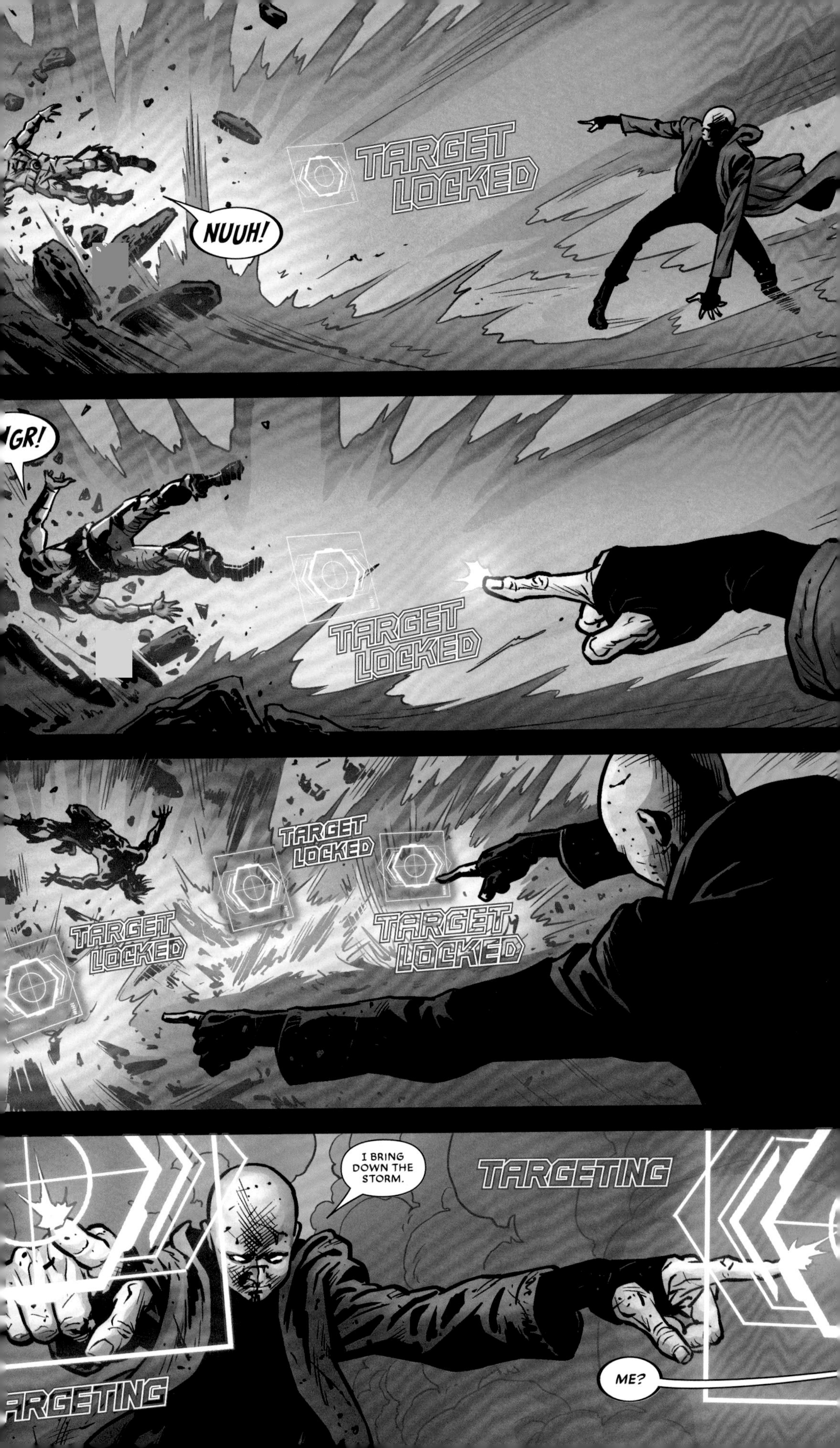
TARGET LOCKED
NUUH!
GR!
TARGET LOCKED
TARGET LOCKED
TARGET LOCKED
TARGET LOCKED
I BRING DOWN THE STORM.
TARGETING
ARGETING
ME?

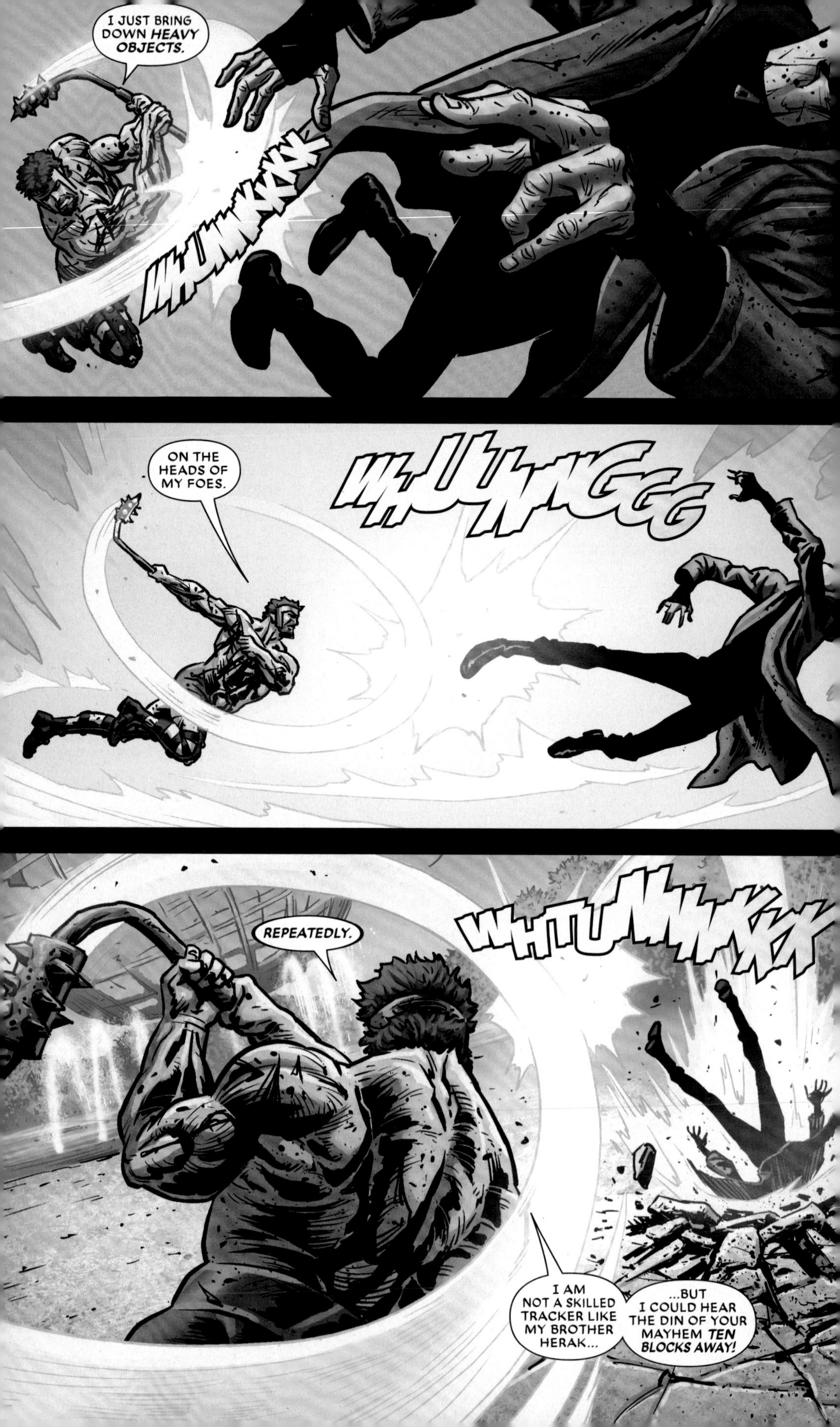
I JUST BRING DOWN HEAVY OBJECTS.
WHUNKKK
ON THE HEADS OF MY FOES.
WHUUNNGGG
REPEATEDLY.
WHTUNNKKK
I AM NOT A SKILLED TRACKER LIKE MY BROTHER HERAK...
...BUT I COULD HEAR THE DIN OF YOUR MAYHEM TEN BLOCKS AWAY!

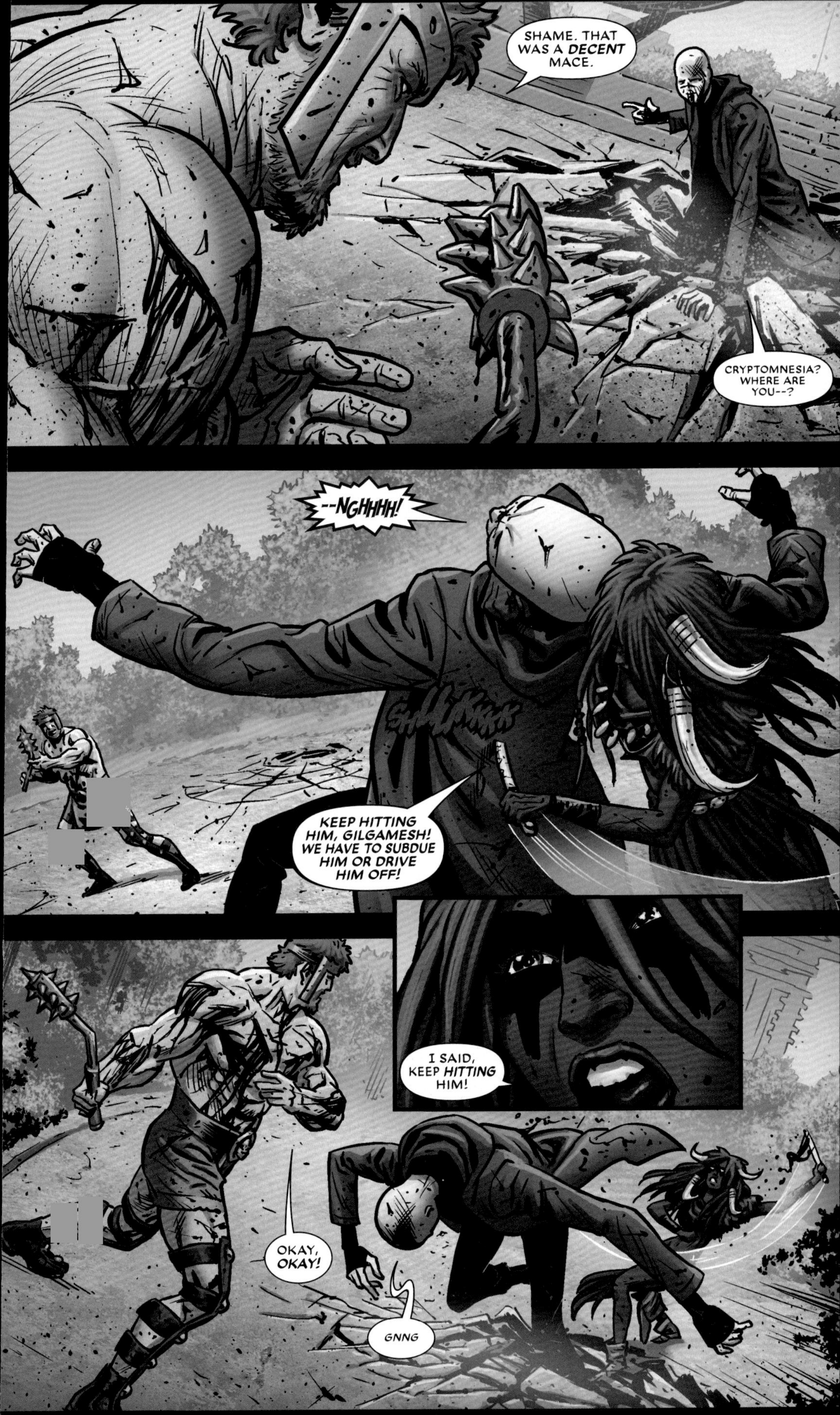
SHAME. THAT WAS A DECENT MACE.
CRYPTOMNESIA? WHERE ARE YOU--?
--NGHHHH!
KEEP HITTING HIM, GILGAMESH! WE HAVE TO SUBDUE HIM OR DRIVE HIM OFF!
I SAID, KEEP HITTING HIM!
OKAY, OKAY!
GNNG

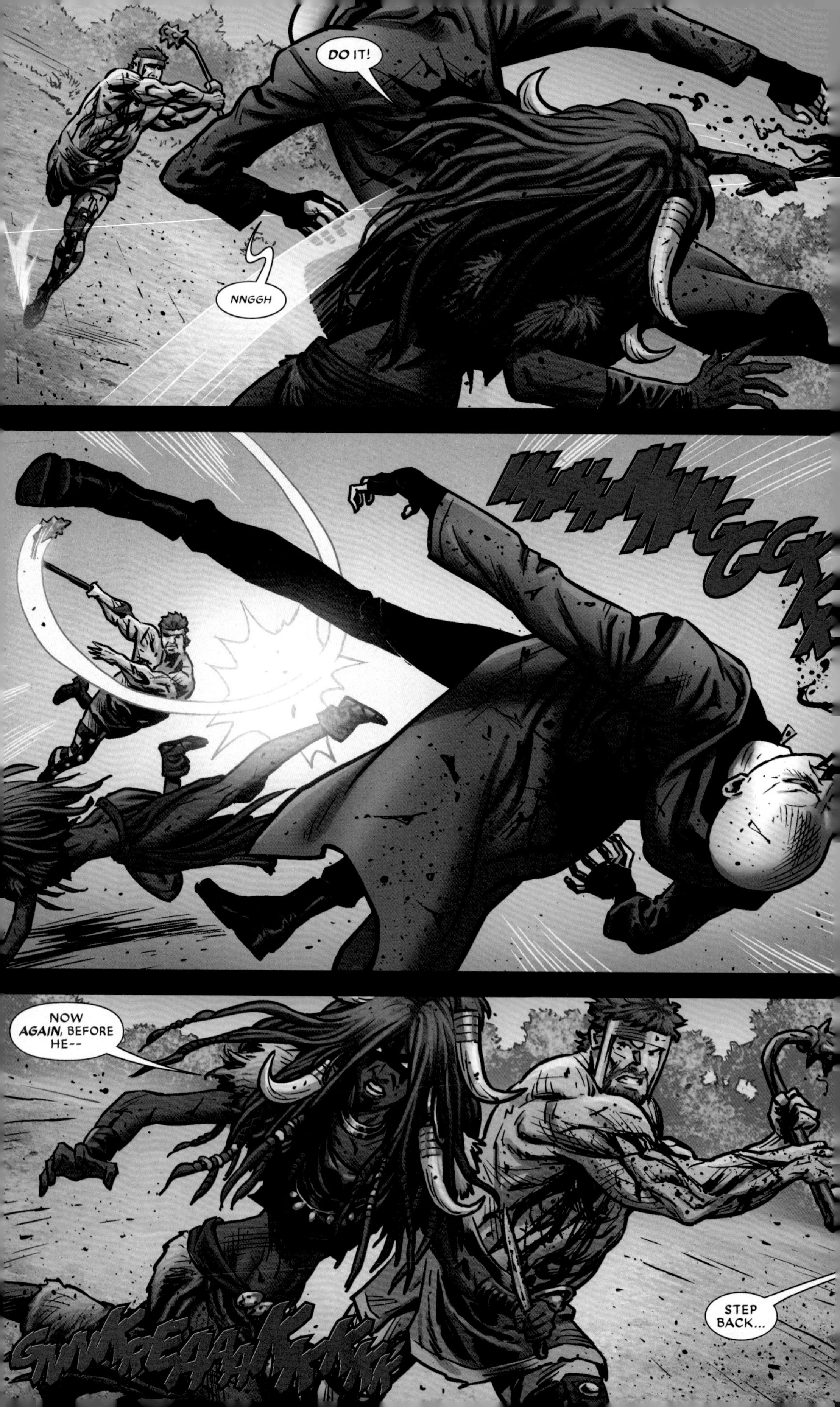
DO IT!
NNGGH
WHHHHNNGGKKK
NOW AGAIN, BEFORE HE--
GWWREAAAHHKKK
STEP BACK...

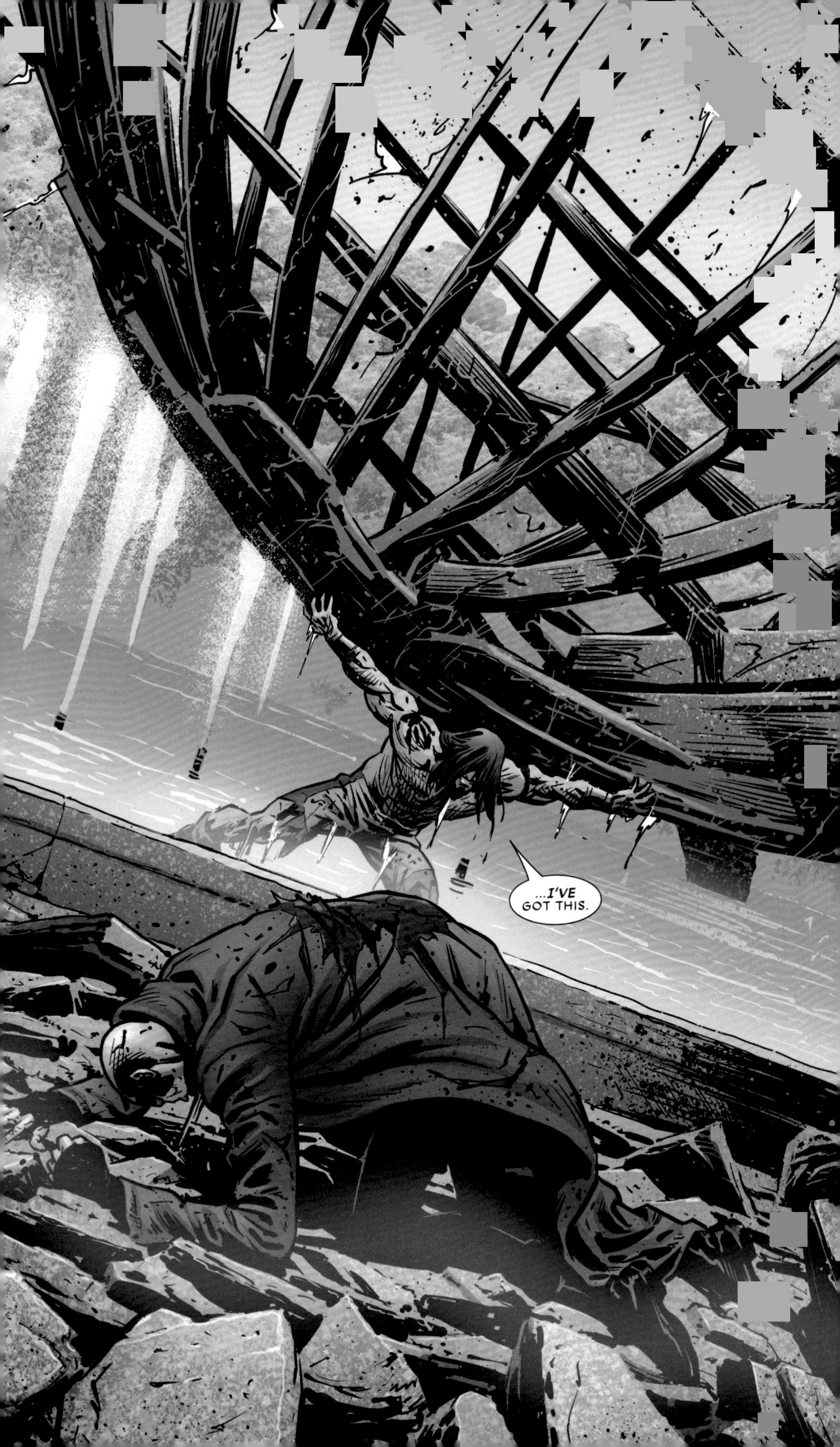
...I'VE GOT THIS.

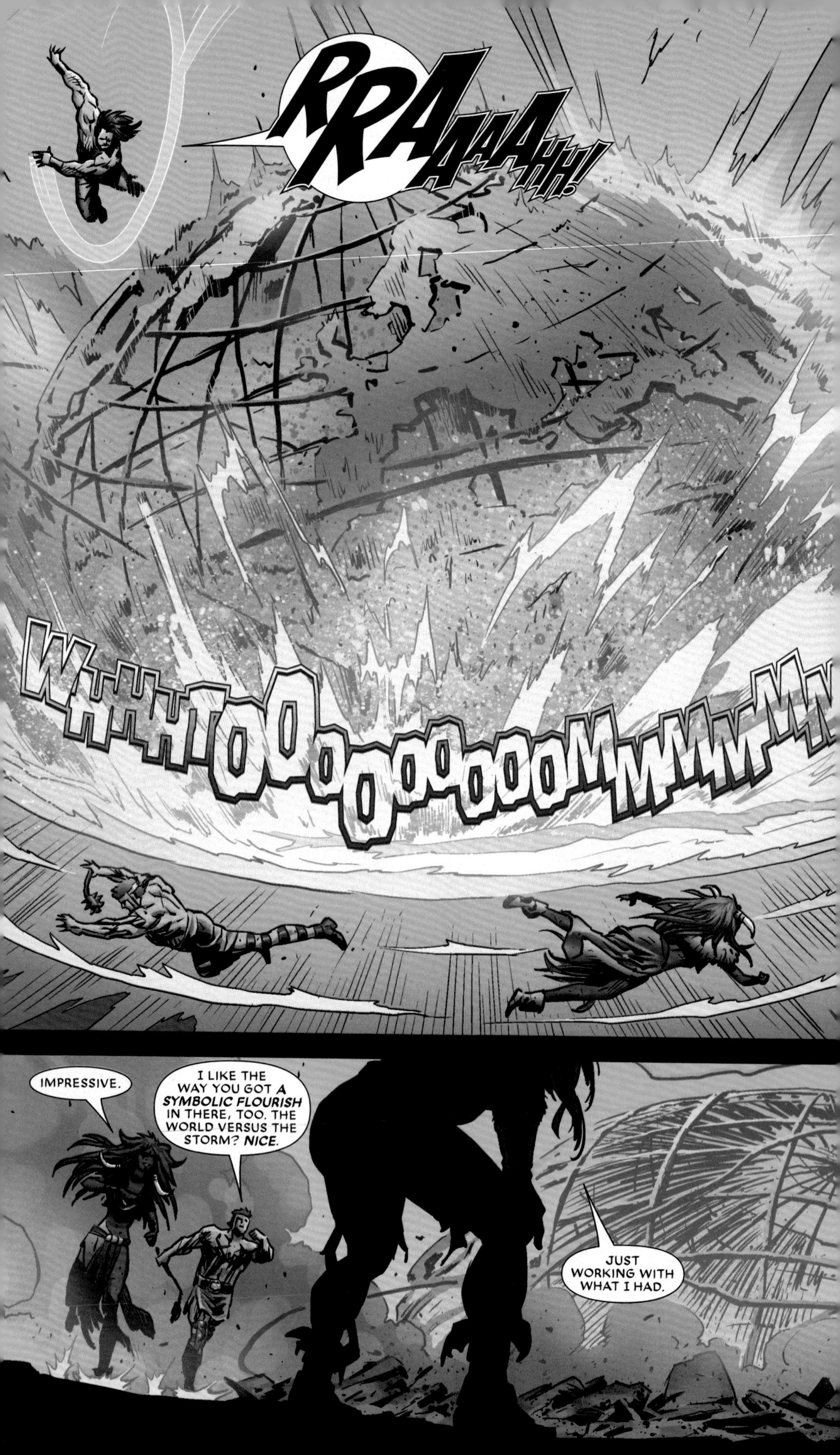
RRAAAAHH!
WHHHOOOOOOOOOMMMMMMN
IMPRESSIVE.
I LIKE THE WAY YOU GOT A SYMBOLIC FLOURISH IN THERE, TOO. THE WORLD VERSUS THE STORM? NICE.
JUST WORKING WITH WHAT I HAD.

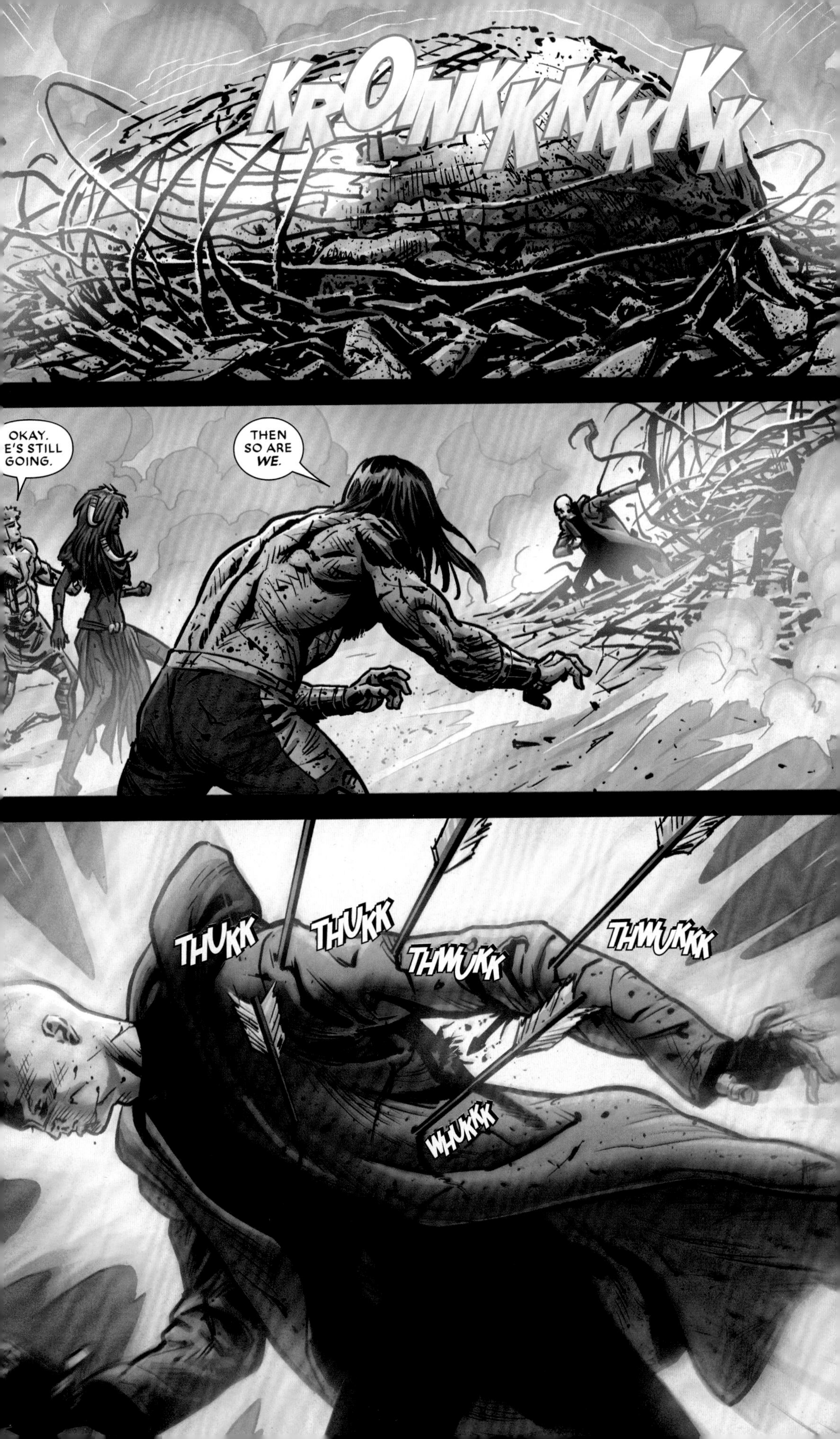

KROINKKKKKKK
OKAY. E'S STILL GOING.
THEN SO ARE *WE*.
THUKK
THUKK
THWUKK
THWUKKK
WHUKKK

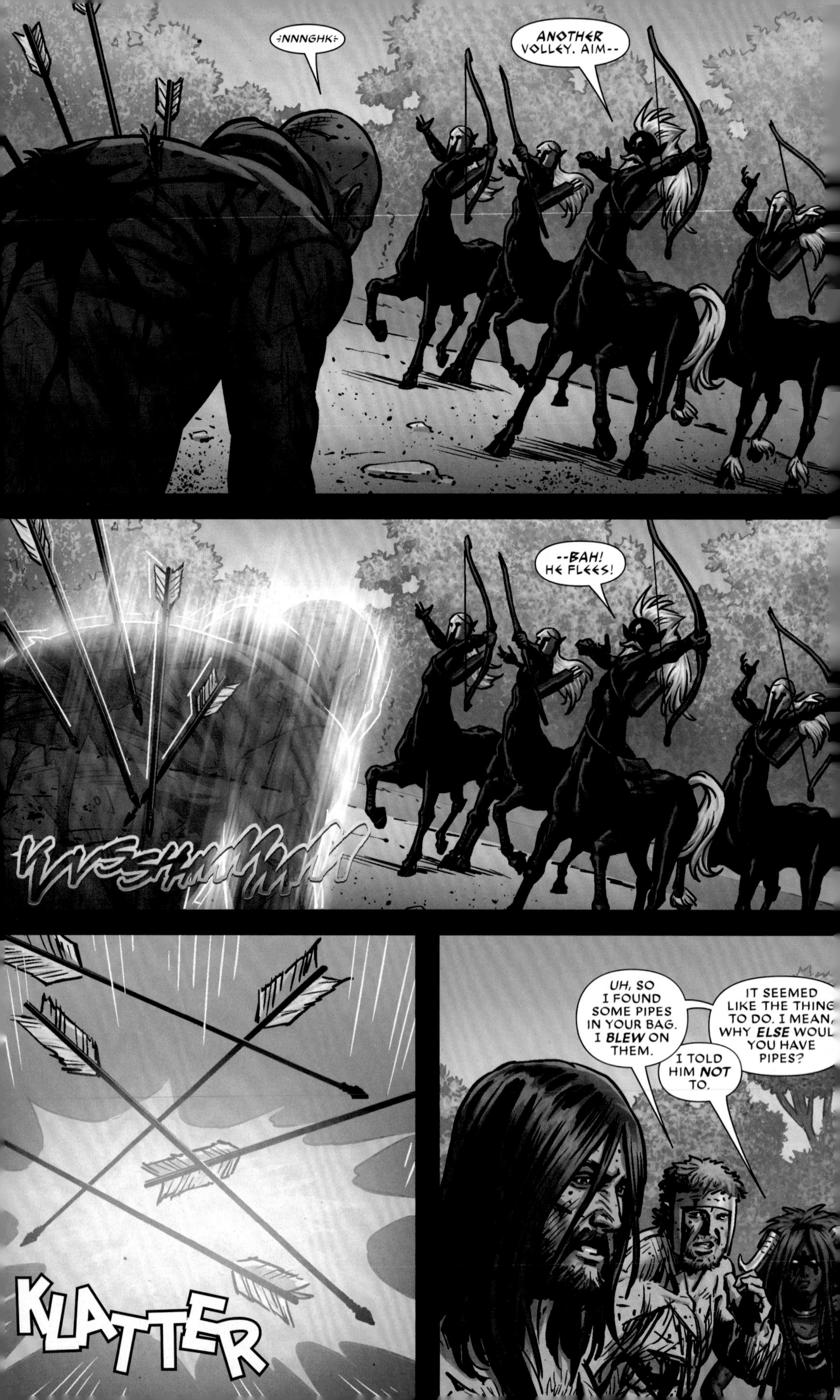

NNNGHK
ANOTHER VOLLEY. AIM--
--BAH! HE FLEES!
KVASHMMMM
KLATTER
UH, SO I FOUND SOME PIPES IN YOUR BAG. I BLEW ON THEM.
IT SEEMED LIKE THE THING TO DO. I MEAN, WHY ELSE WOUL YOU HAVE PIPES?
I TOLD HIM NOT TO.

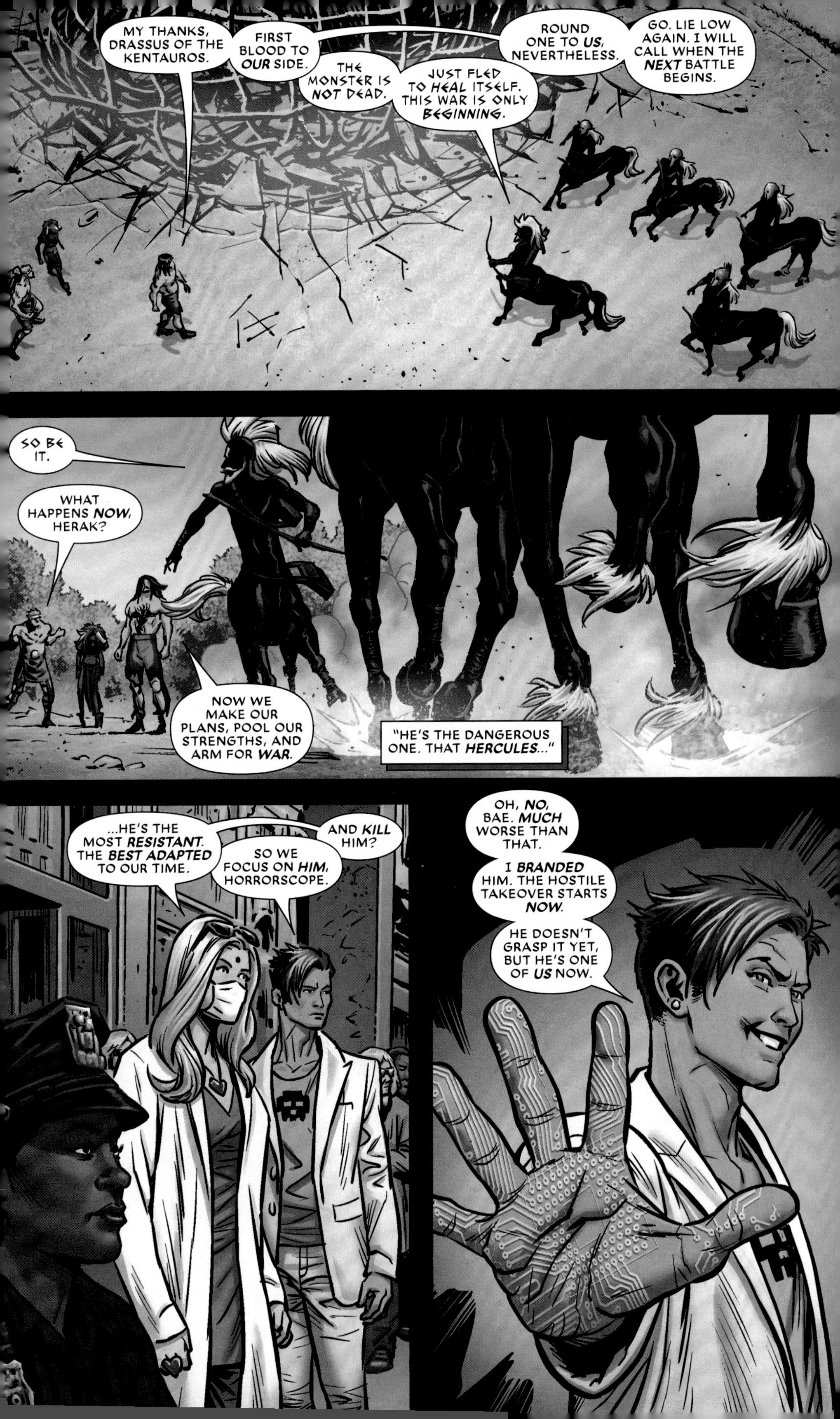

MY THANKS, DRASSUS OF THE KENTAUROS.
FIRST BLOOD TO OUR SIDE.
THE MONSTER IS NOT DEAD.
JUST FLED TO HEAL ITSELF. THIS WAR IS ONLY BEGINNING.
ROUND ONE TO US, NEVERTHELESS.
GO. LIE LOW AGAIN. I WILL CALL WHEN THE NEXT BATTLE BEGINS.
SO BE IT.
WHAT HAPPENS NOW, HERAK?
NOW WE MAKE OUR PLANS, POOL OUR STRENGTHS, AND ARM FOR WAR.
"HE'S THE DANGEROUS ONE. THAT HERCULES..."
...HE'S THE MOST RESISTANT. THE BEST ADAPTED TO OUR TIME.
SO WE FOCUS ON HIM, HORRORSCOPE.
AND KILL HIM?
OH, NO, BAE. MUCH WORSE THAN THAT.
I BRANDED HIM. THE HOSTILE TAKEOVER STARTS NOW.
HE DOESN'T GRASP IT YET, BUT HE'S ONE OF US NOW.

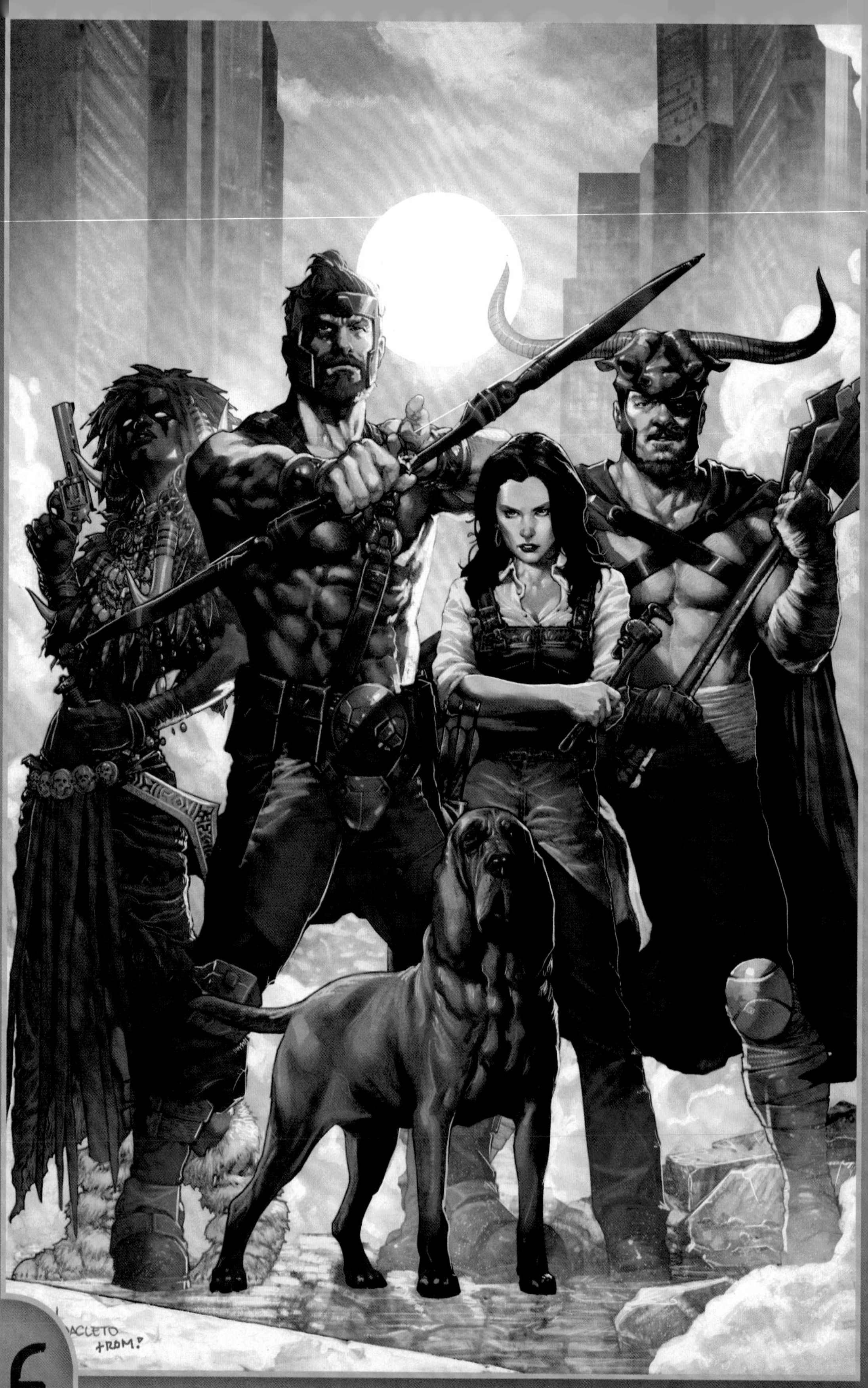

6 HERE'S TO A LONG LIFE

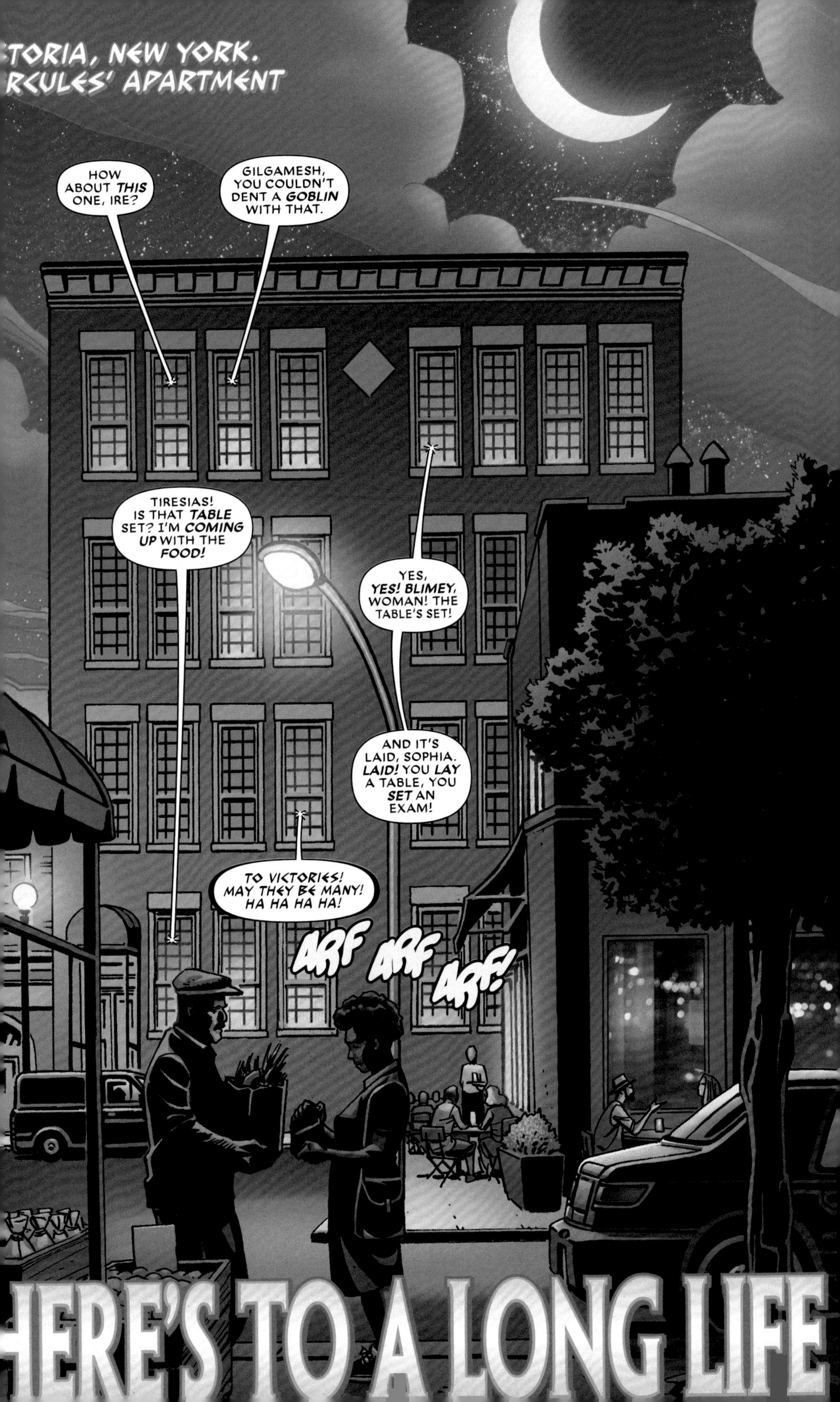
TORIA, NEW YORK.
RCULES' APARTMENT
HOW ABOUT THIS ONE, IRE?
GILGAMESH, YOU COULDN'T DENT A GOBLIN WITH THAT.
TIRESIAS! IS THAT TABLE SET? I'M COMING UP WITH THE FOOD!
YES, YES! BLIMEY, WOMAN! THE TABLE'S SET!
AND IT'S LAID, SOPHIA. LAID! YOU LAY A TABLE, YOU SET AN EXAM!
TO VICTORIES! MAY THEY BE MANY! HA HA HA HA!
ARF ARF ARF!
HERE'S TO A LONG LIFE

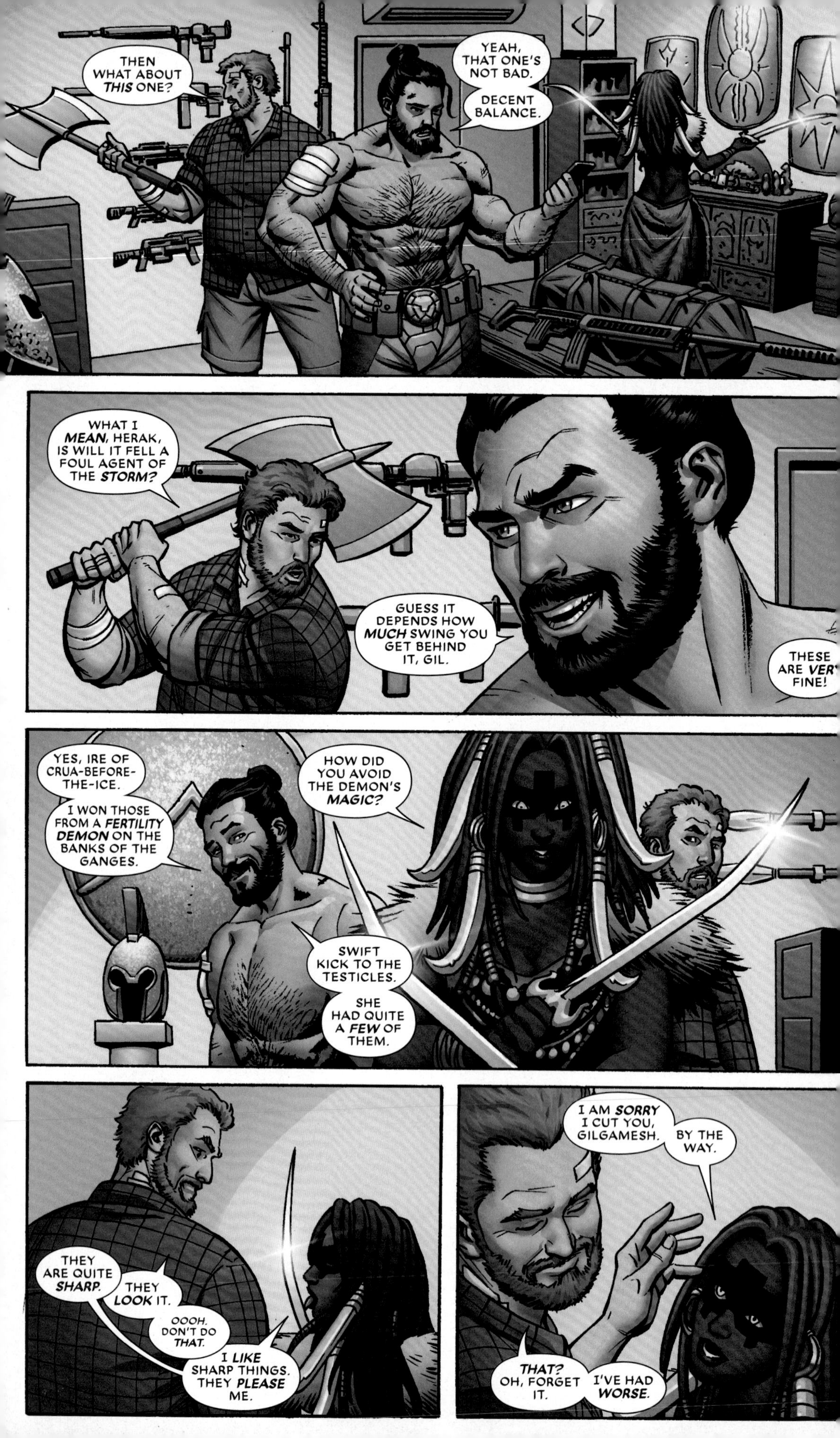
THEN WHAT ABOUT *THIS* ONE?
YEAH, THAT ONE'S NOT BAD.
DECENT BALANCE.
WHAT I *MEAN*, HERAK, IS WILL IT FELL A FOUL AGENT OF THE *STORM?*
GUESS IT DEPENDS HOW *MUCH* SWING YOU GET BEHIND IT, GIL.
THESE ARE *VER* FINE!
YES, IRE OF CRUA-BEFORE-THE-ICE.
I WON THOSE FROM A *FERTILITY DEMON* ON THE BANKS OF THE GANGES.
HOW DID YOU AVOID THE DEMON'S *MAGIC?*
SWIFT KICK TO THE TESTICLES.
SHE HAD QUITE A *FEW* OF THEM.
THEY ARE QUITE *SHARP.*
THEY *LOOK* IT.
OOOH. DON'T DO *THAT.*
I *LIKE* SHARP THINGS. THEY *PLEASE* ME.
I AM *SORRY* I CUT YOU, GILGAMESH.
BY THE WAY.
THAT? OH, FORGET IT.
I'VE HAD *WORSE.*

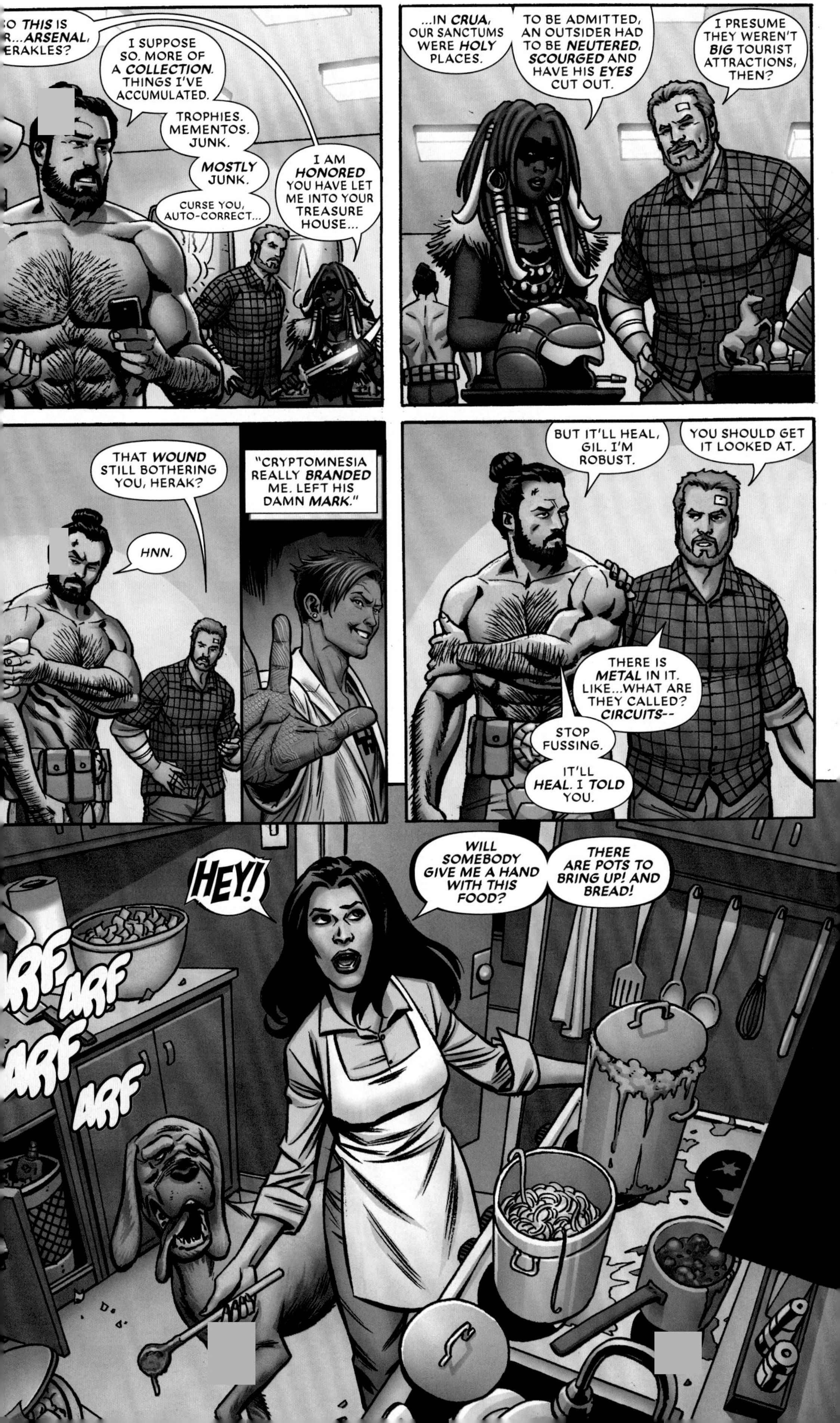

O THIS IS R...ARSENAL, ERAKLES?
I SUPPOSE SO. MORE OF A COLLECTION. THINGS I'VE ACCUMULATED.
TROPHIES. MEMENTOS. JUNK.
MOSTLY JUNK.
CURSE YOU, AUTO-CORRECT...
I AM HONORED YOU HAVE LET ME INTO YOUR TREASURE HOUSE...
...IN CRUA, OUR SANCTUMS WERE HOLY PLACES.
TO BE ADMITTED, AN OUTSIDER HAD TO BE NEUTERED, SCOURGED AND HAVE HIS EYES CUT OUT.
I PRESUME THEY WEREN'T BIG TOURIST ATTRACTIONS, THEN?
THAT WOUND STILL BOTHERING YOU, HERAK?
HNN.
"CRYPTOMNESIA REALLY BRANDED ME. LEFT HIS DAMN MARK."
BUT IT'LL HEAL, GIL. I'M ROBUST.
YOU SHOULD GET IT LOOKED AT.
THERE IS METAL IN IT. LIKE...WHAT ARE THEY CALLED? CIRCUITS--
STOP FUSSING.
IT'LL HEAL. I TOLD YOU.
HEY!
WILL SOMEBODY GIVE ME A HAND WITH THIS FOOD?
THERE ARE POTS TO BRING UP! AND BREAD!
ARF ARF ARF ARF ARF

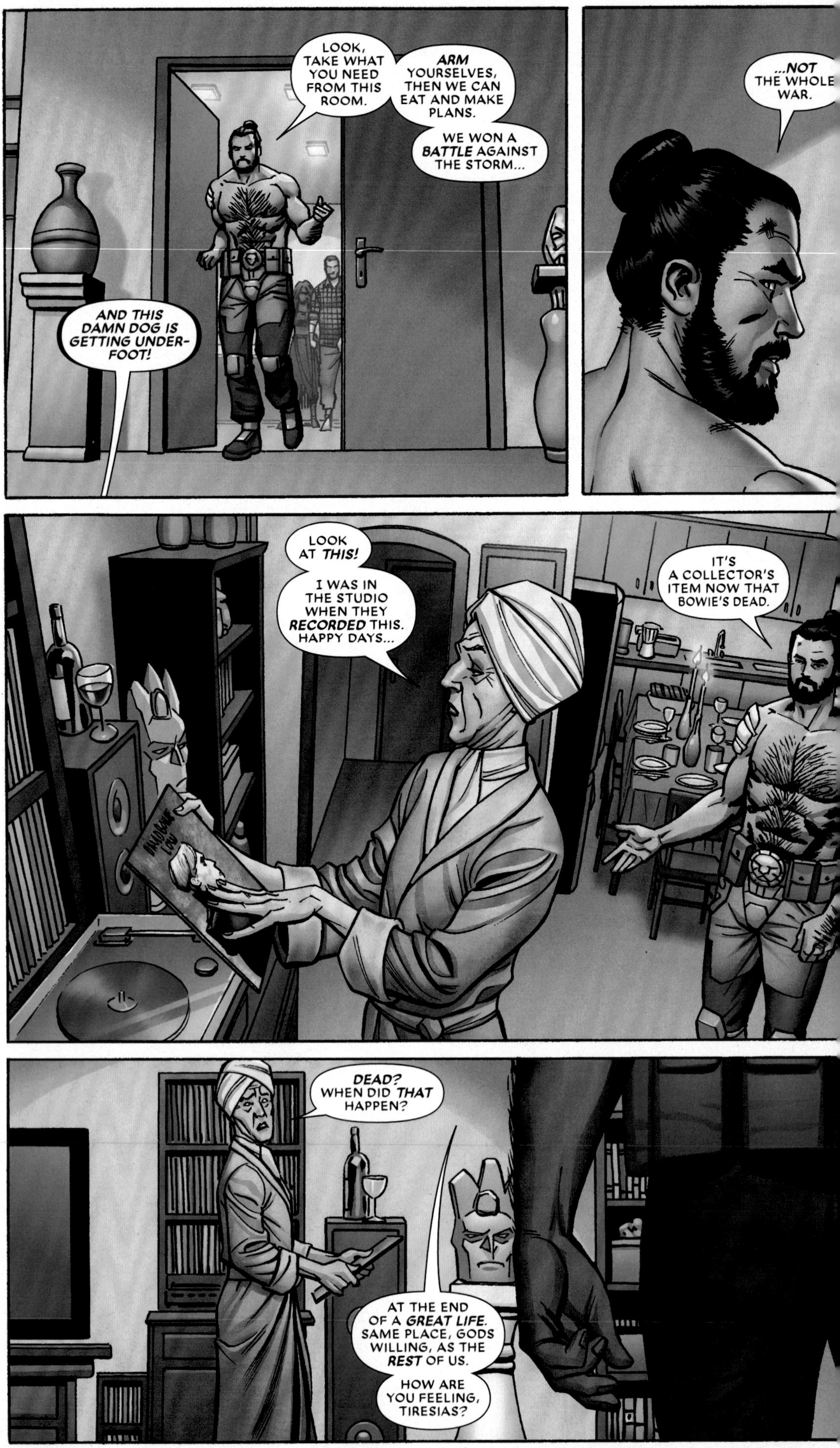
LOOK, TAKE WHAT YOU NEED FROM THIS ROOM.
ARM YOURSELVES, THEN WE CAN EAT AND MAKE PLANS.
WE WON A BATTLE AGAINST THE STORM...
AND THIS DAMN DOG IS GETTING UNDER-FOOT!
...NOT THE WHOLE WAR.
LOOK AT THIS!
I WAS IN THE STUDIO WHEN THEY RECORDED THIS. HAPPY DAYS...
IT'S A COLLECTOR'S ITEM NOW THAT BOWIE'S DEAD.
DEAD? WHEN DID THAT HAPPEN?
AT THE END OF A GREAT LIFE. SAME PLACE, GODS WILLING, AS THE REST OF US.
HOW ARE YOU FEELING, TIRESIAS?

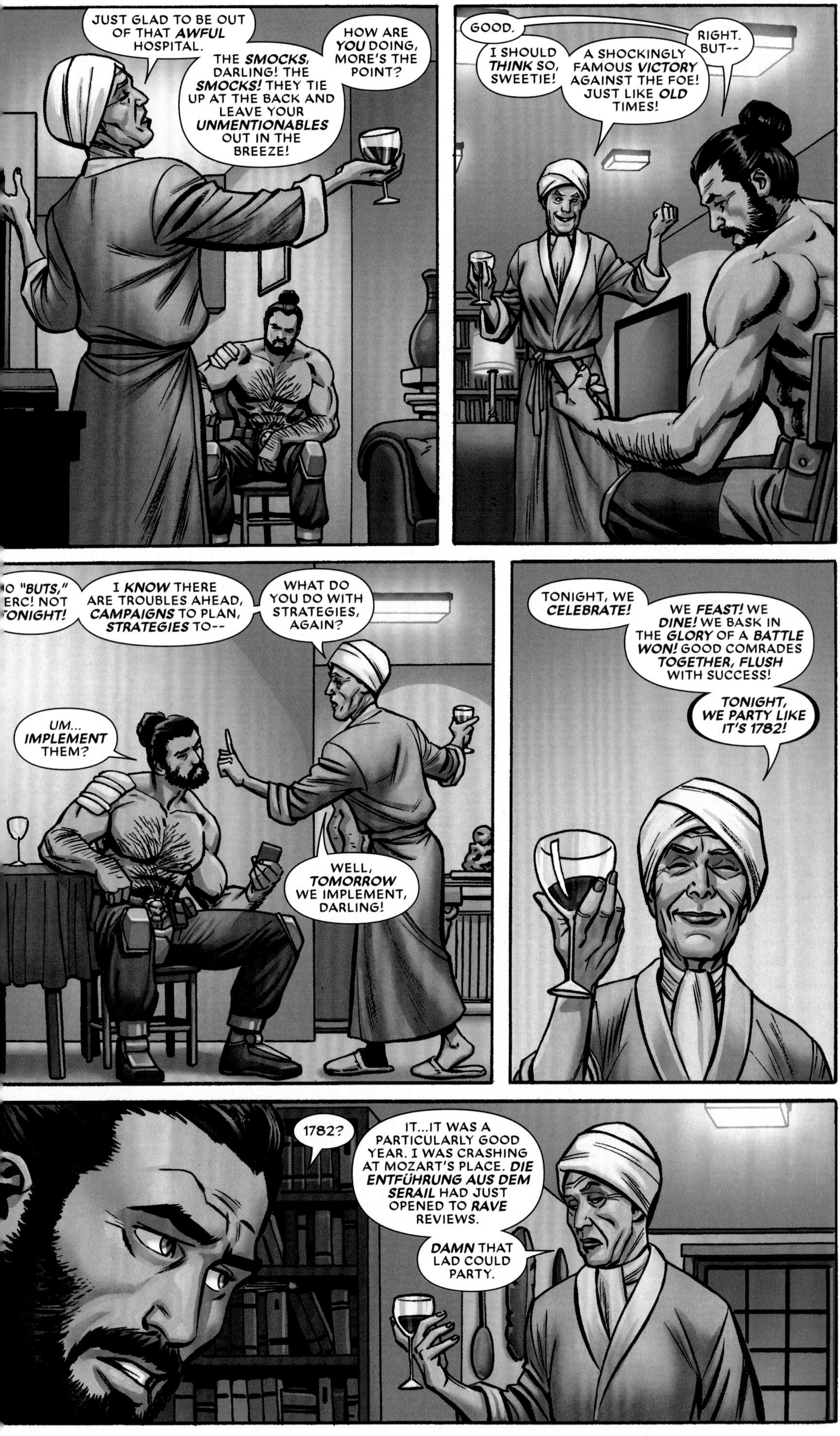
JUST GLAD TO BE OUT OF THAT AWFUL HOSPITAL.
THE SMOCKS, DARLING! THE SMOCKS! THEY TIE UP AT THE BACK AND LEAVE YOUR UNMENTIONABLES OUT IN THE BREEZE!
HOW ARE YOU DOING, MORE'S THE POINT?
GOOD.
I SHOULD THINK SO, SWEETIE!
A SHOCKINGLY FAMOUS VICTORY AGAINST THE FOE! JUST LIKE OLD TIMES!
RIGHT. BUT--
O "BUTS," ERC! NOT TONIGHT!
I KNOW THERE ARE TROUBLES AHEAD, CAMPAIGNS TO PLAN, STRATEGIES TO--
WHAT DO YOU DO WITH STRATEGIES, AGAIN?
UM... IMPLEMENT THEM?
WELL, TOMORROW WE IMPLEMENT, DARLING!
TONIGHT, WE CELEBRATE!
WE FEAST! WE DINE! WE BASK IN THE GLORY OF A BATTLE WON! GOOD COMRADES TOGETHER, FLUSH WITH SUCCESS!
TONIGHT, WE PARTY LIKE IT'S 1782!
1782?
IT...IT WAS A PARTICULARLY GOOD YEAR. I WAS CRASHING AT MOZART'S PLACE. DIE ENTFÜHRUNG AUS DEM SERAIL HAD JUST OPENED TO RAVE REVIEWS.
DAMN THAT LAD COULD PARTY.

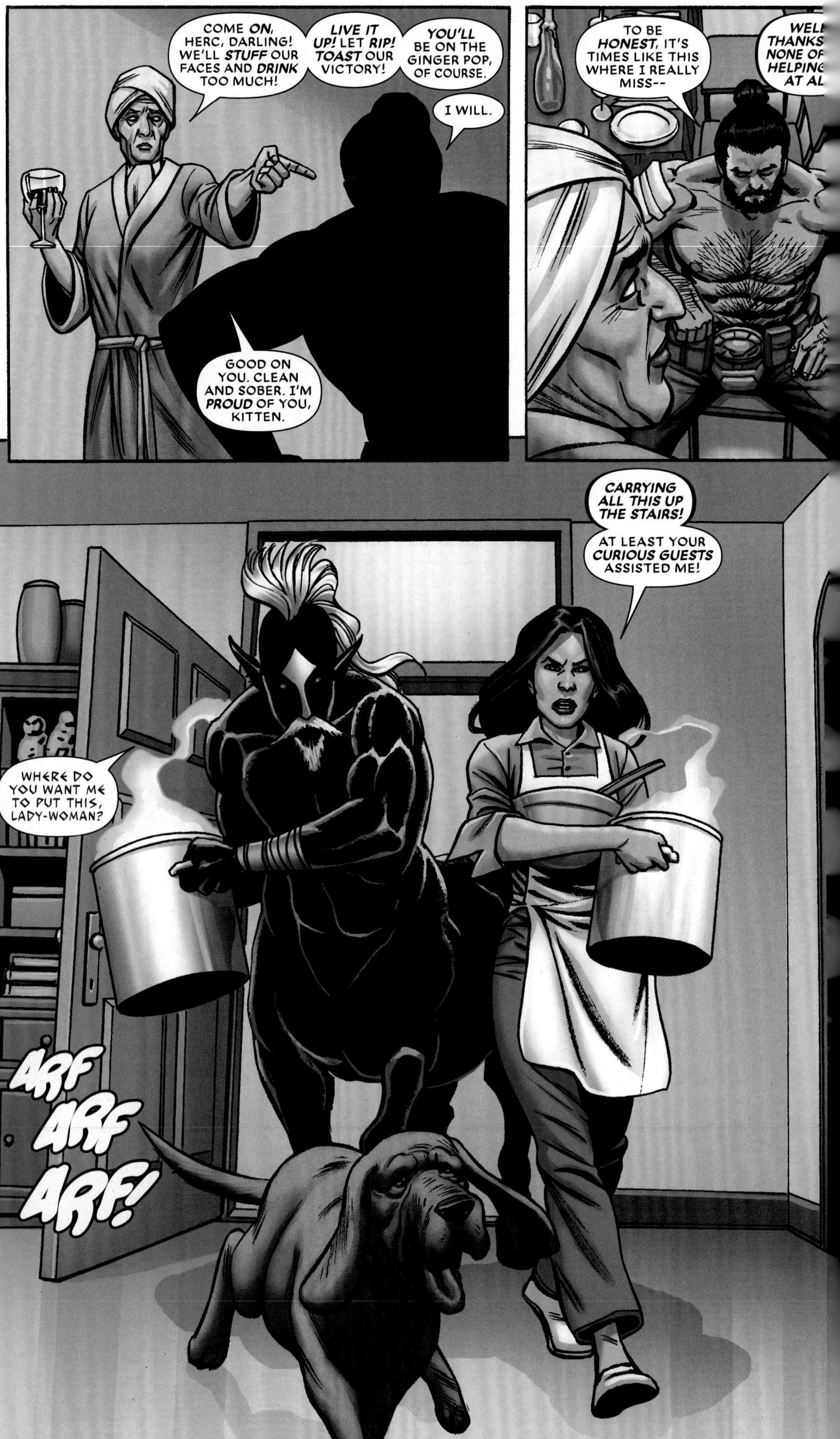

COME ON, HERC, DARLING! WE'LL STUFF OUR FACES AND DRINK TOO MUCH!
LIVE IT UP! LET RIP! TOAST OUR VICTORY!
YOU'LL BE ON THE GINGER POP, OF COURSE.
I WILL.
GOOD ON YOU. CLEAN AND SOBER. I'M PROUD OF YOU, KITTEN.
TO BE HONEST, IT'S TIMES LIKE THIS WHERE I REALLY MISS--
CARRYING ALL THIS UP THE STAIRS!
AT LEAST YOUR CURIOUS GUESTS ASSISTED ME!
WHERE DO YOU WANT ME TO PUT THIS, LADY-WOMAN?
ARF ARF ARF!

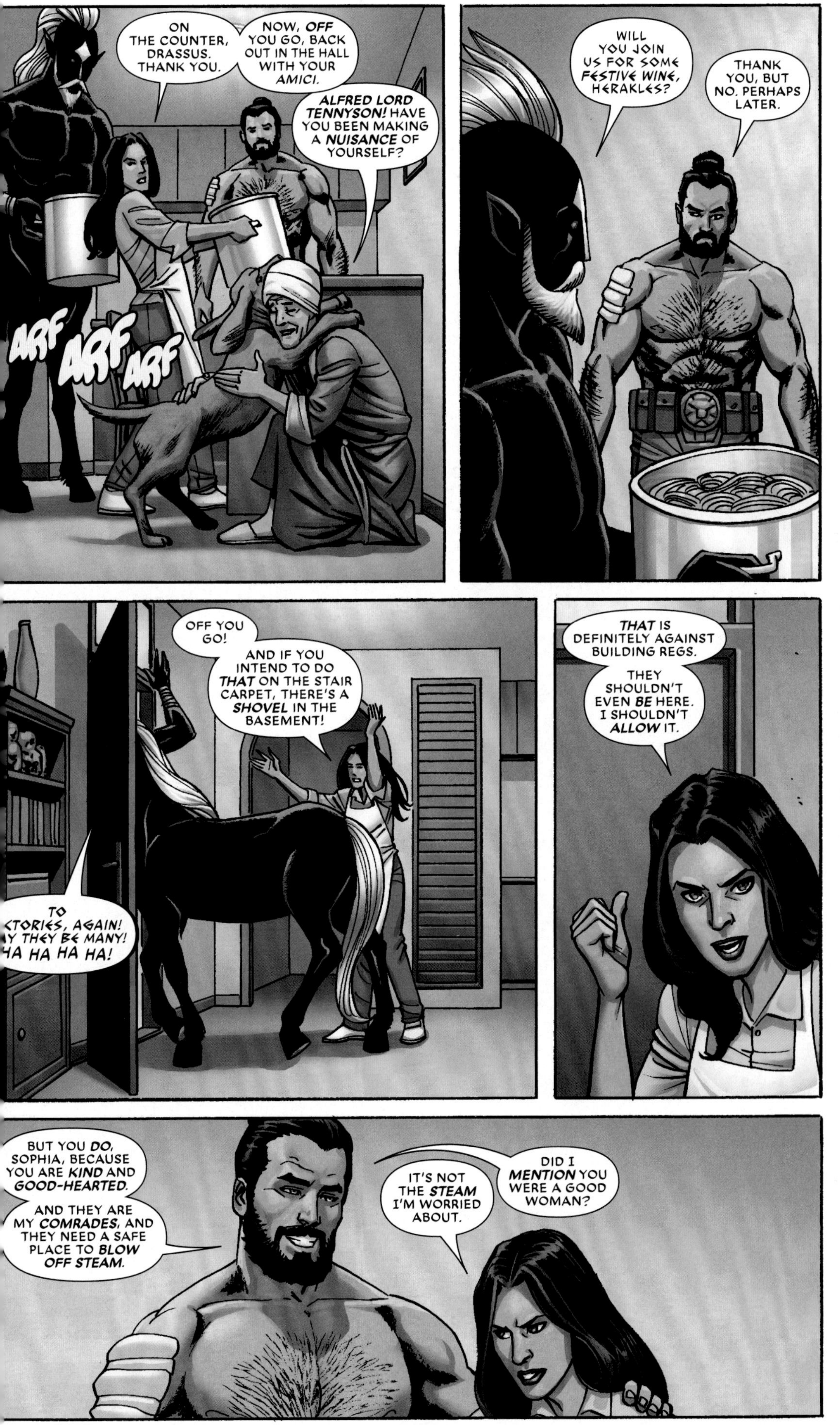
ON THE COUNTER, DRASSUS. THANK YOU.
NOW, OFF YOU GO, BACK OUT IN THE HALL WITH YOUR AMICI.
ALFRED LORD TENNYSON! HAVE YOU BEEN MAKING A NUISANCE OF YOURSELF?
ARF ARF ARF
WILL YOU JOIN US FOR SOME FESTIVE WINE, HERAKLES?
THANK YOU, BUT NO. PERHAPS LATER.
OFF YOU GO!
AND IF YOU INTEND TO DO THAT ON THE STAIR CARPET, THERE'S A SHOVEL IN THE BASEMENT!
TO
CTORIES, AGAIN!
Y THEY BE MANY!
HA HA HA HA!
THAT IS DEFINITELY AGAINST BUILDING REGS.
THEY SHOULDN'T EVEN BE HERE. I SHOULDN'T ALLOW IT.
BUT YOU DO, SOPHIA, BECAUSE YOU ARE KIND AND GOOD-HEARTED.
AND THEY ARE MY COMRADES, AND THEY NEED A SAFE PLACE TO BLOW OFF STEAM.
IT'S NOT THE STEAM I'M WORRIED ABOUT.
DID I MENTION YOU WERE A GOOD WOMAN?

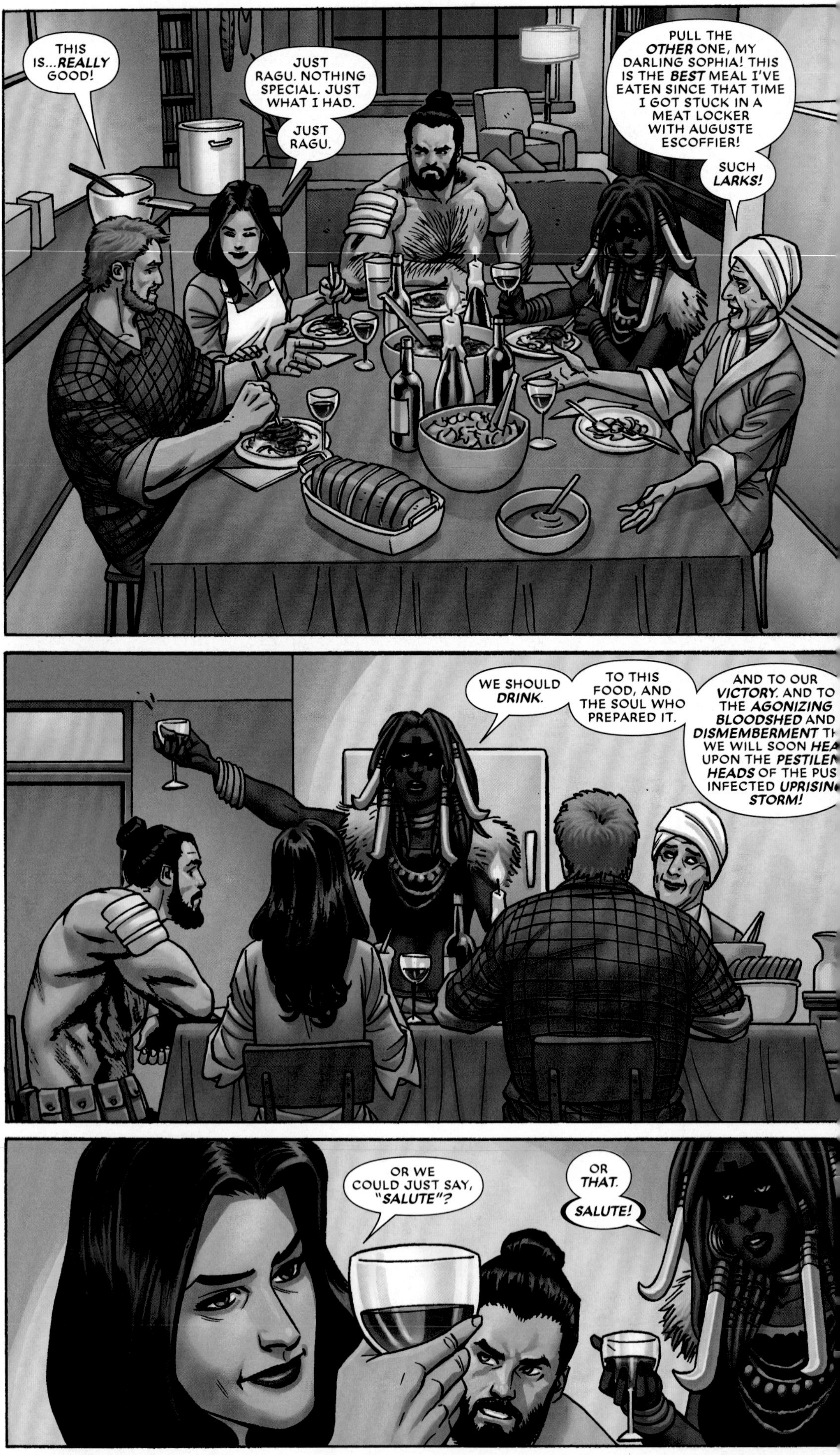
THIS IS...REALLY GOOD!
JUST RAGU. NOTHING SPECIAL. JUST WHAT I HAD.
JUST RAGU.
PULL THE OTHER ONE, MY DARLING SOPHIA! THIS IS THE BEST MEAL I'VE EATEN SINCE THAT TIME I GOT STUCK IN A MEAT LOCKER WITH AUGUSTE ESCOFFIER!
SUCH LARKS!
WE SHOULD DRINK.
TO THIS FOOD, AND THE SOUL WHO PREPARED IT.
AND TO OUR VICTORY. AND TO THE AGONIZING BLOODSHED AND DISMEMBERMENT T WE WILL SOON HEA UPON THE PESTILEN HEADS OF THE PUS INFECTED UPRISIN STORM!
OR WE COULD JUST SAY, "SALUTE"?
OR THAT.
SALUTE!

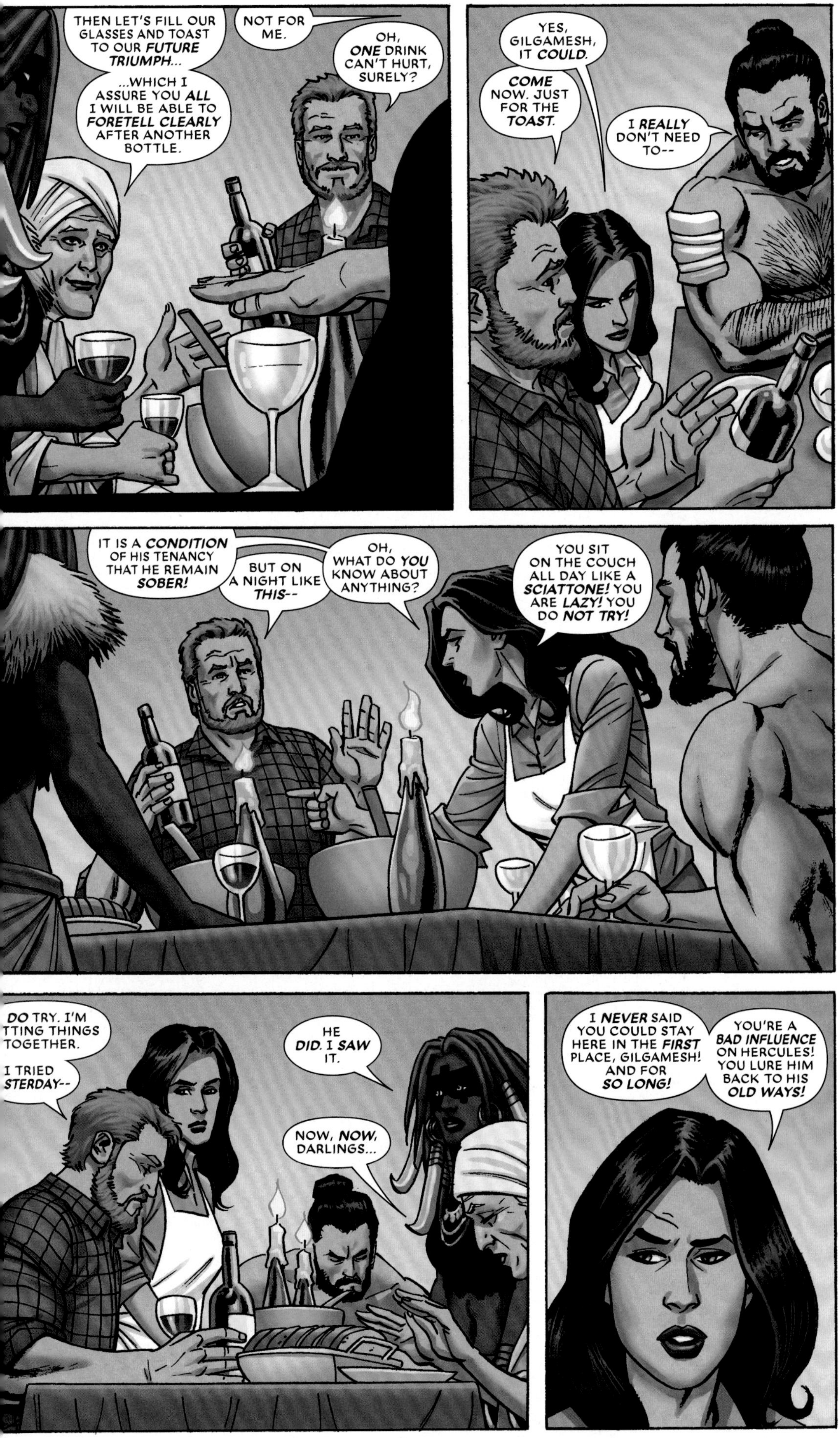
THEN LET'S FILL OUR GLASSES AND TOAST TO OUR *FUTURE TRIUMPH*...
...WHICH I ASSURE YOU *ALL* I WILL BE ABLE TO *FORETELL CLEARLY* AFTER ANOTHER BOTTLE.
NOT FOR ME.
OH, *ONE* DRINK CAN'T HURT, SURELY?
YES, GILGAMESH, IT *COULD*.
COME NOW. JUST FOR THE *TOAST*.
I *REALLY* DON'T NEED TO--
IT IS A *CONDITION* OF HIS TENANCY THAT HE REMAIN *SOBER!*
BUT ON A NIGHT LIKE *THIS*--
OH, WHAT DO *YOU* KNOW ABOUT ANYTHING?
YOU SIT ON THE COUCH ALL DAY LIKE A *SCIATTONE!* YOU ARE *LAZY!* YOU DO *NOT TRY!*
DO TRY. I'M TTING THINGS TOGETHER.
I TRIED STERDAY--
HE *DID*. I *SAW* IT.
NOW, *NOW*, DARLINGS...
I *NEVER* SAID YOU COULD STAY HERE IN THE *FIRST* PLACE, GILGAMESH! AND FOR *SO LONG!*
YOU'RE A *BAD INFLUENCE* ON HERCULES! YOU LURE HIM BACK TO HIS *OLD WAYS!*

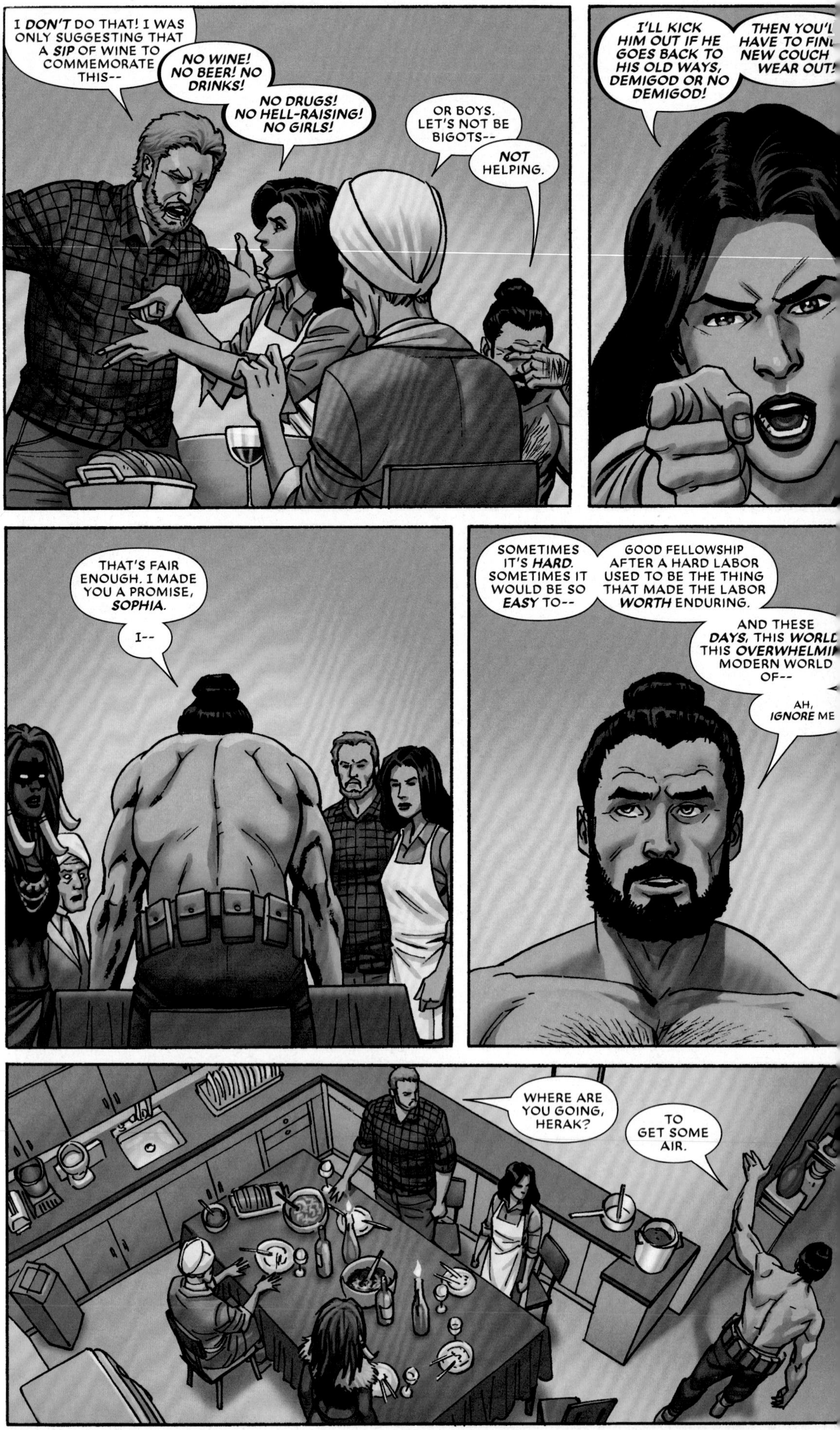
I DON'T DO THAT! I WAS ONLY SUGGESTING THAT A SIP OF WINE TO COMMEMORATE THIS--
NO WINE! NO BEER! NO DRINKS!
NO DRUGS! NO HELL-RAISING! NO GIRLS!
OR BOYS. LET'S NOT BE BIGOTS--
NOT HELPING.
I'LL KICK HIM OUT IF HE GOES BACK TO HIS OLD WAYS, DEMIGOD OR NO DEMIGOD!
THEN YOU'L HAVE TO FINI NEW COUCH WEAR OUT!
THAT'S FAIR ENOUGH. I MADE YOU A PROMISE, SOPHIA.
I--
SOMETIMES IT'S HARD. SOMETIMES IT WOULD BE SO EASY TO--
GOOD FELLOWSHIP AFTER A HARD LABOR USED TO BE THE THING THAT MADE THE LABOR WORTH ENDURING.
AND THESE DAYS, THIS WORLD THIS OVERWHELMI MODERN WORLD OF--
AH, IGNORE ME
WHERE ARE YOU GOING, HERAK?
TO GET SOME AIR.

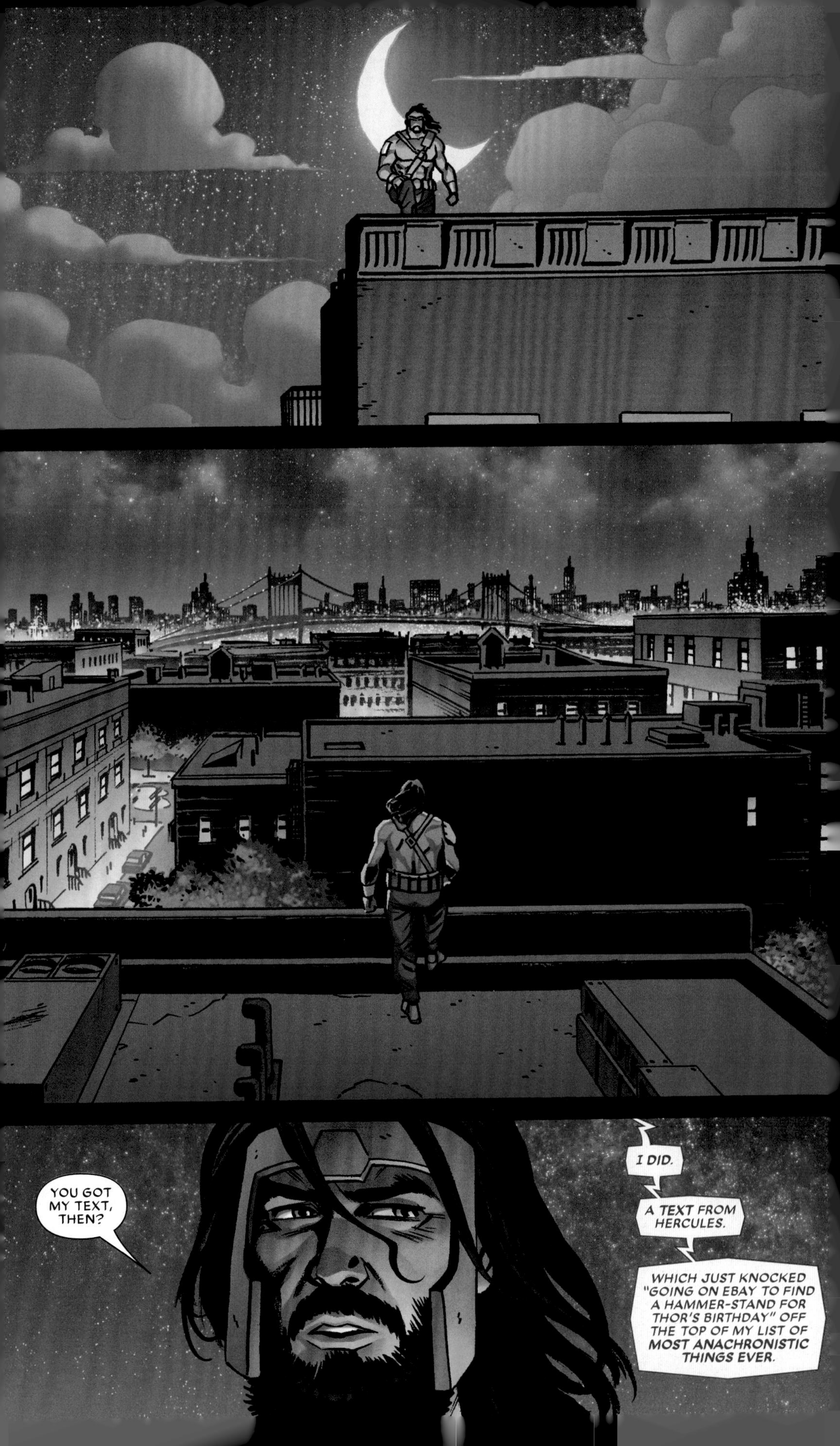
YOU GOT MY TEXT, THEN?
I DID.
A TEXT FROM HERCULES.
WHICH JUST KNOCKED "GOING ON EBAY TO FIND A HAMMER-STAND FOR THOR'S BIRTHDAY" OFF THE TOP OF MY LIST OF MOST ANACHRONISTIC THINGS EVER.

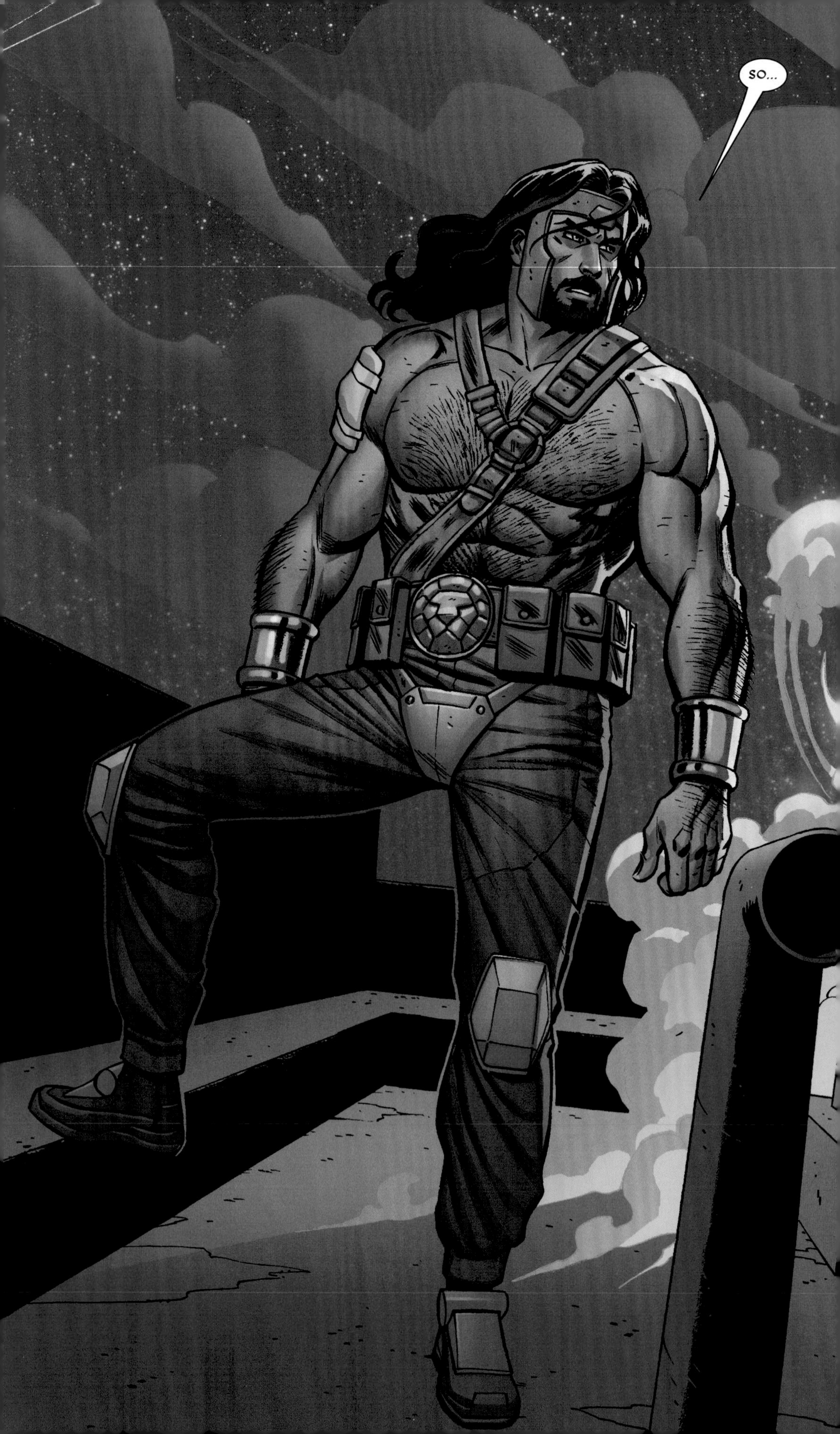
SO...

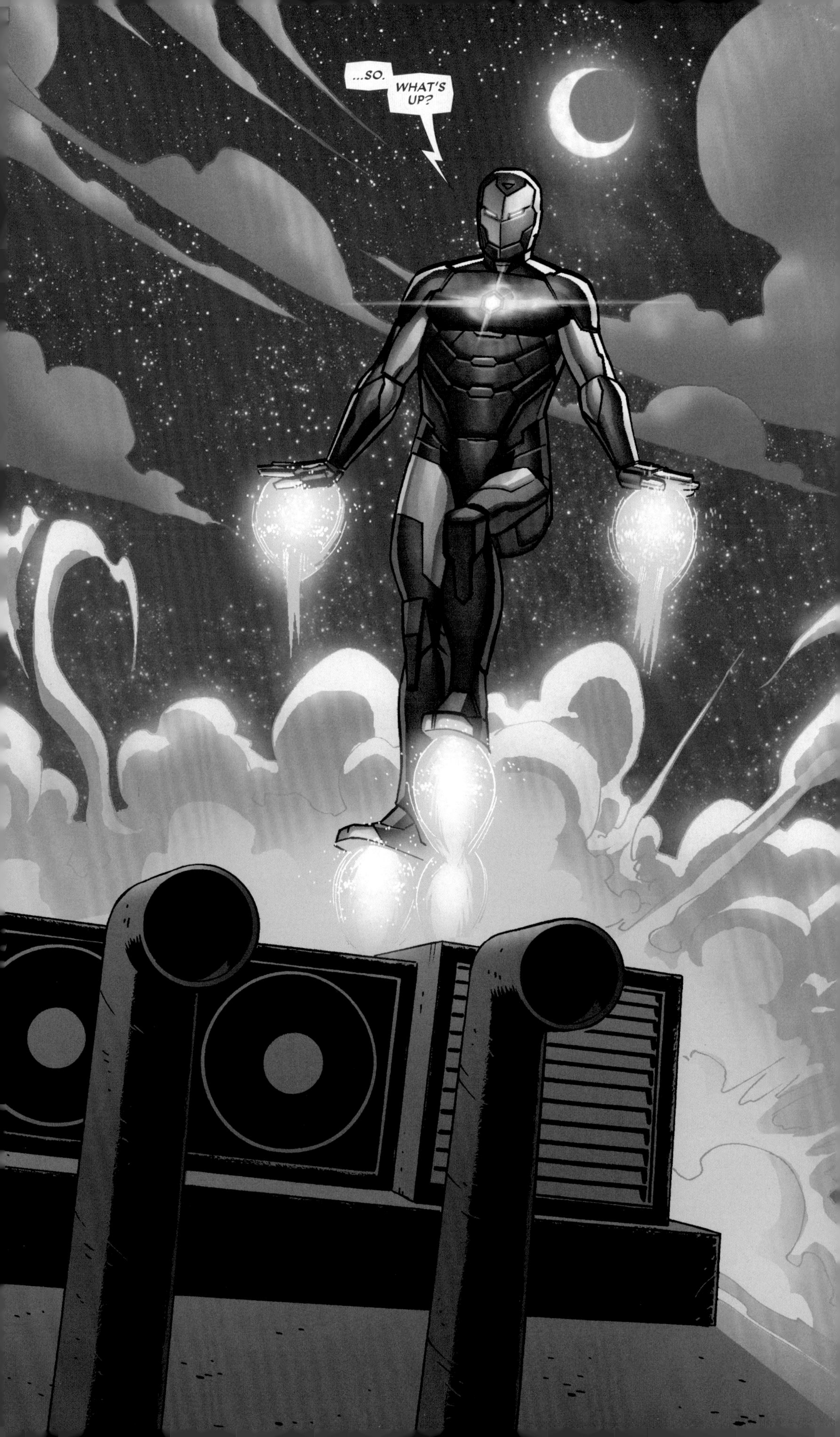
...SO.
WHAT'S UP?

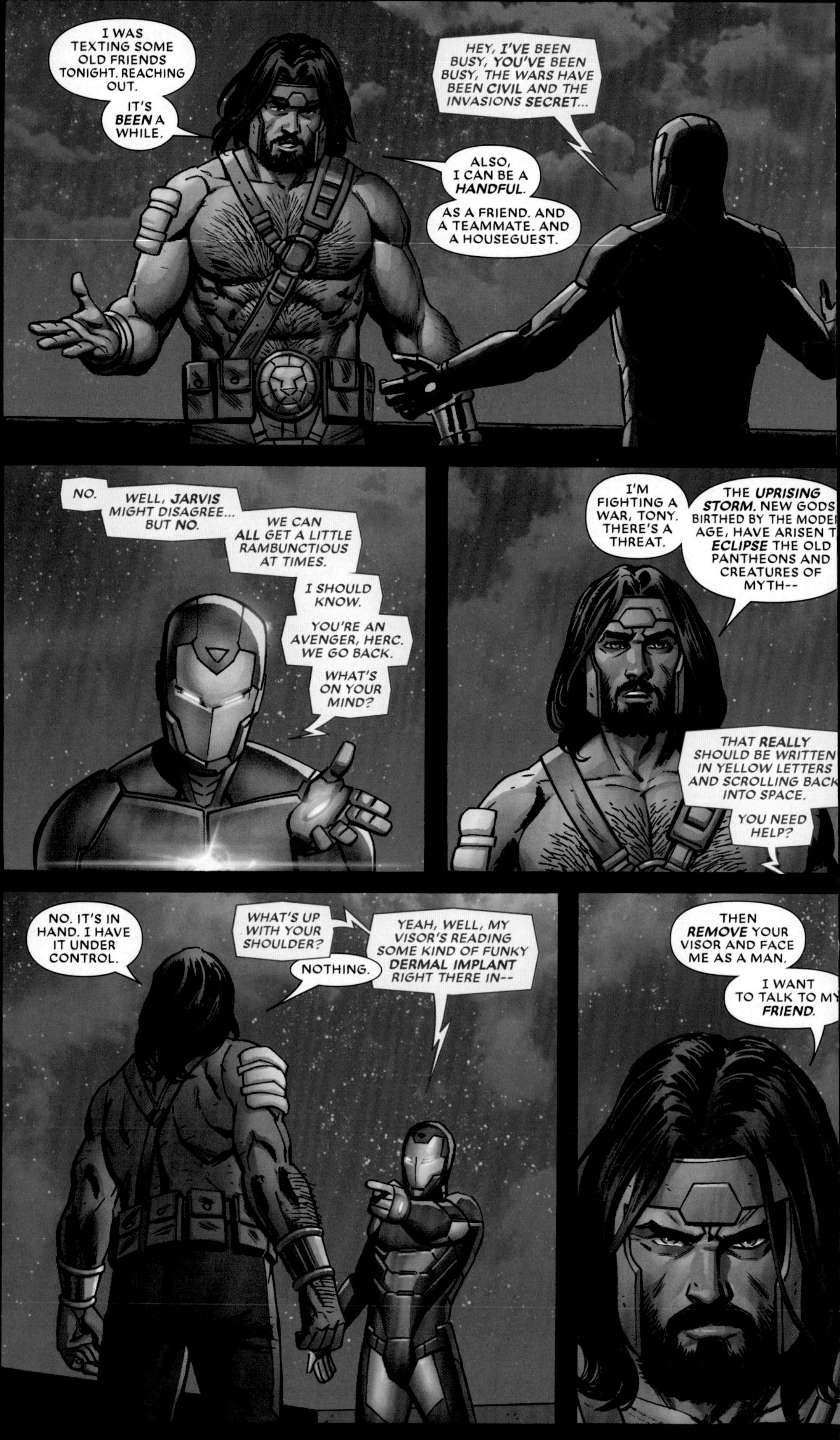
I WAS TEXTING SOME OLD FRIENDS TONIGHT. REACHING OUT.
IT'S *BEEN* A WHILE.
HEY, *I'VE* BEEN BUSY, *YOU'VE* BEEN BUSY, THE WARS HAVE BEEN *CIVIL* AND THE INVASIONS *SECRET*...
ALSO, I CAN BE A *HANDFUL*.
AS A FRIEND. AND A TEAMMATE. AND A HOUSEGUEST.
NO.
WELL, *JARVIS* MIGHT DISAGREE... BUT *NO*.
WE CAN *ALL* GET A LITTLE RAMBUNCTIOUS AT TIMES.
I SHOULD KNOW.
YOU'RE AN AVENGER, HERC. WE GO BACK.
WHAT'S ON YOUR MIND?
I'M FIGHTING A WAR, TONY. THERE'S A THREAT.
THE *UPRISING STORM*. NEW GODS BIRTHED BY THE MODE AGE, HAVE ARISEN T *ECLIPSE* THE OLD PANTHEONS AND CREATURES OF MYTH--
THAT *REALLY* SHOULD BE WRITTEN IN YELLOW LETTERS AND SCROLLING BACK INTO SPACE.
YOU NEED HELP?
NO. IT'S IN HAND. I HAVE IT UNDER CONTROL.
WHAT'S UP WITH YOUR SHOULDER?
NOTHING.
YEAH, WELL, MY VISOR'S READING SOME KIND OF FUNKY *DERMAL IMPLANT* RIGHT THERE IN--
THEN *REMOVE* YOUR VISOR AND FACE ME AS A MAN.
I WANT TO TALK TO MY *FRIEND*.

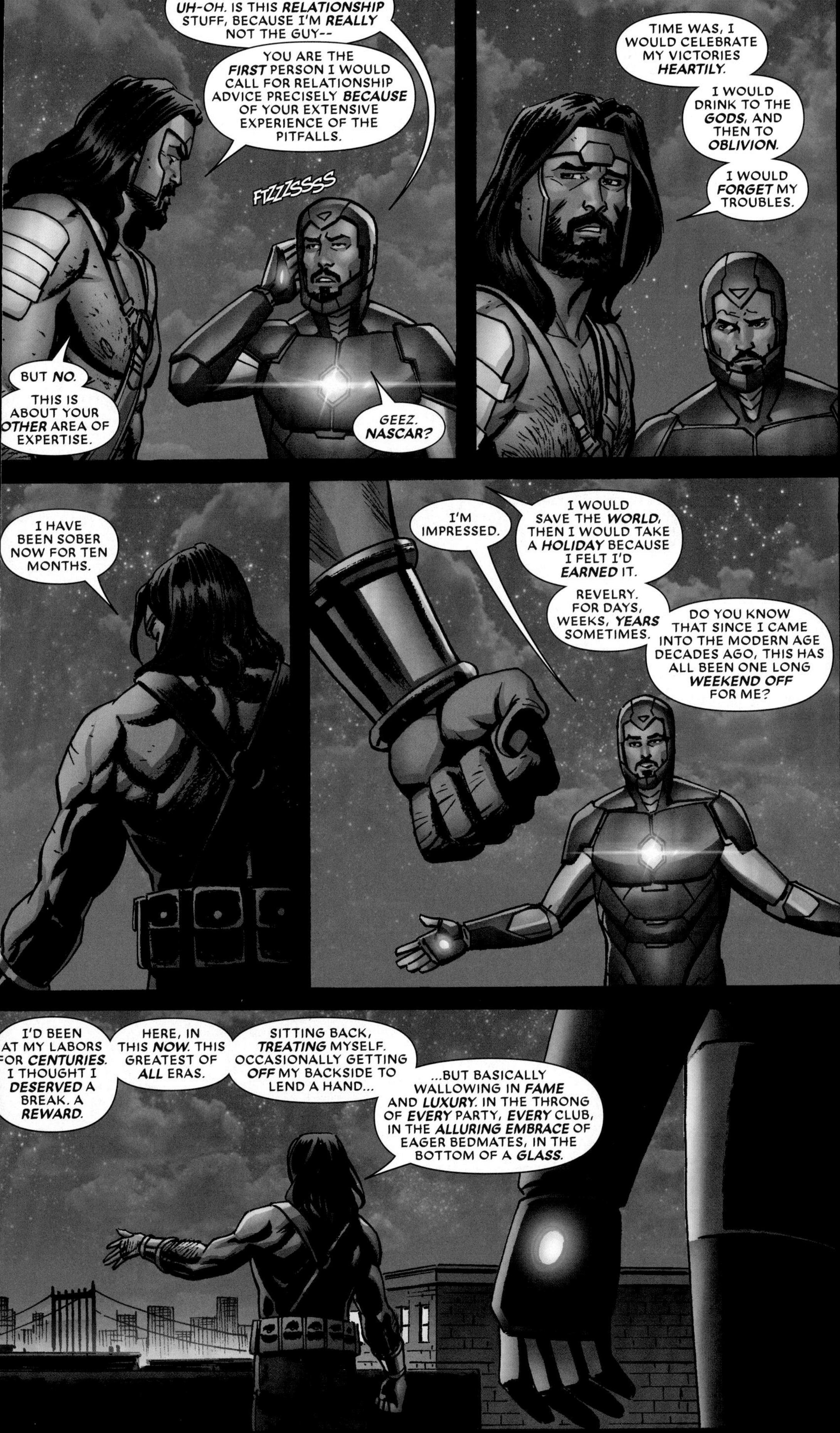
UH-OH. IS THIS RELATIONSHIP STUFF, BECAUSE I'M REALLY NOT THE GUY--
YOU ARE THE FIRST PERSON I WOULD CALL FOR RELATIONSHIP ADVICE PRECISELY BECAUSE OF YOUR EXTENSIVE EXPERIENCE OF THE PITFALLS.
FTZZZSSSS
BUT NO.
THIS IS ABOUT YOUR OTHER AREA OF EXPERTISE.
GEEZ. NASCAR?
TIME WAS, I WOULD CELEBRATE MY VICTORIES HEARTILY.
I WOULD DRINK TO THE GODS, AND THEN TO OBLIVION.
I WOULD FORGET MY TROUBLES.
I HAVE BEEN SOBER NOW FOR TEN MONTHS.
I'M IMPRESSED.
I WOULD SAVE THE WORLD, THEN I WOULD TAKE A HOLIDAY BECAUSE I FELT I'D EARNED IT.
REVELRY. FOR DAYS, WEEKS, YEARS SOMETIMES.
DO YOU KNOW THAT SINCE I CAME INTO THE MODERN AGE DECADES AGO, THIS HAS ALL BEEN ONE LONG WEEKEND OFF FOR ME?
I'D BEEN AT MY LABORS FOR CENTURIES. I THOUGHT I DESERVED A BREAK. A REWARD.
HERE, IN THIS NOW. THIS GREATEST OF ALL ERAS.
SITTING BACK, TREATING MYSELF. OCCASIONALLY GETTING OFF MY BACKSIDE TO LEND A HAND...
...BUT BASICALLY WALLOWING IN FAME AND LUXURY. IN THE THRONG OF EVERY PARTY, EVERY CLUB, IN THE ALLURING EMBRACE OF EAGER BEDMATES, IN THE BOTTOM OF A GLASS.

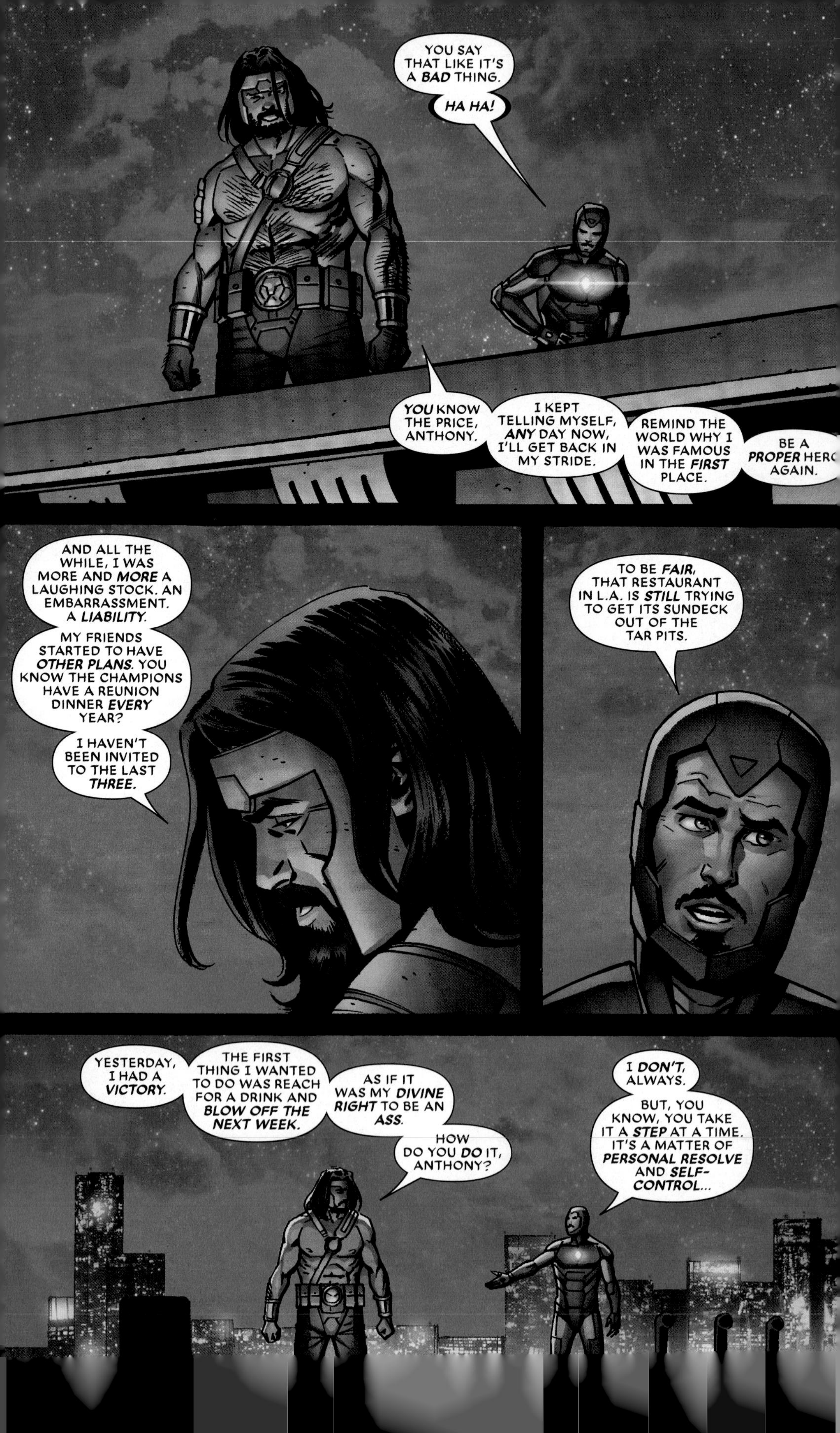
YOU SAY THAT LIKE IT'S A BAD THING.
HA HA!
YOU KNOW THE PRICE, ANTHONY.
I KEPT TELLING MYSELF, ANY DAY NOW, I'LL GET BACK IN MY STRIDE.
REMIND THE WORLD WHY I WAS FAMOUS IN THE FIRST PLACE.
BE A PROPER HERO AGAIN.
AND ALL THE WHILE, I WAS MORE AND MORE A LAUGHING STOCK. AN EMBARRASSMENT. A LIABILITY.
MY FRIENDS STARTED TO HAVE OTHER PLANS. YOU KNOW THE CHAMPIONS HAVE A REUNION DINNER EVERY YEAR?
I HAVEN'T BEEN INVITED TO THE LAST THREE.
TO BE FAIR, THAT RESTAURANT IN L.A. IS STILL TRYING TO GET ITS SUNDECK OUT OF THE TAR PITS.
YESTERDAY, I HAD A VICTORY.
THE FIRST THING I WANTED TO DO WAS REACH FOR A DRINK AND BLOW OFF THE NEXT WEEK.
AS IF IT WAS MY DIVINE RIGHT TO BE AN ASS.
HOW DO YOU DO IT, ANTHONY?
I DON'T, ALWAYS.
BUT, YOU KNOW, YOU TAKE IT A STEP AT A TIME. IT'S A MATTER OF PERSONAL RESOLVE AND SELF-CONTROL...

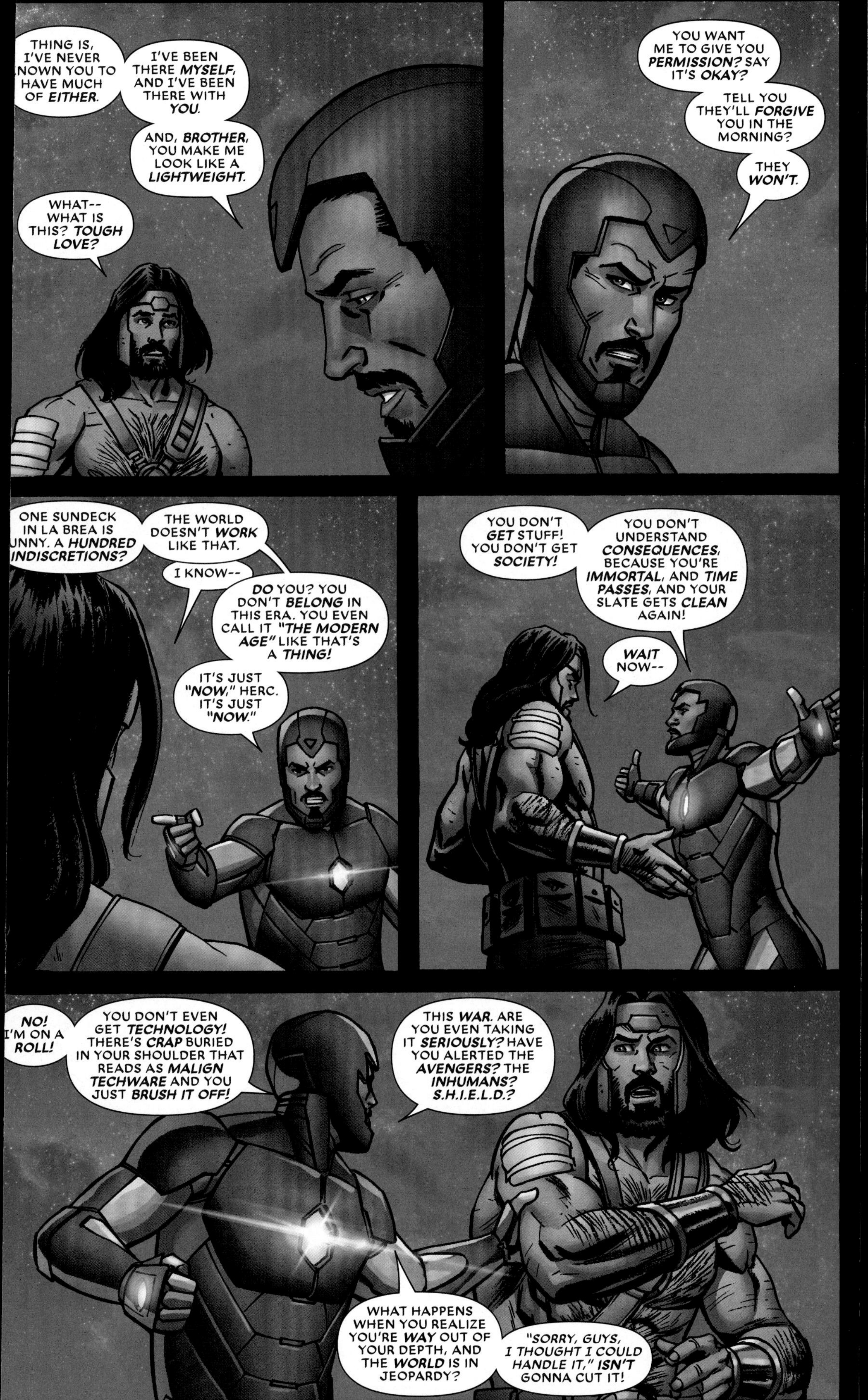
THING IS, I'VE NEVER KNOWN YOU TO HAVE MUCH OF EITHER.
I'VE BEEN THERE MYSELF, AND I'VE BEEN THERE WITH YOU.
AND, BROTHER, YOU MAKE ME LOOK LIKE A LIGHTWEIGHT.
WHAT-- WHAT IS THIS? TOUGH LOVE?
YOU WANT ME TO GIVE YOU PERMISSION? SAY IT'S OKAY?
TELL YOU THEY'LL FORGIVE YOU IN THE MORNING?
THEY WON'T.
ONE SUNDECK IN LA BREA IS FUNNY. A HUNDRED INDISCRETIONS?
THE WORLD DOESN'T WORK LIKE THAT.
I KNOW--
DO YOU? YOU DON'T BELONG IN THIS ERA. YOU EVEN CALL IT "THE MODERN AGE" LIKE THAT'S A THING!
IT'S JUST "NOW," HERC. IT'S JUST "NOW."
YOU DON'T GET STUFF! YOU DON'T GET SOCIETY!
YOU DON'T UNDERSTAND CONSEQUENCES, BECAUSE YOU'RE IMMORTAL, AND TIME PASSES, AND YOUR SLATE GETS CLEAN AGAIN!
WAIT NOW--
NO! I'M ON A ROLL!
YOU DON'T EVEN GET TECHNOLOGY! THERE'S CRAP BURIED IN YOUR SHOULDER THAT READS AS MALIGN TECHWARE AND YOU JUST BRUSH IT OFF!
THIS WAR. ARE YOU EVEN TAKING IT SERIOUSLY? HAVE YOU ALERTED THE AVENGERS? THE INHUMANS? S.H.I.E.L.D.?
WHAT HAPPENS WHEN YOU REALIZE YOU'RE WAY OUT OF YOUR DEPTH, AND THE WORLD IS IN JEOPARDY?
"SORRY, GUYS, I THOUGHT I COULD HANDLE IT," ISN'T GONNA CUT IT!

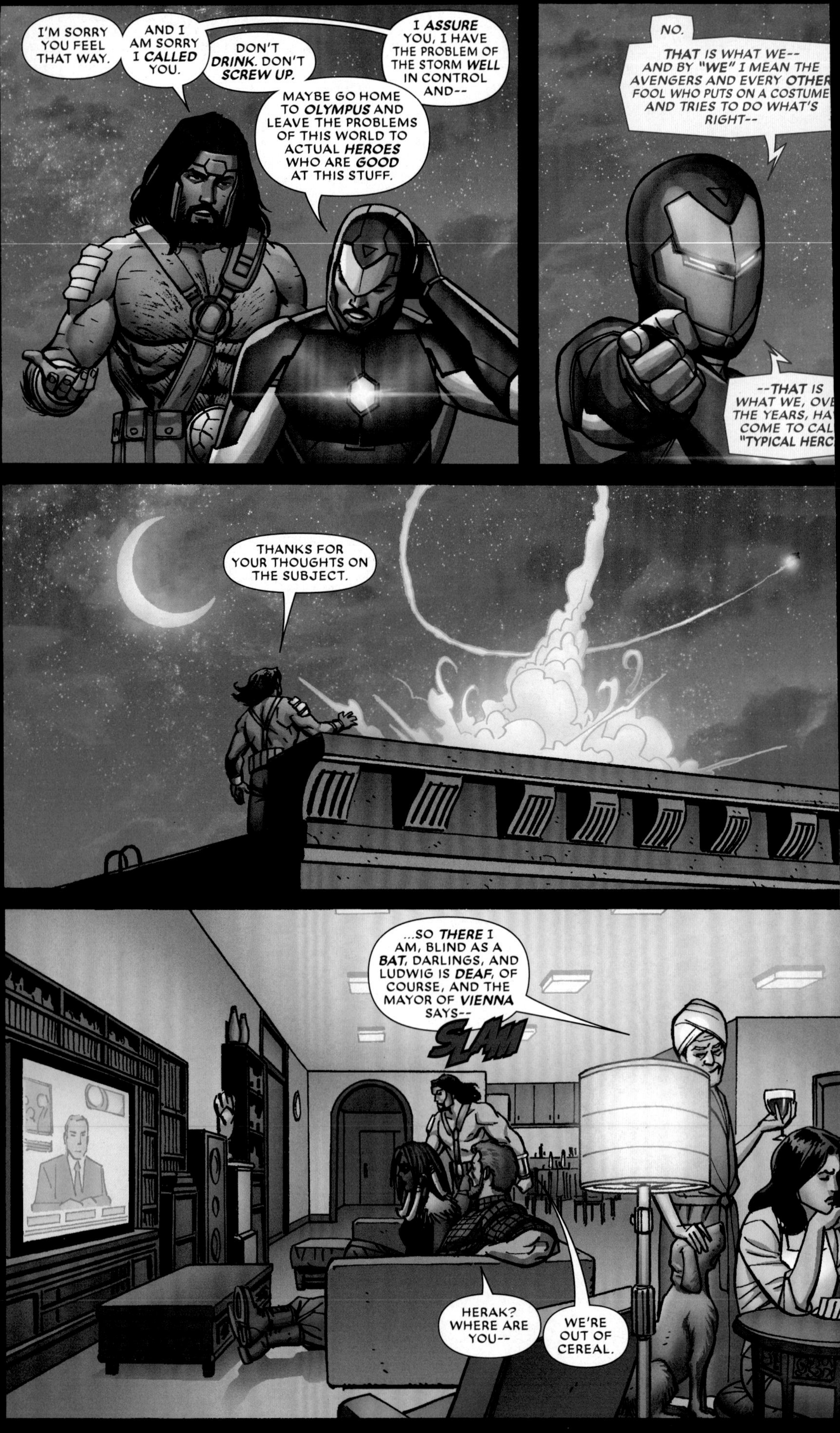

I'M SORRY YOU FEEL THAT WAY.
AND I AM SORRY I CALLED YOU.
DON'T DRINK. DON'T SCREW UP.
I ASSURE YOU, I HAVE THE PROBLEM OF THE STORM WELL IN CONTROL AND--
MAYBE GO HOME TO OLYMPUS AND LEAVE THE PROBLEMS OF THIS WORLD TO ACTUAL HEROES WHO ARE GOOD AT THIS STUFF.
NO.
THAT IS WHAT WE-- AND BY "WE" I MEAN THE AVENGERS AND EVERY OTHER FOOL WHO PUTS ON A COSTUME AND TRIES TO DO WHAT'S RIGHT--
--THAT IS WHAT WE, OVE THE YEARS, HAV COME TO CAL "TYPICAL HERC
THANKS FOR YOUR THOUGHTS ON THE SUBJECT.
...SO THERE I AM, BLIND AS A BAT, DARLINGS, AND LUDWIG IS DEAF, OF COURSE, AND THE MAYOR OF VIENNA SAYS--
SLAM
HERAK? WHERE ARE YOU--
WE'RE OUT OF CEREAL.

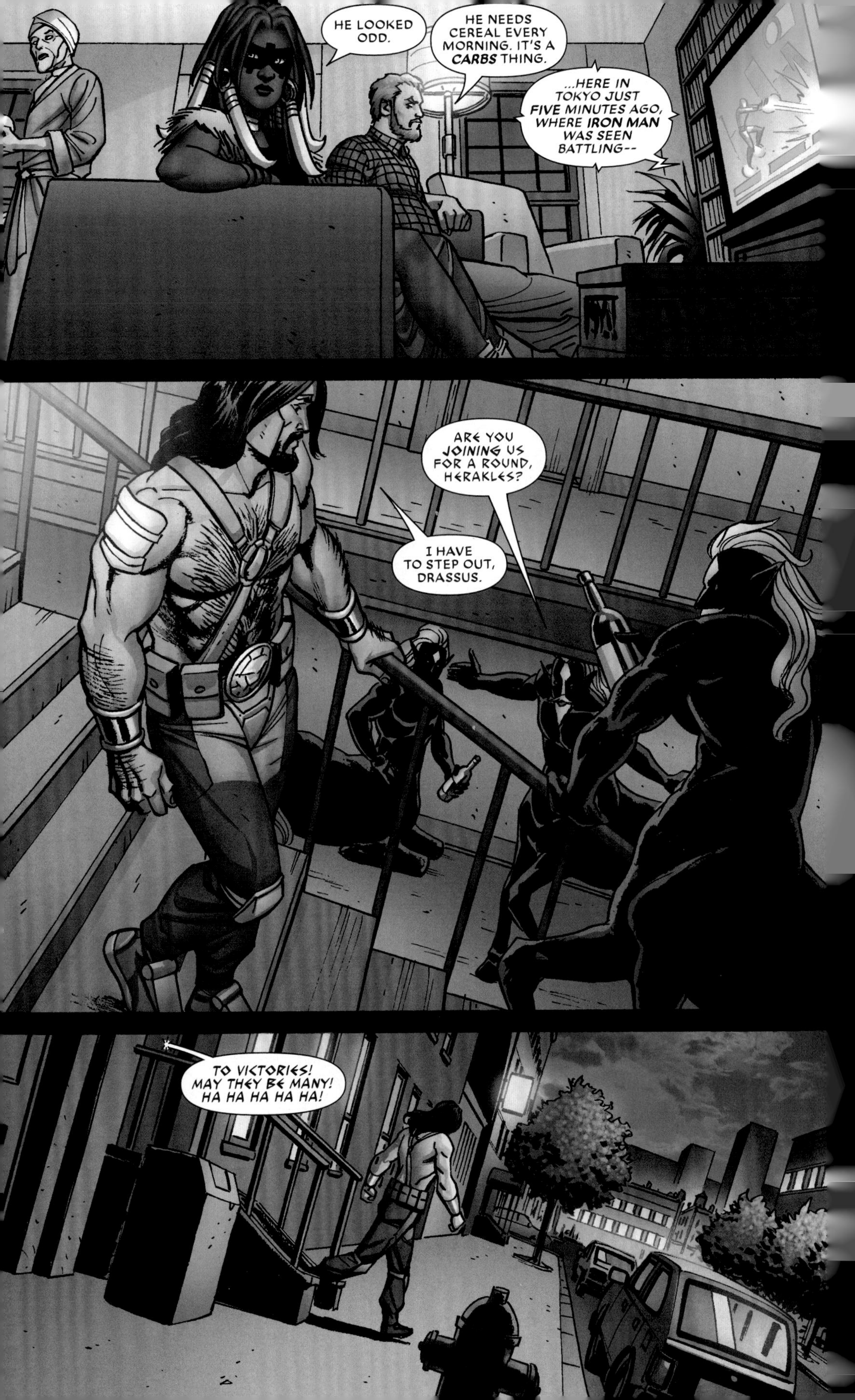
HE LOOKED ODD.
HE NEEDS CEREAL EVERY MORNING. IT'S A CARBS THING.
...HERE IN TOKYO JUST FIVE MINUTES AGO, WHERE IRON MAN WAS SEEN BATTLING--
ARE YOU JOINING US FOR A ROUND, HERAKLES?
I HAVE TO STEP OUT, DRASSUS.
TO VICTORIES! MAY THEY BE MANY! HA HA HA HA HA!

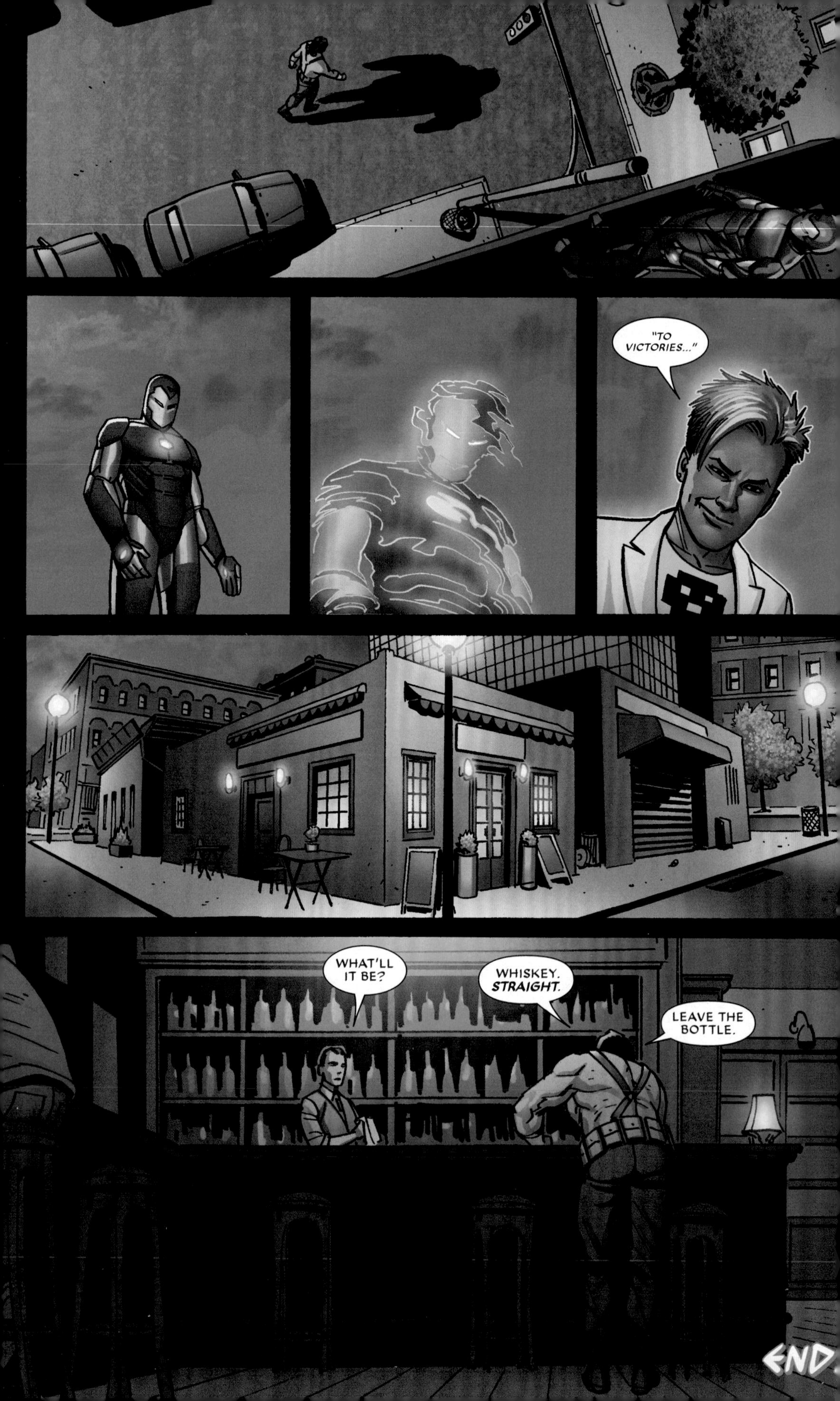
"TO VICTORIES..."
WHAT'LL IT BE?
WHISKEY. *STRAIGHT.*
LEAVE THE BOTTLE.
END

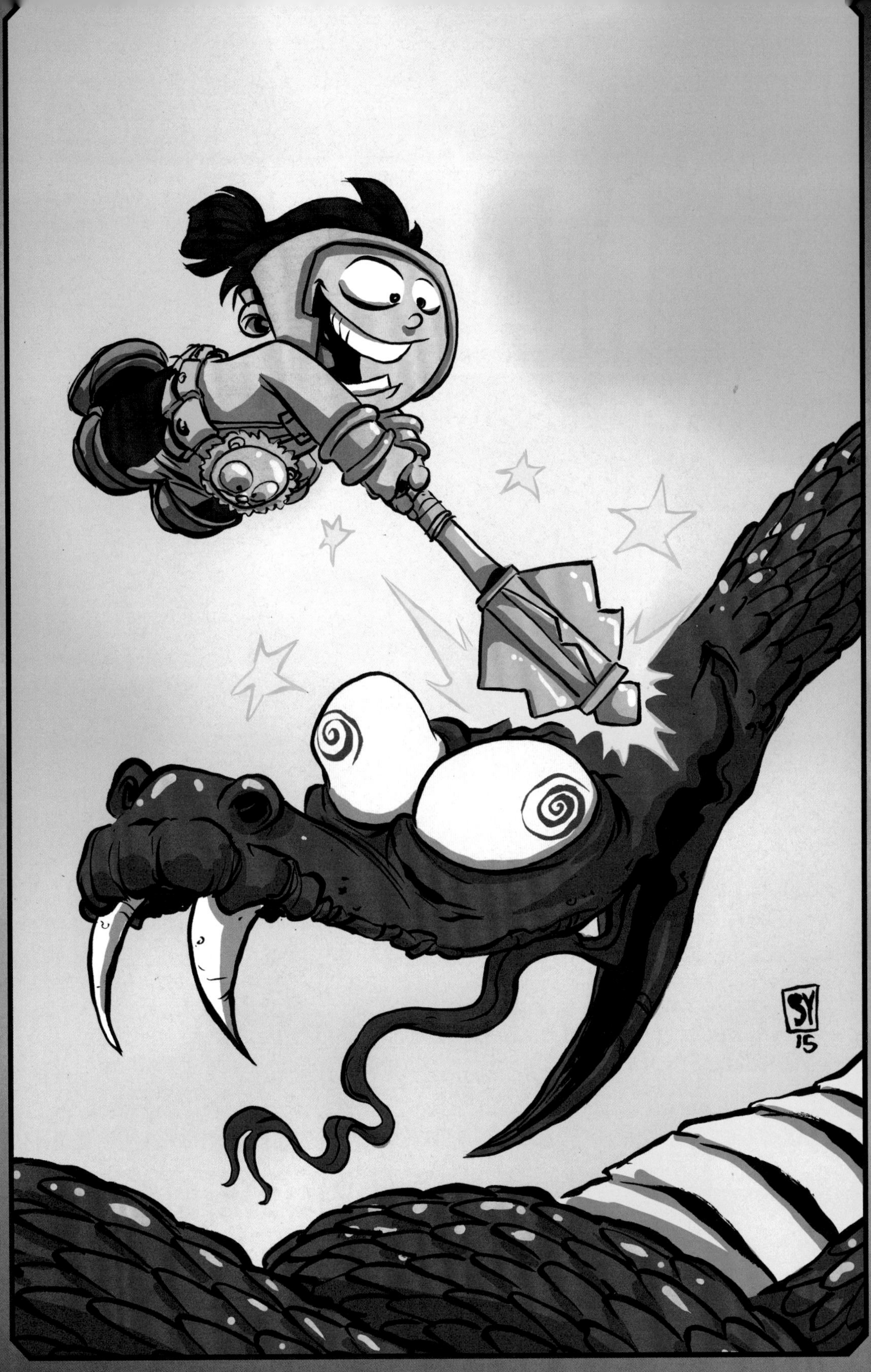
SY
'15

No. 1 VARIANT BY SKOTTIE YOUNG

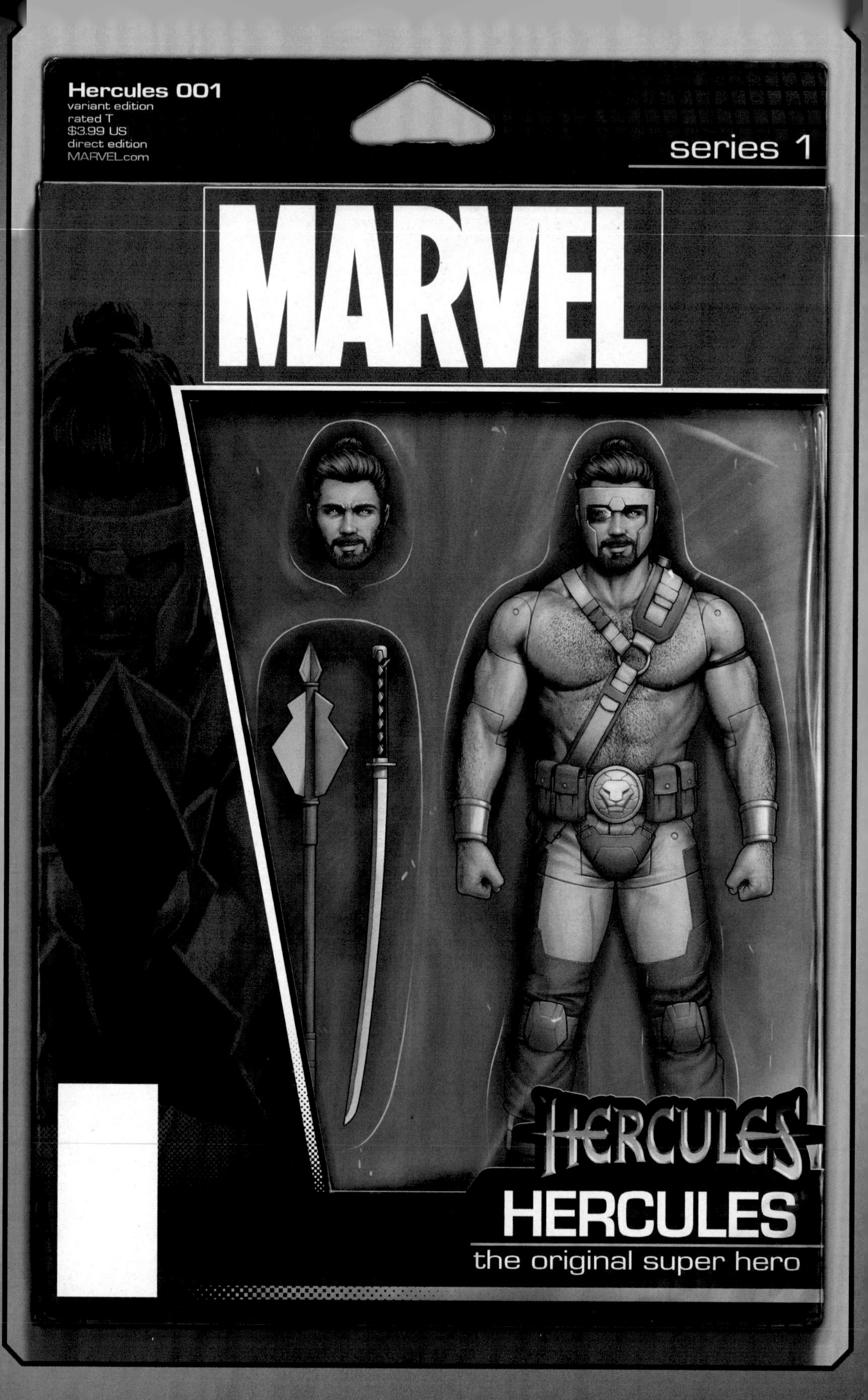
Hercules 001
variant edition
rated T
$3.99 US
direct edition
MARVEL.com
series 1
MARVEL
HERCULES
HERCULES
the original super hero

No. 1 ACTION FIGURE VARIANT BY JOHN TYLER CHRISTOPHER

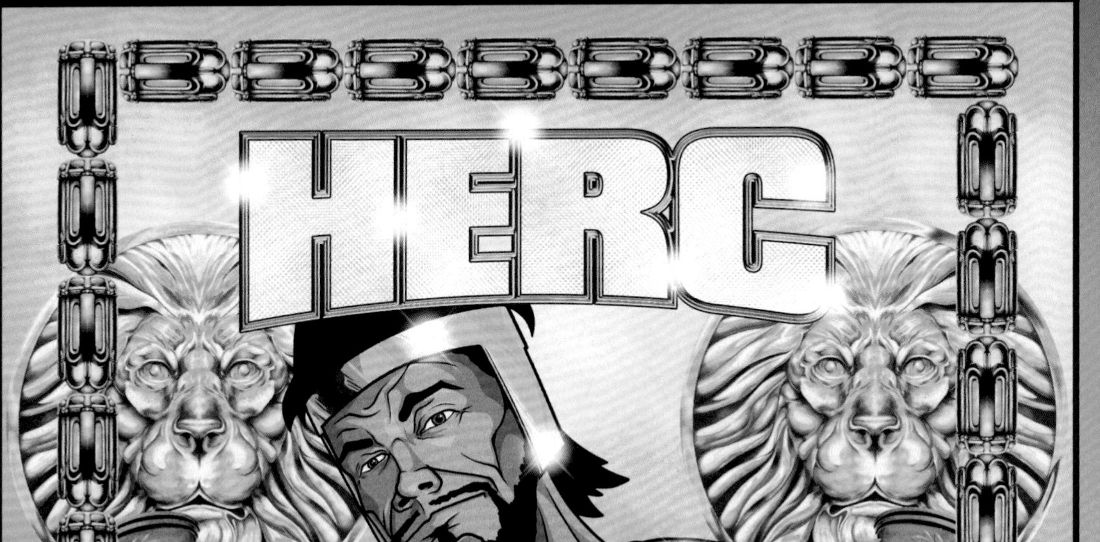
HERC
OLYMPIC
FLAME

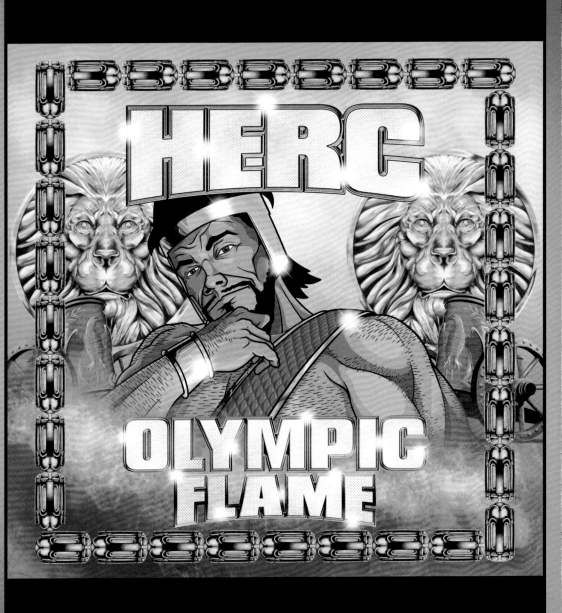

No. 1 HIP-HOP VARIANT BY THEOTIS JONES

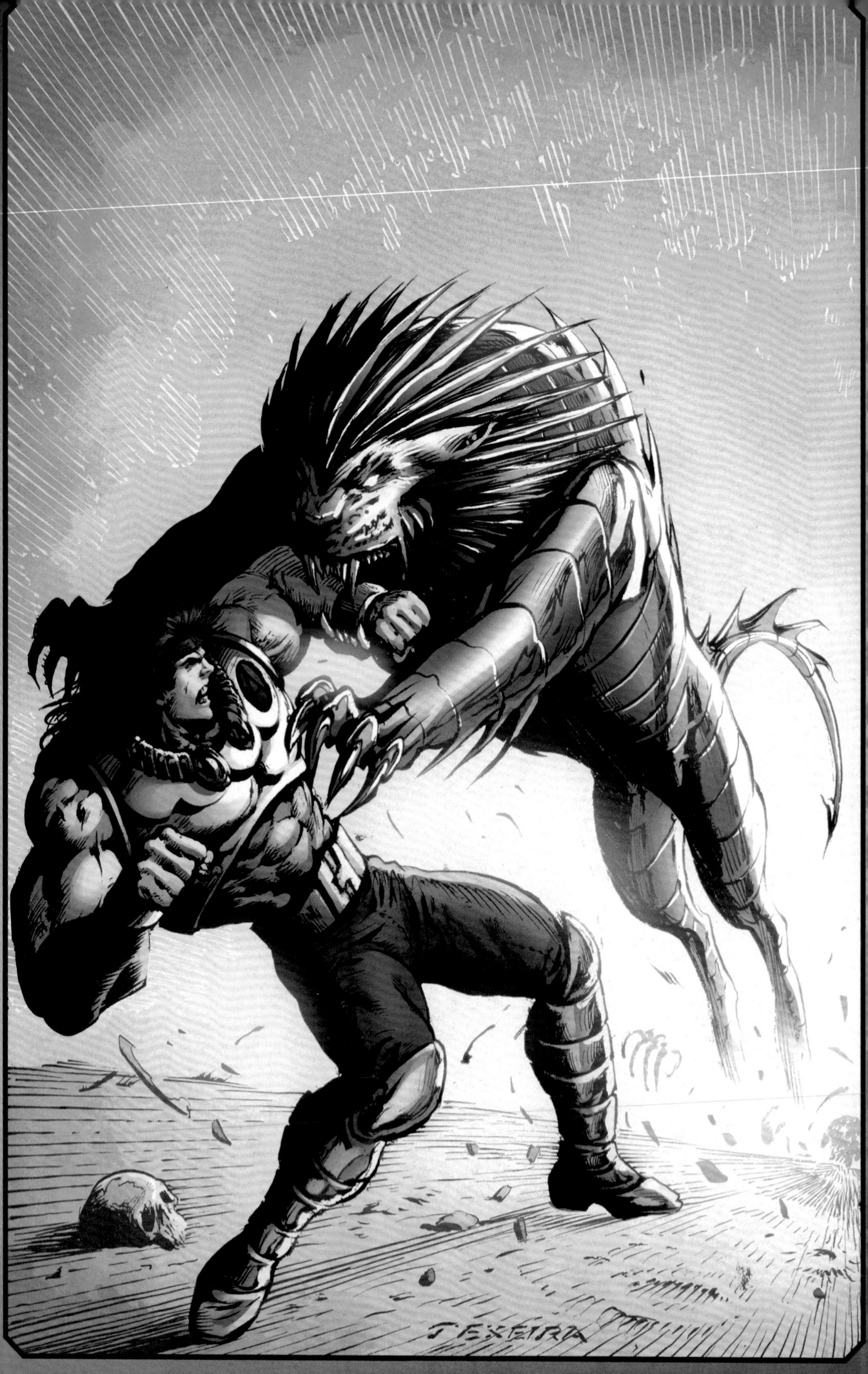
TEXEIRA

No. 2 MARVEL '92 VARIANT BY MARK TEXEIRA

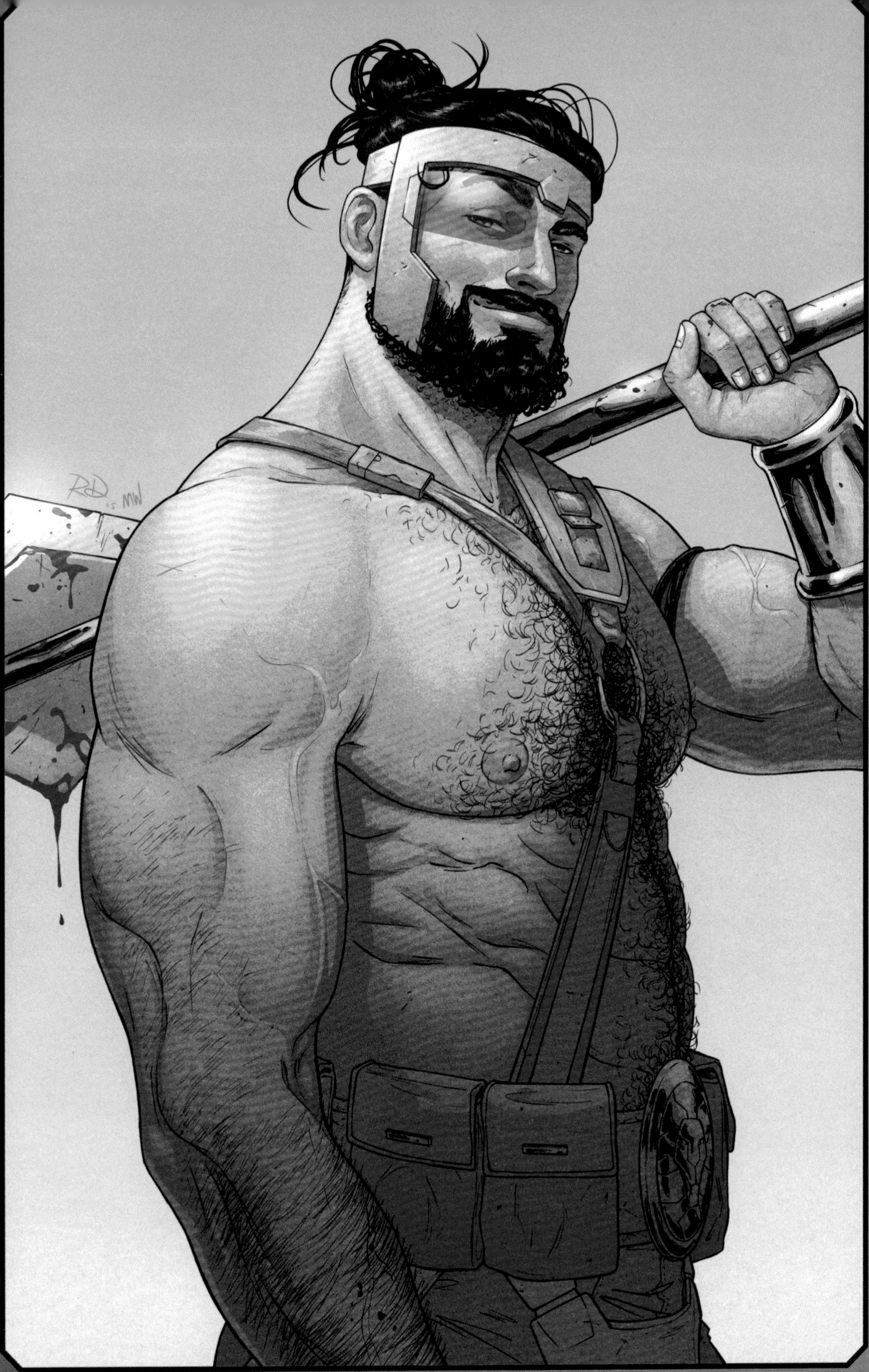
RD '15 MW

No. 2 VARIANT BY RUSSELL DAUTERMAN & MATTHEW WILSON

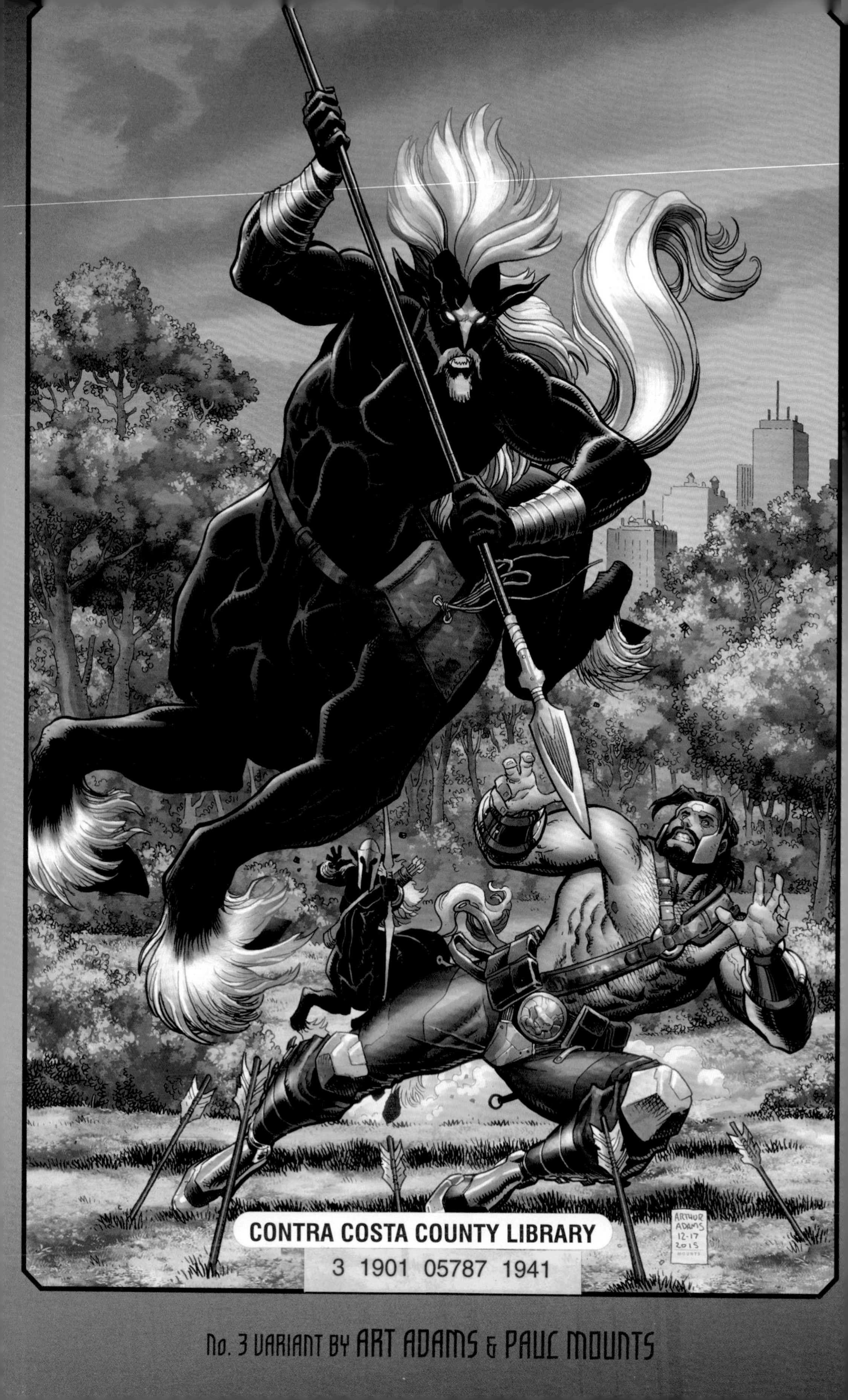
ARTHUR
ADAMS
12-17
2015
MOUNTS

No. 3 VARIANT BY ART ADAMS & PAUL MOUNTS